*The X Factor:*
*An American*
*Cultural Dilemma*

16 May 90
To Barbie & Bobby
Read, learn & inwardly digest
Neil M. Fleishman

# THE X FACTOR

## An American Cultural Dilemma

Neil M. Fleishman

VANTAGE PRESS
New York / Washington / Atlanta
Los Angeles / Chicago

*Excerpts cited from Dr. William H. Reid's* The Psychopath: A Comprehensive Study of Antisocial Disorders and Behaviors, *Brunner-Mazel, 1978; and Dr. Hervey Cleckley's* The Mask of Sanity, *5th ed., Mosby, 1976, used by permission. Excerpts taken from:* Journal of Medical Science; Journal of Psychiatry; The New York Times, *19 April 1981;* Vancouver Province, *7 April 1981;* The Journal of Nervous and Mental Disease, *1960, the William & Wilkins Co.;* Modern Clinical Psychiatry, *9th ed., W.B. Saunders & Co.; used by permission. Credit for the use of material is also given to Associated Press and United Press International, Inc.*

FIRST EDITION



Published by Vantage Press, Inc.
516 West 34th Street, New York, New York 10001

Manufactured in the United States of America
ISBN: 0-533-06460-0

Library of Congress Catalog Card No.: 84-91375

To Hervey Milton Cleckley, M.D. (1903–1984)

To each of us on first looking into
Cleckley's *The Mask of Sanity*

Like stout Cortez when with eagle eyes
He stared at the Pacific—and all his men
Look'd at each other with a wild surmise—
Silent, upon a peak in Darien.

*All women become like their mothers. That is their tragedy. No man does. That's his.*

—Oscar Wilde

*Children begin by loving their parents; after a time they judge them; rarely, if ever, do they forgive them.*

—Oscar Wilde

# CONTENTS

# FOREWORD

I first met Mr. Neil Fleishman in 1982, after a couple of telephone calls from Vancouver. He had wanted to come to Omaha to discuss his project and manuscript with me. That was flattering, but odd. Here was a private attorney, willing to spend good money to fly (with his wife) several thousand miles, to talk with someone who would almost certainly disagree with many of his premises and poke holes in his logic.

My vision was clouded by my own past experience. Here in academe, one soon gets used to the fact that our highly touted academic freedom and open exchange of ideas is a myth. We all too often study that which is comfortable. We do research in ways shaped by those who finance us. And we publish that which will further our professional security—cleverly disguised as scholarly careers—in journals whose editorial boards (of which I am often a member) look more for statistical significance and party line than for new thought. This is not all bad. There are some 400 million people in Canada and the United States, about two-thirds of whom want to get into print. One can become overwhelmed by ideas that are silly, being sold as innovative. But we often have trouble separating the potentially good from the bad.

*The X Factor* contains, in my view, both wheat and chaff, but it is not silly. I will risk a little career security (Oops! I mean, scholarly reputation) on that. *The X Factor,* as a lot of other Neil Fleishman activities, is flamboyant. It is seductive. It is at times maddening and at all times controversial. It may well be valuable.

So read this book, then let me know whether it's mostly wheat or mostly chaff. Let Neil know, too. He's interested, although your opinion will not temper his enthusiasm in the least.

William H. Reid, M.D., M.P.H.
Professor of Psychiatry
University of Nebraska Medical Center

# ACKNOWLEDGEMENTS

The author firstly acknowledges the collaboration with J. Barrie Bentz, M.D., friend and physician, whose guidance and medical knowledge has been a *sine qua non* in the preparation and completion of this work; he has given unstintingly of his time and effort in his deep concern for the family and its disruptions; to Dr. William H. Reid, M.D., M.P.H., Professor of Psychiatry, University of Nebraska Medical Centre, Omaha, Nebraska, whose advice and allowance of the use of the Medical Library at Omaha has proved fruitful; to George and Barbara Armstrong, a special acknowledgement for just being there; and lastly and foremost of all to the late Dr. Hervey Milton Cleckley and his charming widow, Emily. Dr. Cleckley for his unfailing courtesy and willingness to listen and advise on new and startling concepts—to Dr. Cleckley it was never said better than Catullus—"*Atque in perpetuum, frater, ave atque vale.*"

# INTRODUCTION

In this work the author is presenting the relationship between man and woman, and more particularly husband and wife, which relationship can be well expressed by using Antonio Vivaldi's title to his Opus 4 as an analogy, that is, The Conflict between *Invention* and *Harmony*. That is, *Harmony* to be the hoped-for natural state of being between a husband and wife and *Invention* being man's work superimposed upon this harmony to alter it, to change it, to destroy it, to do with it whatever either one of the partners will.

And what of this state between man and woman, husband and wife? Perhaps in all of recorded literature it has never been better expressed than was done by Geoffrey Chaucer in *The Canterbury Tales*, and more particularly in "The Wife of Bath's Tale." To quote now from Neville Coghill's translation in the Penguin series:

> "My liege and lady, in general," said he,
> "A woman wants the self-same sovereignty
> over her husband as over her lover,
> And master him; he must not be above her.
> That is your greatest wish, whether you kill
> Or spare me; please yourself. I wait your will."

How perceptive this was of Chaucer when we read the translator's comments on page 12:

> All Chaucer's heroes regard love when it comes upon them as the most beautiful of absolute disasters, an agony as much desired as bemoaned, ever to be pursued, never to be betrayed.
>
> This was not in theory the attitude of a husband to his wife. It was for a husband to command, for a wife to obey.

Chaucer, in his genius, has given a curious twist to "The Wife of Bath's Tale," a twist that is as relevant today as it was in Chaucer's time and in times immemorial. It is this mastery over man the Wife of Bath has wanted all her life and has attained in her five marriages, but at a great and incalculable cost to her. This desire has not brought her reciprocal love nor has it provided her with eternal youth that she so desires, nor has granted to her such beauty as will attract men forever. These are the factors over which she has never had any control. Nor has she been able to attain that ideal happiness throughout her life. Her character is rooted in deep-seated ideals, but on the surface gives her continuous assertion of authority over men and her experience in the marriage bed. And with her worldly bravado, she has not been able to hide her idealistic wishes. With all her desire for mastery over man, she still obviously seeks a sixth husband and remains undaunted in the face of what surely must be impossible conditions imposed by the nature of the relations between the sexes. At the end she says,

> And may Christ Jesus send
> Us husbands meek and young and fresh in bed,
> And grace to overbid them when we wed.
> And—Jesu hear my prayer!—cut short the lives
> Of those who won't be governed by their wives;
> And all old, angry niggards of their pence,
> God send them soon a very pestilence!

With her dauntlessness and her refusal to be abashed by life as it really is, we realize that she will eventually gain her sixth husband, but that fleeting, nebulous concept of happiness will ever elude her.

And, of course, the conflict has continued unabated from Chaucer's time to the present. And certainly prior to Chaucer's time to the time writ upon the Tablets of Hammurabi, but nevermore in all history has a conflict been so pointed as it was with the appearance of August Strindberg on the scene. Strindberg's years are 1849 to 1912. And without any doubt, he now appears as one of the remarkable personalities of modern times in the Western world. He was an enormously accomplished man in the Western world, in fact, one almost could state, a genius, to use this much abused word. He was an accomplished linguist, having studied a dozen or more languages, was fluent in Chinese, Hebrew, and Sanskrit. An accomplished musician, he had attempted medicine, teaching, and acting, and failed in everything, save and except that in which he excelled, writing. His volume of work was enormous, encompassing some fifty-five volumes, but it is for his plays that he is most remembered, and the greatest of these plays is perhaps *The Father*, first produced in 1887.

At a first reading, Strindberg appears to be the out-and-out rebel, the out-and-out outcast of society, the man struggling in vain against society's strictures. Upon a closer reading and a sounder knowledge of what Strindberg was not only attempting to do, but which he successfully did do, one must come to a different conclusion. Strindberg was an accomplished and exact delineator of a society of which he formed a part, and of a particular society of which he became one of the nineteenth century's outstanding victims.

*The Father* is a drama surrounding the efforts of the wife to completely destroy her husband by inserting in his mind doubts as to paternity of his beloved daughter, employing as it were, the old biblical concept that every child has but one mother but a thousand fathers. The wife uses this as an onslaught against a super-sensitive husband, so much so that it destroys him in the end and with the ending of the play he dies, constrained in a straitjacket and of a stroke. What Strindberg has done in his play is to delineate the compleat psychopath in the character of Laura, the wife. The captain, the husband, is delineated as the once again compleat victim, and if it were ever to be shown, it is shown here. In truth, the victim needs the psychopath as the martyr needs his tormenter. Here is used the translation by Elizabeth Sprigge, contained in *Modern Drama,* Alternate Edition, edited by Otto Reinert, and published by Little, Brown and Company, Boston, 1966. From Act Two:

> *Captain:* You always dominated me. You could hypnotize me when I was wide awake, so that I neither saw nor heard, but simply obeyed. You could give me a raw potato and make me think it was a peach; you could make me take your ridiculous ideas for flashes of genius. You could corrupt me—yes, make me do the shabbiest things. You never had any real intelligence, yet, instead of being guided by me, you would take the reins into your own hands. And when at last I woke to the realisation that I had lost my integrity, I wanted to blot out my humiliation by some heroic action—some feat, some discovery—even by committing hara-kiri. I wanted to go to war, but I couldn't. It was then that I gave all my energies to science. And now—now when I should be stretching out my hand to gather the fruit, you chop off my arm. I'm robbed of my laurels; I'm finished. A man cannot live without repute.

And then at the end of Act Two:

> *Laura (retreating):* Your own. The one in which you told the doctor that you were mad. *(He stares at her in silence.)* Now you have fulfilled the unfortunately necessary functions of father and breadwinner. You are no longer needed, and you must go. You must go, now that you realise my wits are as strong as my will—you won't want to stay and acknowledge my superiority.

And then toward the ending of Act Three, there is this rationalization by Laura, showing as Dr. Cleckley has shown, a complete and utter lack of insight into what her conduct has produced:

> *Laura:* But I didn't mean this to happen. I never really thought it out. I may have had some vague desire to get rid of you—you were in my way—and perhaps, if you see some plan in my actions, there was one, but I was unconscious of it. I have never given a thought to my actions—they simply ran along the rails you laid down. My conscience is clear, and before God I feel innocent, even if I'm not. You weighed me

down like a stone, pressing and pressing until my heart tried to shake off its intolerable burden. That's how it's been, and if without meaning to, I have brought you to this, I ask your forgiveness.

And then, almost at the end of the play:

*Doctor:* If this be so, of which I am as poor a judge as of the cause of his illness, in any case my skill is at an end. Try yours now, Pastor.

It has been said that Strindberg suffered from a persecution complex and suffered with hallucinations attendant upon this so-called complex. However, no one has been ever able to ascertain whether or not he was clinically insane. The greatest stigma that has been attached to Strindberg, of course, has been to label him a misogynist. To have attended a performance of *The Father* presented before a group of university students was most illuminating. To them, these young *avante garde* students, led mostly by young women students, dishevelled, both in appearance, mentality and emotion, thought the play itself hilarious and consumed the time by loud laughs, brays, and other forms of emptyheadedness. This occurred as late as the year 1980.

The conclusion must be that Strindberg is so important to the understanding of the role of the psychopathic wife in the marriage that some critical relevance should be shown. *The Father* was first presented on the stage in the United States of America in the year 1912, and it was his first play to have been so presented. Reference is made here to the book *August Strindberg, The Strindberg Reader,* edited and translated by Arvid Paulson, published by Phaedra, Inc., New York, 1968, and more particularly at the end of the book from page 437 on. The editor states that *The Father* "has generally failed because of having been produced as a melodrama instead of as a furious tragedy." *The Father* is neither a melodrama nor a furious tragedy. It is quite clearly and simply an exposé by Strindberg of the role of the psychopathic wife in the matrimonial holocaust, because in truth the holocaust is what the marriage in *The Father* is all about.

Another reviewer of the day said of the play, "No more sinister picture of malevolent womanhood has ever been staged." Another reviewer writes, "It is an awful conflict between a man and a woman, with the playwright bitterly arrayed against the latter." Of course to me it is none of these things. It is simply another example of a Mount Everest. The problem is to be surmounted and the conscionable dramatist Strindberg surmounts the problem without sinister malevolence in the scales, without setting himself up as the arbitrator between good and bad in a man or the woman. Again in 1931 another reviewer calls *The Father,* "Strindberg's insanely bitter diatribe against women." In 1949 one reviewer, George Jean Nathan in the *New York Journal-American,* came as close to anyone as putting has putting his finger on the attributes of Strindberg.

> In its almost every detail—psychological, psychopathic, dialogic, dramaturgical—the play remains more modern than any of the numerous later ones it inspired.

That *The Father* still remains a source of not misunderstanding but non-understanding, can be shown in the latest review by Walter Kerr, in the *New York Times,* Sunday, 19 April, 1981. In a review under the heading "Theatre," Walter Kerr is quoted:

> Just as Ibsen often made monkeys of his men, Strindberg too devoutly made witches out of his women.
>
> She is at her very best, I think, toward the evening's chilling end as she reassures her now permanently disabled husband (a stroke, while straightjacketed) that whatever she has done to him has been innocently done. She feels no guilt, she tells us. And it is plain that she doesn't. Because we have watched her drive a man wild by persuading him that he's not the father of his own child, and because we must give credence to the actress's disavowal of responsibility for the lie told and the evil done, we're forced to face what the play does say: Women are born untrustworthy—not to say irrational—and don't you go bothering Strindberg with any of this women's lib guff.

Well, of course, no one is driven to the ineluctable conclusion that women are untrustworthy. What Strindberg showed is that *this* woman was the way she was and, as we understand now, that she was the essential and true psychopath at work in her path of destruction. It has been mentioned by reviewer after reviewer that which struck the Victorian audiences adversely and ran a thrill of horror through the audiences was the extreme violence of the play, violence being shown by the captain throwing a lamp at his wife, Laura. In retrospect, and looking at the work presented in this book, one can see just how little violence was really portrayed by Strindberg. The violence really portrayed by him was one of the psyche, not of material.

It is worthwhile now to inquire into the state of the marital scene as it is in the United States of America. To begin, there is the article that appeared in the *Los Angeles Times* on Friday, 7 July 1972, then entitled *Alarming Rise in Broken Marriages,* by William Hines. This alarming rise in broken marriages is revealed in the latest monthly vital statistics report from the National Center for Health Statistics, a Bureau of the Department of Health, Education, and Welfare.

> It seems likely that the disproportionate number of divorces in California results from the State's "no-fault" law which recognizes "irreconcilable differences" as the only ground. This in turn would suggest that if more States go the no-fault route, as has been suggested by many legal reformers, a higher proportion of marriages will be dissolved.
>
> In 1950 the national divorce-marriage ratio was 231, just a shade over half what it is today. During the next decade the change was small,

with a ratio 246 in 1955 and 258 in 1960. By 1967, five years ago, the ratio was at 333 and beginning to climb rapidly, reaching 428 in 1971 and 455 this year.

The highest ratios of divorces to 1,000 marriages were reported by Montana, 803; Oregon, 768; California, 755; Alaska, 703; Florida, 685; Washington, 656; Colorado, 596; Ohio, 593; Delaware, 571; District of Columbia, 569; Arkansas, 538; Kansas, 532; Maine, 523; and Oklahoma, 519.

It is also instructive and interesting to note that in 1980 in the State of California, for the first time the number of divorces exceeded the number of marriages. From the published study entitled *Divorces by Marriage Cohort,* published by the United States Department of Health, Education, and Welfare, Public Health Service, in August 1979, the following extracts throw some light on the social trend developing in the United States of America.

During all periods of increase the percent change was usually higher for divorces than for marriages, and the difference was particularly pronounced in the years 1963–73 when marriages increased 38.1 percent but divorce 113.8 percent. The cumulative result of these differences was that during the entire 1922–75 period annual marriage totals increased 90 percent, from 1,134,151 to 2,152,662, and divorce totals grew almost 600 percent, from 148,815 to 1,036,000.

On page 21, Table 5, headed Marriages, Divorces, and Percent change from preceding year (See attached Schedule "A" in the appendix).

Surely an enlightening group of statistics with which one must struggle in order to comprehend what is happening in modern United States society. On inquiry into the causes of marital discord, it is to be found in this appendix that the theories and ideas advanced are as varied as the sands of the sea. When one considers each and all the rest seriatim, it cannot be said which are right, which are wrong. Perhaps there is some validity, in what amount we cannot say, in each and every idea put forward. There appeared by a United Press Dispatch from Philadelphia, 23 April 1981, an item entitled "Long Life can be Fatal to Wedlock." We print the whole of this article out of sheer interest:

Higher divorce rates are one result of North Americans' longevity, says a researcher who claims many marriages cannot stand an extra two decades until "death do us part."

"Longevity has added as much as a quarter of a century of close living to many marriages," Dr. Holger Stub, a researcher in the field of social gerontology at Temple University, said Wednesday.

"This alone exposes marriage to a phenomenal increase in disruptive influences and culminates in high divorce and separation rates."

Stub, who spent a year studying the consequences of longevity, said even though marriages may now have a potential length of 50 years, many won't last half that long.

"Like the policeman, mailman, secretary or soldier who returns from one career and takes up another, increased longevity allows men and women virtually to bargain for two marriages, one for the young family years and another for the post-parental period," Stub said.

"It is not merely a possibility but is actually taking place." Stub said a "relatively large minority" of husbands and wives separate at middle age, after their children have grown and left home, and remarry "by plan and design." He said the prospect of a long life "changes the whole perspective of what people feel they can do with the rest of their lives.

"The increased length of life allows new kinds of steps, alternatives and decisions for human beings," Stub said. "It was not long ago that a woman was old at 45 and a man was old at 50. Now you think about 70 as being old. When the definition of old age goes higher and higher, it allows you a whole lot of leeway."

In a stunning reversal of form, Betty Friedan, the author of *The Feminine Mystique,* who needs no further introduction, has been reported recently as recanting and in fact following her Road to Canossa.

"We almost threw the baby out with the bath water and put feminism in conflict with the family.

"In addition," she said, "women in their 20s and 30s are facing very great conflicts because they are falling into superwoman traps.

"Young women who should benefit by the avenues opened to them by the older generation of feminists soon discover there are no role models and that social structures are not there to follow."

Friedan blamed extremist, "amazon separatists," for reacting to feminism by treating women as an oppressed class and preaching down with home and family. "Consequently," she said, "young women face new problems and receive a confusing set of messages which, in turn, have produced a new myth—the 'either or' syndrome.

"This new, young woman says, 'Don't talk to me about children.' But the life sensitivity, the biological life roots of women cannot be denied."

Friedan said the first waves of feminism failed to come to terms with the family.

Upon realizing this, she said she "went back to my drawing board" to design some new concepts. "We must come to terms with the family. It isn't about to disappear."

Friedan said that the "four-square" family unit of father, mother and two children now is in the minority in the U.S. and 83 percent of the population is living in different forms of families.

"The family is the root of our society and of human autonomy. Any movement to equality and independence is immeasurably strengthened by the family."

Friedan now finds herself in the position of royal food taster, who at last has tasted of the bitter fruits and, in fact, examplifies the former and late Secretary of State Dean Acheson's great and disturbing remark in another context, but by analogy here applies, "Great Britain has lost an empire but has not yet found a role."

The opposite side of the spectrum of Betty Friedan is, of course, Phyllis Schlafly. Once again a name so well known to the people of the United States that she needs no further introduction. The note by Associated Press Dispatch of Washington, D.C. on Thursday, April the 23rd, 1981, headlined "Women bring harassment upon themselves: Schlafly." The following statements made by Mrs. Schlafly were made for a United States Senate Labor Subcommittee. The subcommittee had hearings at which an inquiry had been made into the effect of sexual harassment and sex discrimination on the job, which women in the United States allegedly had to undergo. Says Mrs. Schlafly, "Mrs. Schlafly contended, however, that those who raise the issue of sexual harassment on the job are a threat to the American family."

> "The feminist goal is to induce all wives and mothers out of the home and into the workforce," she said.
>
> Mrs. Schlafly, a fervent opponent of the Equal Rights Amendment, so angered feminists with her testimony that she was hissed for saying:
>
> "The most cruel and damaging sexual harassment taking place today is the harassment by feminists and their federal government allies against the role of motherhood and the role of the dependent wife."
>
> Meanwhile, Mrs. Schlafly said she was far more concerned about those who urge combat roles for women in the military and policies that prohibit women from resigning from the armed forces to start a family.
>
> She said the Pentagon should reverse its policies of opening more jobs to women and should "Keep women out of places where they don't belong, such as on ships of the U.S. Navy, and in military barracks where there is nothing between sleeping servicemen and servicewomen except maybe a curtain."
>
> She said affirmative action programs that seek to increase the percentage of women in specific jobs deny "breadwinner" husbands jobs, raises and promotions.
>
> "It is time to reassert the dignity and social good of the male provider role," she told the subcommittee.

Mrs. Schlafly was answered by the *New York Times* in an editorial in the Sunday Edition of April 26, 1981.

> Phyllis Schlafly, of Alton, Ill., is the founder and chairman of an organization opposed to the Equal Rights Amendment. A veteran debater, she is formidably articulate—and this week she muddied the waters of a Senate Labor Committee hearing on sexual harassment in the workplace by slinging mud on other women.
>
> "When a woman walks across the room," Mrs. Schlafly testified, "she speaks with a universal body language that most men intuitively understand. Men hardly ever ask sexual favors of women from whom the answer is 'No.' Virtuous women are seldom accosted by unwelcome sexual propositions or familiarities, obscene talk or profane language."

> Mrs. Schlafly's words are all too reminiscent of that old and terrible response to rape: "She must have asked for it." They evoke as well a time when women, teenagers especially, believed themselves to be at fault for every elevator pinch, subway snuggle or muttered invitation. Follow Mrs. Schlafly's logic and the young girl who comes home crying because a strange man said something bad to her on the street is, *ipso facto,* not "virtuous."
>
> Given her previous pronouncements on the roles of men and women, Mrs. Schlafly's statements are scarcely a surprise. What is a surprise is that she was asked to air them before a Senate committee. Unlike the other witnesses, Mrs. Schlafly did not come armed with studies, statistics and expert knowledge of the subject under discussion. All she presented were her opinions, and it is regrettable that she had so tall a soap box for so mean a message.

However, what the *New York Times* does is to misstate Mrs. Schlafly's main thrust and in doing so demeans itself as a newspaper and shows the great august *New York Times* oft hones its knife to suit its own purpose.

Another interesting comment appeared recently in the press:

> And when *Dressed to Kill* ran, the Ridge was picketed by a women's group who claimed the film was sexist. When Schein talked to them, they gave him garbled accounts of scenes that weren't in the movie. He found out that not one of the intrepid ladies could admit to having seen the film.
>
> They refused his offer to sit in on the movie for free and present their judgments to the audience, but they did go on picketing and threatened violence against the theatre. Where were they when the movie ran earlier at a major downtown cinema? Schein wonders.

What then of these who scoff at, laugh at, and hiss one of the world's truly great works of art, such as Strindberg's *The Father*? What then is the effect of those who hiss at Mrs. Phyllis Schlafly who is testifying before a committee of Congress? What then of the mindless, poor things who picket a theatre and a film of which they have no knowledge, but which film itself, *Dressed to Kill,* portrays some of the agony of the modern American housewife. What more can be said of those who seem possessed of a Messianic complex?

It suggests that these people live on the outskirts of, or completely outside, the boundaries of a well-organized society, or a well-organized social order. It may be the question, what is the necessity or what is the desirability of the well-organized social order? The answer is that without well-organized social order, there is social chaos. In the chapters that follow is postulated that which results from a disintegrating social order, and that is social chaos. Sooner or later this chaos is going to have to be dealt with by the country as a whole or in whatever countries it does appear.

The crushing statistics from the Department of Health and Welfare that we have set out have had some impact in the United States of

America, and it was the former President Carter who in his campaign speeches in 1976 over and over referred again to the fact that the American family was in trouble. Apparently this observation gave great credit to the former president, but little credit to the professionals working in the field of the family. In the summer of 1980, in the *New Republic,* on 28 June, 1980, Diane Ravitch writes in an article entitled, "In the Families Way":

> Some American families are in trouble, but most are not. About 90 percent of all Americans are residing as members of families related by blood, marriage, or adoption (another eight percent are single persons). Forty-seven million families (out of a total of fifty-seven million families) are composed of the conventional, husband-wife relationship. We have been told repeatedly that 40 percent of all marriages end in divorce, but that statistic means that for every 10 couples who married last year, four couples get divorced; alongside that information must be added the fact that 80 percent of all married couples have never been divorced.

What the author of that quotation, Diane Ravitch, misses and misconceives is the accumulative effect of the statistics given out by the Department of Health and Welfare in 1972 and again the quotations for the 1979 publication; although the State of California places only third in a ratio of divorces to marriages, it must be remembered in perusing these statistics that California is the most populous state in the Union and therefore every year a great number of women and children are turned out into a cruel hostile world by the process of divorce, and it must be said that these women and these children are truly the dispossessed of our modern society.

One of the factors contributing towards the break-up of the American marriage must be the biological factor. It is a sad commentary to notice that by and large the American female tends to age badly, to which remark and observation the usual rejoinder is, "So what? So do men." The obvious answer to this is that a man can grow old, looking like King Kong, and still remain cock-of-the-walk, if you will forgive the mixing of metaphors. After all, it is his world to do with as he wishes, but it is not a woman's world in the same sense. Laws are made by men for men in a man's world. To observe how badly the average American woman ages means not only physically, but emotionally as well. This emotional aging accentuates the problem, and in fact and in truth becomes the main issue. What follows from this problem, follows directly as a result of this age itself, this age of lessened responsibilities and of the feeling of the right to do one's own thing, to use the popular phrase. Both male and female lack the desire to conform to what has been for countless generations accepted as conduct to be adhered to, and for the man seeking to do his own thing means that he seeks his company and his pleasures elsewhere. As far as the woman is concerned, this is a good deal more difficult to accomplish, as a good many, if not most, divorced women find out after they have been divorced. Out there is a world totally hostile to them, as divorced women, and totally unreceptive to their desires and their needs, and as must be reiterated, most of these divorced women eventually find out this in a fashion not conducive to their being at ease in a new type of social milieu.

Then there is the disparity of age. It is one of My cardinal Rules of marriage, and that is, that no marriage has much survival potential where the wife is older than the husband. This is a biological factor that has become a law, not just a theory. The French have a saying that every man should marry a woman half his age plus seven years. Whether this is true or not, there is no way of establishing, but it does command some sort of attention as emanating from a people who in story and in history have been well versed in the ways of love.

Another biological factor that impinges on the relations of husband and wife are the respective life expectancies of each. The life expectancy of females is now seventy-eight years of age and for males seventy years. And this disparity is increasing over the years. The gulf is widening. A medical practitioner who is interested as well in family problems has this to say:

> "Doctor, tell me, where are all the men for these women who are finding themselves out in the world alone after divorce or upon widowhood?"
>
> "There simply aren't many."
>
> "Well, Doctor, where are they all?"
>
> "They are all dead or disinterested."
>
> "Why?"
>
> "It is stress that is killing them nowadays. It is the men who are having the heart attacks in great numbers, not the women. You know, it is not only stress in the man's occupation, that is his job or his business or his profession, that works havoc on him. It is stress within the four walls of the matrimonial home. This is doing away with him at such a relatively early age and leaving a great mass of unattached, uncared-for women of all ages."

Speaking biologically of men and women, there are certain unalterable facts. Now, as it has been since the dawn of history, it must become worthy of consideration that as long as women menstruate, impregnate, and lactate, they will always be at a disadvantage in this world. The hollering, the screaming, and the jumping of three feet in the air when attendant on the use of this epigram will only accentuate that these are part of the unalterable facts of biology and to which attention must be paid instead of the little that is being paid now.

*The X Factor:*
*An American*
*Cultural Dilemma*

# I

# THE AMERICAN CULTURAL DILEMMA

With the ending of World War II in 1945, there materialised in the whole of the "Western World" the social upheavals and consequent need for adjustments, resulting as they have from the dawn of recorded history following every major clash of arms. Social effects have been considered in many studies to be those arising from economic or geographical hardships, i.e., postwar inflation, unemployment, crop failures, resulting in not only hunger, but in driving the rural populace to the large population centres, the cities.

Looking back to the ending of World War I (until 1939 called the Great War), the historical effects can be seen much more clearly than those that are much too simply called the social effects. This earlier conflict provided the last chapter to what was, perhaps, Napoleon's greatest accomplishment: the ending of the institution of feudalism in Western continental Europe. He blasted that thousand and more year old concept from the scene from out of the mouths of his cannon. The clash of ideologies, exemplified by the rise of socialism and the demands made by the working classes against those of the managerial class, again the ideological ferment provided by the triumph of Communism in Russia, by the aggrandisement of capital and the consequent rise of machine use in industry and agriculture, providing other ideological clashes. These have been held by many scholars of the time to be social in nature.

With the ending of the first worldwide conflict in 1918, America, which for the first time had involved itself in large-scale foreign intervention, finally came of age. It was finally seen and accepted that the decade of the eighteen-nineties had provided the conclusion of the American empire movement westward to the Pacific. America had at last become a member of what, as will be seen later, the West-European-American Culture. Not just a bare member, but the most powerful and the most influential. It used to be said that "When the Czar of Russia sneezed, all Europe caught a cold." Now it was differently said that "When America deliberated, the rest of the world held its breath with either unconcealed gloom or gleeful anticipation."

With the ending of World War I, as it became quickly to be named, and which impinged on, but did not necessarily involve, all four corners of the globe, there followed the disastrous inflation of central continental Europe: the ongoing destruction there and the triumph of the Communist state; and finally the Great Depression, coming on hard in the United States and spreading worldwide. There was in America from the time of the ending of the conflict and the onset of the Depression, the Harding "Era of Normalcy," and attended in America by few urgent social pressures.

## SEVEN FACETS OF GENIUS USHERING IN THE TWENTIETH CENTURY THAT EITHER CONTRIBUTED TO OR ILLUMINATED THE DESTABILIZATION OF THE THOUSAND-YEAR, WEST-EUROPEAN–AMERICAN CULTURE

*Primus inter pares* of the twentieth century genius must be Albert Einstein. With the publication of his First Theory of Relativity in 1905, he ensured that pure science would never again follow the Newtonian paths. With The General Theory of Relativity, there developed $E = mc^2$. There followed Max Planck, Niels Bohr, Ernest Rutherford, Lisa Meitner, Enrico Fermi, Hans Bethe, Edward Teller, and then came Hiroshima.

On the 29 May, 1913, a riot took place at the Theatre des Champs-Elysees in Paris. This was the audience reaction to the first performance of Igor Stravinski's *Le Sacre du Printemps (The Rite of Spring),* Pierre Monteux conducting. But music was never the same again, nor would the human ear be attuned to listen in quite the same fashion.

A revolution in the analysis of thought process, of mind control, of the transforming of thoughts into action, was first initiated with the appearance in 1900 of *The Interpretation of Dreams,* by Sigmund Freud. His was the prime influence in the exploration of the unconscious. Freud has impinged on each and every facet of twentieth-century thought. Many psychoanalytical schools have been founded on the original Freudian base. Since this work is an extension of Dr. Cleckley's work, *The Mask of Sanity,* it might be appropriate to give the words of Dr. Cleckley as related to this author in August of 1983: "Every phase of psychiatry today makes due acknowledgement of its debt to Freud and I envisage that all phases of psychoanalysis will be back to the concepts of Freud in twenty years. He, unfortunately, is accepted as the only answer."

In February of 1922, there rolled from the press of Shakespeare and Company, Paris, a novel of almost one thousand pages in length.

This was the record of a single day, June 16, 1904, in the life of a Dubliner, Leopold Bloom. With this singular *tour de force,* being essentially a great affirmation of life, the author, James Joyce, changed the whole course of literature. But dealing with more than just words, James Joyce provided a new, exciting and, yes, revolutionary rationale of the twentieth century.

Working in France from the years 1905–1908, Alfred Binet produced the first of the comparative intelligence tests, which, when combined with the research of Dr. L. H. Terman working at Stanford University, in 1937 came to be known as the Stanford-Binet Intelligence Test, or, in simpler terms, establishing the principle of the IQ. This has led to latter day postulations of the relationship of the IQ to genetical structure as exemplified by the work of Jensen, Eysenck, and Shockley.

The sixth, and perhaps the least appreciated facet of twentieth century genius, was the monumental work of Dr. Hervey Milton Cleckley, M.D., which, when first published in 1942, gave to America the first expose of the psychopath, both at play and at work, so to speak. The first and the succeeding editions have shown and explained much in human conduct and response that was formerly incapable of explanation. Dr. Cleckley was the first to realize just how few clinical psychiatrists would be convinced of his own observations. It is axiomatic that the physician must know the cause of illness or aberrant behaviours and must equally strive to heal that illness or restrain from aberrant behaviour. With the psychopath, as so clearly demonstrated by Dr. Cleckley, neither hope could be fulfilled. The psychiatrist, first and foremost a physician, with rare exceptions, has not interested himself in the area of psychopathy.

With the manuscript completed by the time of the outbreak of the Great War of 1914, and with publication in 1918, Oswald Spengler launched his monumental study of world cultures and philosophy of history. *The Decline of the West* has since withstood all assaults on the validity of its premise.

> "In this book is attempted for the first time the venture of predetermining history, of following the still untravelled stage in the destiny of a Culture, and specifically of the only Culture of our time—the West-European-American." (Oswald Spengler, *The Decline of the West* [New York: Alfred A. Knopf, 1932], p. 32.)

In bare essence, what Spengler asserts that the only culture on this planet, which comprises civilization and sociality both, has lost its sense of purpose, and each member of it is at a certain stage of life uncertain of his own direction; he gropes and feels his way. For this cultural loss of purpose, there has been substituted the panacea of all decaying cultures, *panem et circenses* (bread and circuses). Therein lie the seeds of the Decline of the West, and the end of the West-European-American Culture.

However, social unrest and disorder, in its enormity and intensity never conceived in the aftermath of World War I prevailed after the second world conflict. The Spenglerian concept of *panem et circenses* as applying to the destruction of this earth's one culture extended logically to the waging of wars between the member states that are integral members of this one culture. War is a Spenglerian form of *panem et circenses.*

Great family disorders took place both during and after the 1939–1945 conflict. The forced migrations of countless millions from one end of the European continent to the other during the war took place; males were wrenched from their homelands and taken to one country or another to serve as forced labour, with no concern for the wives and children involuntarily abandoned as a result. Further disorder and family separation by the mass conscription of men of all countries, and taken from their family homes thereby, created a further large group of father-abandoned children. Each casualty in the many armies involved left all the more children without a returning father figure.

The war's aftermath in many lands continued in a relentless fashion to provide more forced migrations, both back to the original homelands and from them. Families were again shattered.

Although the circumstances in the United States during these war years from Pearl Harbour to Hiroshima were similar in some respects to those of the European theatre, that is, embodying the separation of fathers and families, there was one interesting difference. True, the American draft took millions of men from their homes, separated them from their families, sent them scattered over the seven seas to serve, or posted them to various training bases throughout the continental United States. Of equal import was the great migration of the industrially unskilled workers from the farms of the Midwest, from the share-croppers from the fields of the Southeast and Deep South, and from the countless small towns of the nation. From these well-settled homes, husbands and fathers in their hundreds of thousands left wives and family behind to staff the vastly expanding industrial war plants from Pacific to Atlantic and mainly in the Northern belt of the land. If not alone, then with the uprooting of settled families to the already overcrowded cities of the North. To work the twenty-four hour shifts in the steel mills of Gary, Indiana, in the Midwest, to the gigantic mills of Pittsburgh, Pennsylvania, in the East, and to the Kaiser Permanente mills lately erected in the Far West, they came. Likewise to build the bombers and fighters in the warplane factories at Willow Run, Michigan; Everett, Washington; and to the huge automotive and tank plants. Whatever the statistics, whatever the numbers, many families were left without the male figure, and left to subsist on service allottments or monies diverted back home. For the first time in American history, on such a large scale, rural America left the security of the land and crowded into the large and impersonal giant cities. Where cities did not exist they were created. A further, and, as transpired, an irrevocable disruption of predominantly close family units, resulted from world conflict within culture itself. Granted this one-world culture, a form of *panem et circenses,* difficult to comprehend, but nonetheless logically assertable.

Up to and including the decade of the nineties, the effective relief from developing social pressures in America had, of course, been the expansion of Empire westward. With the almost unlimited lands available to the burgeoning population, the problem of *lebensraum,* with which Germany had become so hag-ridden, did not haunt the body politic of the United States.

Another factor inhibiting serious social and family pressures was the fact that America was by and large a highly dedicated religious country, that religion to a great extent being Protestant. Both the Old and New Testaments were the life guides of an essentially Fundamentalist America. Sorrows and grief that today spell almost certain disaster to the cohesiveness of the family in this country were borne with a stoicism worthy of and comparable to the Lamentations of Jeremiah and the Sorrows of Job. The acceptance of suffering on earth, in this life, that is, were to be redeemed by visions of life-everlasting promised in the New Testament.

One can but compare the result of a family tragedy, i.e., the loss of a child in that film shown in 1980, *Ordinary People,* where the mother cannot cope with this loss and splits the family by desertion and abandonment. Compare this with life in America in the eighteen-nineties that can be found in that now classic publication, *Wisconsin Death Trip:*

> . . . the presence of such epidemic diseases as diphtheria, smallpox and cholera. These diseases were awful and perverse not only because they paralyzed and destroyed whole countries, but because they inverted a natural order—that is, they killed the youngest before the oldest; they killed the ones who were to be protected before their rightful protectors; they killed the progeny before the forebears; they killed the children before their parents. When such diseases created circumstances of fate so grotesque, so perverse that they permitted parents to outlive their infants, they permitted them to live on not only in grief but in guilt, since it was they who had failed to maintain the immortality of their genes. You should know a second thing before you read the accounts: these writings transformed what were private acts into public events. In a time that was disjointed by a depression as epidemically fatal and grotesque as the most contagious disease, these articles created temporary but intimate bonds between creatures who had been separated and divided by a selfish culture of secular Calvinsim.

Yet, in spite of all, people endured, families endured. It was only when the unbearable onslaught of circumstances pushed people over the brink of reason that they committed these mind-boggling acts on themselves or others.

The unrelenting strictures of Calvinism helped provide the bond that held families together, no matter what the need or the urge for any individual of that entity to opt out, save for the most compelling of reasons amounting to a virtual loss of reason.

By the end of the decade above, the circle had closed, and Spengler was now able to include this most representative of the modern Western industrial states as the linch-pin of West-European-American Culture. The rigid class-and-caste systems that had bedevilled, and in fact still bedevil, the majority of the entities comprising the one culture, had been eliminated in this, probably the first of the truly egalitarian civilizations within a culture.

In America following the second world conflict, the reconstitution of the family unit in the fashion long established and accepted appeared to come about with the return to their homes of the millions of servicemen. But, these few years that the men had been absent from the family unit had seen the greatest technological advances yet recorded in the history of man. In addition, major political decisions had greatly affected the economics of family life. Purely and simply it had come about by legislative enaction that the women of the family were no longer at the mercy of their repressive or totally neglectful men. Nor were the children.

The number of divorces had by and large stabilized during these war years, in an America devoted wholeheartedly to the winning of this war. Such were the riches of this subcontinent, and where this largesse was not given by nature, man did not hesitate to create. There can be little doubt that wealth was the steel mills of Gary, Indiana, the soy bean field of Illinois, the Liberty ships of the Kaiser yards, the bomber plants of Willow Run, Michigan, and finally, amongst many other unnamed miracles of industrial production, the uranium creators of Oak Ridge, Tennessee, and Hanford, Washington. To those who have propounded that Russia had the capabilities of winning this war alone, America must say, "No way." In all certainty America's enemies in Europe and Asia failed to join in laughter at that quaint apocryphal piece of wit, "Orville, them things will never fly."

The force of the foregoing lies in the fact that the effects of this country's great industrial production was such that total mobilization of all America's resources was not needed to prosecute this effort. It was only the men who were needed to staff the industrial plants, to man the ships, guns, planes, tanks, and infantry slit trenches. Yes, yes, Rosie the Riveter was indeed there, and with what elan the Office of War Information was able to show the world that this was indeed America's total effort.

Spengler, were he living today, would only give vent to admiration when he wrote in 1917,

> Since the Napoleonic era the old civilized consensus has mingled unwelcomed with the new-civilized Western "society" of the cities and

> has taken their economic and scientific methods into use with the cool superiority of age. A few generations later, the Japanese, also a very old intellect, did the same, and probably with still greater success (Spengler, p.323).

America gave itself over in unrestrained joy to the return of its husbands and fathers, the bulk of whom had left involuntarily. These men were returning to a social order now in the throes of turmoil, one example being that the long-accepted concept of the nuclear family had been subject to such strain that it was doubtful whether or not the long-absent husband and father now returning was going to cement together that which was on the verge of disintegration. To hold the family together was going to take many major adjustments. Husbands and fathers could not conceive the necessity and little understood the demands that made such necessary. Those of the wives who demanded something different in their lives, were ill equipped to express what it was. The adjustment problems became insurmountable. Neither husband or wife was in a sense a victim. These were things that they were doing to themselves, things of a complexity beyond the understanding and control of either. The children of the war years, they were the true victims. Not so much the boys; they had matured earlier. Most were ready to go out into the world at an earlier age than had their fathers or grandfathers. The outside world seemingly presented no problem. Girl children, on the other hand, became involved in the emotional turmoil of their mothers. America had not opened its doors to the would-be independent woman. Economically, socially, and by cultural patterns of generations, she remained tied to the husband figure, and by association, the daughter to the father figure.

One outstanding feature of the immediate postwar years and the attempts at the readjustments within the family, was the startling "baby boom." The main burden of forgiving the transgressions, real or imagined, by either spouse during these years of separation, fell perforce, upon the wife, as a natural concommitant of her economic dependency and her cultural indoctrination. Economically, this was even more so, in face of the fact the woman as a whole had played a relatively minor part in the pursuit of the war effort. Total mobilization of America's resources, using both male and female, was never envisaged. The marketplace was not yet open to the American woman, and she remained dependent on the man who provided.

The complaints made by one spouse regarding the marital conduct of the other during these first postwar years were largely traditional. To her, he had become a "no good chippy chaser" and a "no good drunken bum." To him, she was "whoring around." As if programmed, a man would enter in upon what began to seem an universal routine. "Why that goddam bitch—she screwed around with everything in sight before I married her and she's doing the same thing now." Said often enough by the raging husband, and loud enough for the whole neighbourhood to hear, this not only to wife, but by transference later to daughter, produced a trauma that was impossible to heal.

"A man may sleep with a hundred women and he remains the jolly dog; but let a woman sleep with any than her husband and she remains the eternal whore." It is this cancer gnawing at so many men's minds: the loss of his wife's virginity to someone other than he, before the marriage, that eats at him. Someone other than he has manhandled his property. Fortune has decreed that he purchase a used car, but he longingly looks at this pristine beauty of his dreams—the new car. Othello, and his paranoid belief in the treachery of Desdemona, has much to offer in comparison with today's ever-suspecting male. Biblical and other less-industrialized societies have much to commend in the bringing of the virgin to the marriage bed. The double standard has been deeply ingrained in all cultures since day of the Cro-Magnon. The drive to change this state of affairs, commendable though it may seem to many, presents the same problems in attempting to legislate against human nature.

To the casual observer, it seemed unlikely that any great changes in the social order of things were about to take place. To those willing and privileged to see, there were certain and undeniable portents of a gathering storm. These were first felt following the period of the mid-nineteen-sixties.

Of a sudden it appeared that the "battered wife" syndrome was making its appearance as a major factor breaking up the American home. Large bureaucracies came into being to help the beleaguered wife to cope with this new brutality. "Hey, any woman who knows what she wants, can always get her husband to punch her out." Provocation by the wife was fast becoming an art form, worthy of inclusion in the annals of "The Human Comedy."

## SCENARIO NUMBER ONE

> ". . . the Defendant has physically assaulted and harmed me in the past, most recently last September when he shoved me on the ground and put his foot in my neck. . . ."

> "I, the defendant, have never physically assaulted the plaintiff, my wife. Somewhat unbelievably so, I draw attention that my wife is a blue belt karate expert, this being a higher qualification of karate, and that she has received a one year minimum of karate training. With respect to the incident of September last, she became irrational and emotionally upset during a discussion of our matrimonial problems, and made me the victim of her karate expertise. She decked me and then called the cops to look at this unconscious bum out cold on the floor who was her husband. The cops and the judge just laughed at me."

There followed for the first time, and in ever-increasing numbers, the involuntary abandonment of the marital scene by the husband, but more to the issue here, of the daughters. The state was itself now formulating policy to break up homes by enforced separation of the spouses. It was not sanctified by law that the judge might look at the question of provocation. But there was no law that the daughter in the home could not look, and draw her own conclusions, as she invariably did. Daddy's gone. An index of the father-daughter syndrome in the making.

Keeping pace with the rise of brutality in the home, were the startling allegations of child abuse within the secure home. Abuse, if you please, by the father upon the daughter. Vast bureaucracies were formed to cope with this new social disaster. Abuse centres were set up over the nation, and "Dial an Abuse" became a commonplace.

## SCENARIO NUMBER TWO

I turn now to the real issue at trial, access rights of the husband, to which the wife is totally opposed, alleging a danger to the child of sex abuse. Her charges are of a most serious kind, being of a criminal nature of father against daughter, buggery and incest. There was certainly no problem in this area before separation. Mr. W. has always had a father's love for his daughter. Nothing in the way of complaint until Mrs. W. claims that in June of 19– after the separation the two-year old child complained to her that "Daddy hurt my bum." On cross-examination the wife said she was alarmed about what counsel put to her as Force 10 on the Richter scale, but not a word of complaint to her husband. She says the second incident occurred in March 19– after a visit to the father. Katie told her something about Dad having done something to her "puss." And then later Katie said to her mother, "Come and take a bath with me like Daddy does."

I must say I am disturbed by all these charges. Why would the mother wait ten months to confront the father and then tell him on the telephone to talk to a lawyer about these allegations. By that time on advice, the wife had gone to the family sexual medical team at the hospital so designated by the state and its bureaucracy for that purpose. There had been insufficient evidence to lay any complaint, according to the doctor who saw Katie on the first occasion; and up until April certainly not any sufficient evidence to lay any direct complaint against the father. This medical council was asked to investigate and the husband did attend one session. In this session the Team seemed to work from the angle that the abuse had taken place and he should continue with interviews and receive treatment. Apparently that was the approach also of Dr. R., in the husband's assessment. The husband on the stand under oath completely denies these accusations, states that he is shocked and sickened by them and wants to be allowed to see his daughter again. He seeks the access rights that he has been denied by the wife since last March.

My assessment of this allegation is this: It is a serious charge requiring strict proof before I would accept that as valid. I am impressed with the sincerity of the natural love and affection for his daughter and

> not a perverted one. The whole development of this sexual abuse charge in the middle of litigation, when the wife at trial admits that she does not need her husband, she doesn't need or want him to see the child, smacks of, and I don't think this is unfair, a fertile imagination.

"A fertile imagination" of a certainty. It must be something more. Paranoia? No. Schizophrenia? No. Manic depressive, or any one other of a host of mental illnesses? No. This is the Western World and the very foundations of Spengler's aptly found West-European-American Culture. The only hope can be that the X Factor in the above will not destroy the husband as well. Katie, the daughter, is surely doomed.

## THREE OF THE ETIOLOGICAL FACTORS CONDUCIVE TO THE APPEARANCE OF THE X FACTOR IN AMERICAN CULTURE

### NUMBER ONE

The first of these was the assassination of President John F. Kennedy in November of 1963. This can be said to have been the crystallizing factor, the catalyst, or, if you will, the rationalization for much of the spousal unrest that followed. It was driven home to much of the American public for the first time that the effect of an act so cataclysmic could be unbearable. America had already suffered the death of Abraham Lincoln, but at that time the spirit of fortitude in the fact of omnipresent adversity and now lacking in the latter half of the twentieth century, prevailed. For the first time, the American people stumbled on the pathway of its self-confidence. For the first time, America sensed with foreboding that its destinies lay without its own control. How inappropriate became that old aphorism, "No assassination ever changed the course of history." Camelot in the world outside the home had been destroyed by the idiotic actions of one man, or as a large segment of the American public came to believe, by a conspiracy of many. Here was the X Factor as it applied to the man directing his animus against organized society. How frail after all this seemed the ideal of Camelot in the individual household.

It was President Kennedy alone who saw that this the American Culture had lost its sense of purpose and had attempted to restore it, to give it a new and positive meaning. This much can be said of his whole-hearted endorsement of the Peace Corps, that given the same support as rearmament, it could have placed Western Culture back on the path to rejuvenation, or at the very least pointed the way. Many Americans believed at the time of his death and many believe today, that with John F. Kennedy fulfilling his second term, as he was sure to do, and with his brother Robert succeeding him, that there would have been no Viet Nam. Along with contemporaneous unseating of the male in the household, King Arthur as head of the nation of Camelot was dead.

Weep for Ione
Dead the long year.

## NUMBER TWO OF THE POSSIBLE ETIOLOGICAL FACTORS LEADING TO THE X FACTOR

The second of these energizing factors impelling discontent in the family home and leading to the advocacy of permanent separation of the spouses as being the only solution to constant discord, was the rise in America of the expectations of womanhood. Specifically, the emergence of Woman's Liberation as a vivid and vital weapon to effect social change. Not that the demands made upon a largely male-dominated culture for change were to be brought about by gradual, well-considered progressive movement. Rather these demands were presented by highly capable, and one must say, genetically advantaged females in the forefront of the movement. "I want it, and I want it now."

That this strident demand for equality of the sexes was for something more than just bare social change was not at first apparent. The true import was in time to unfold and to present to a largely unaware America that something much more than bare social change was at stake. What was being brought into focus was a cultural upheaval, a desire and an attempt at a cultural revolution. Albeit, this unwittingly.

To drive home the basis for this thesis, it is instructive to note that this West-European Culture had its origins during the latter part of the reign of Charlemagne and following his death, to be more exact, in about the year A.D. 900. As such, it has subsisted, developed, and to receive its final contribution from what America had to offer. This has been a culture brought to fruition and existing for over a thousand years. Spengler holds the apogee of this culture to have been in the time following the Baroque Era and at the specific time when Beethoven wrote his quartets. This would bear dating between 1798 and 1827.

But to digress, this would place the framing and presentation of the American Constitution within this time span. The members of the Continental Congress who conceived this document were men steeped in the history and culture of both the Greek and Roman cultures as well as the Renaissance and the Reformation. These latter already having formed part of the West-European Culture. These were men at home with the thinking of Aristotle, Seneca, Cicero, Dante, Shakespeare, and Martin Luther, to name a very few. They were keenly prescient of the later dictum of Lord Acton:

> Power tends to corrupt; absolute power corrupts absolutely.

These men were also able to foresee Santayana's later caution:

> Those who cannot remember the past, are condemned to repeat it.

Thus they penned what next to the Bible must be the noblest work of man. They provided caution in the changing of the division of powers, both as it related to the political and personal.

To these framers of the Constitution, it was clearly apparent that the relationship of man to woman, the rights and duties of one to the other, had literally been established from the dawn of recorded history. Applying the simple basics, man's duties were threefold: to put a roof over the heads of his family, to put food on the table, and to protect his family from marauding tribes.

Woman's duties were twofold: to give man his pleasure, and the word "pleasure" must be taken in its full, almost generic sense. Amongst other things, it was a man's pleasure that he should receive woman's unquestioning obedience. Secondly, it was woman's duty to raise his children, with the culturally accepted emphasis on the qualifying word, "his."

This historical, and as it came to be, cultural balance in the relationship of man to woman was dictated by the law of necessity; all existence was perilous, be it at the whims of nature or of man. Be that as it may, the dominant fact of male supremacy had been accepted in the West-European Culture for a thousand years, and for all cultures past. Through the years there had been some flashes of insight into the problem of co-existence between the sexes: Chaucer, that most acute delineator of the social scene, described the strange dichotomy that has bedevilled the relationship of man and woman through the ages. In *The Canterbury Tales,* and specifically in "The Wife of Bath's Tale," the young knight when asked to say what it was that woman holds most precious above all else, answers:

> My liege lady, in general, woman wants dominion over her husband as well as her lover, and to be master of them both.

Then too, there is Ibsen and Nora and her strivings and yearnings for a new freedom. Food for thought is Spengler's acid comment:

> Nora is the very type of the provincial derailed by reading (Spengler, p.33).

The problems of the Woman's Liberation Movement and of the proponents of the Equal Rights Amendment to convince the American public that a change in the Constitution is necessary for women to achieve their place in the sun has been carried forth with a stridency worthy of a Messianic mission, and has often led to an unsettlement in a large number of the homes of this nation.

No matter the assertion that change is being sought by peaceful means in a free society. The real import of the demands for these wrenching changes is that of a war of counter-culture, a revolution by way of internecine warfare against one that has subsisted for a thousand years. This culture has dictated the supremacy of the male both as husband in the marital relationship and as *paterfamilias,* that is, as head of the family. What is lacking in the desires and plans of those who advocate such drastic and immediate change is the ability to spell out what of value is to be substituted for that culture that has given so much of value.

What fails to be reconciled is the force of Victor Hugo's illuminating statement:

> A revolution is an idea whose time has come

with the equally incisive:

> All revolutions devour their young.

The pursuit of *Liberté, Egalité, Fraternité* in the French Revolution gave vent to the cry:

> O Liberty, what sins are committed in thy name.

In Russia there was substituted for the dream of a new day dawning for the working classes, the dictatorship of the proletariat.

How inappropriate it would be in this largely democratic, tolerant and free society:

> What this country needs is a benevolent dictator. Make me dictator and I'll be benevolent for six months. Then heads will roll.

The decline of the West-European-American Culture as predetermined by Spengler has already commenced with agonizing reality. The rise of the single-parent phenomenon, and in the main of the female single parent, will, with a certainty produce eventual havoc in this country that may well be uncontrollable. In the offspring of the female single parent could conceivably be sown the seeds of the potential Baader-Meinhoffs in this country. Then it may well come true that:

> The barbarians may yet cross the river and topple Rome.

It is not the bare fact of the emergence of the single female parent, or the approbation and indeed almost sanctification by a goodly portion of this social order of the eighties, that should cause concern. Rather it is her alienation from the Culture of the West and, most important, of the alienation of the daughters from what has always been one of the stabilizing factors in the girl-child's life, the father figure.

A further destructive element injected into the behaviour pattern of this country has been the unwavering pursuit of the Liberation's movement in the championing of the absolute of women in choosing to consider the using of their own bodies as they will in an unfettered and absolute manner, this obviously in regard to the matter of abortion on demand. At law, this was first established in the landmark decision of the Supreme Court in *Roe v. Wade* in the early seventies, and followed in June of 1983 wherein was held with greater force that the individual states might not tamper with these rights at will.

It is not the physical act of the performance of the abortion itself that gives offense to this country's social structure as a part of Western Culture, but under the guise of "planned parenthood" a euphemistic and hypocritical approach at its most charitable. What is repugnant is the sanctification by operation of law of the right of any woman to engage in an idle act of sexual intercourse (that which in Yiddish would be called a *shtoop* with all the accompanying curl of the lip in an opprobrious manner sufficient to the act thereof) with no regard to this action's effect on the social order as a whole. Here is seen the current social disease, the instant-gratification syndrome: "I want sexual intercourse and I want it now; I want relief from the consequences of my action, and I want it now."

The primate ape has the banana and must eat it now. The ape is unable to resist instant gratification and unable to defer this present gratification for future benefit. It has long been held as sacred that the human being, higher in the evolutionary scale, is able to discriminate. That any person, male or female, should be held liable for his or her actions, has long been one of the fundamental concepts of this our present culture.

More to the point and leading to the production of the X Factor in our Culture is the utter demeaning of the role of the male with respect to woman's relationship in this act of conception. The result is to refute the role of the male in such a vital segment of human activity.

If any comfort may be derived from the conclusion that the onward drive of the Women's Movement is without regard to the social and cultural consequences, then it might be conceivably found in the words uttered lately, and perhaps too late, of Betty Friedan, one of the gurus of Liberation:

> The author of *The Feminine Mystique*, which became the bible of the woman's movement in North America during its growth in the 1960's, said recently new problems have surfaced distorting what was intended in the first stages of that movement. Betty Friedan said in an interview

that in the dedication to bring equality to women "we almost threw the baby out with the bath water" and put feminism in conflict with the family. Friedan said that the "four square" unit of father, mother and two children now is in the minority in the U.S. and 83 percent of the population is living in different forms of families (Report of an interview *Canadian Press,* April 7, 1981).

To confess error is perhaps noble. But the consequences of the unforeseeability of what Betty Friedan and her associates initiated are incalculable. As Von Moltke said in another context:

> All war plans disintegrate with the firing of the first shot.

The firing of the first shot in this context was the unexpected and uncontrolled onrush of technology, which has made such a vast proportion of the populace, both male and female, surplus to the establishment. Because of this machine and electronic advance in technology, an even greater percentage of teenagers find themselves with no viable role to play in this twentieth-century world. The now liberated women and men are now competing in the marketplace for the same right to attain and maintain this vital role. This, of course, to the hazard and detriment of the male, the father figure, who formerly was granted the role, almost in its entirety, of the breadwinner. Hence has come a further destabilizing factor in the American family unit.

## NUMBER THREE OF THE ETIOLOGICAL PROBLEMS LEADING TO THE X FACTOR

By the end of the decade of the nineteen-sixties, and well into the nineteen-seventies, and running parallel to the first two of the etiological factors already postulated, America was beginning to reap the whirlwind of a great technological advance that had promised to be such a boon and great step forward for mankind. This country was leading the world in the development and application of all phases of this monumental discovery, namely, television. Of all the factors conducive to the emergence of the X Factor, it can be advanced with some degree of credulity that none was more pervasive and conducive to the destruction of the nuclear family than this, the greatest of the technical hopes of the postwar world. The good that television was capable of performing was not interred with its bones. It has been said the influence of the early Walt Disney shows contributed greatly to the reduction of cruelty to animals in France.

To the rest of the world without exception, America represented the attaining of Paradise, not unlike the Moslem and his *hegira* to Mecca. Where else were the streets paved with gold, and where else could the labourer and peasant rub shoulders in equality with the aristocrat? The largesse and abundance, which had for so long excited the interest and desires of the other world, now became visible to all. American social and political institutions, surely serving their own people better elsewhere in the world, were now vividly illuminated visually and audibly, surely all of great benefit to all mankind.

Americans knew all these great things about themselves and did not need reminding of the greatness of their social and political institutions. What America wanted to see and hear was the portrayal of a slice of the real America. Insidiously, and "by stealth and guile," through what had become its most influential media, America got what it wanted to believe was an accurate portrayal of itself.

Newton Minow's description, in fact condemnation, of television as "a vast wasteland" was surely misapplied. Instead, it was a garden overproductive of rank and foul growth that in its insidious fashion seeped into the minds of the American families.

When the state of the human mind enters the picture, it is well to pause and consider the modern psychiatric approach and attitudes to the three etiological factors being under discussion. Too often the psychiatrist misses the forest for the trees, zeroing in on individual minutiae and giving little or no consideration to the total social cultural picture.

It is at this juncture that the person of Karl Kraus leaps to mind. He was that well-known pre-World War I rabble-rouser, who through his publication, *The Torch,* carried on an enormous feud with Sigmund Freud. Although he died at the height of his powers in Vienna in 1936, his name lives. Not too long ago Princeton University announced a complete republication of *The Torch.* But, whatever else he might have accomplished, he immortalized himself in two magnificent quotations, the first of which was,

> Psychiatry is the sickness of which it purports to be the cure.

This, as one might say, "pointed barb," when presented to a seminar of a psychiatric association produced among the assembled members a mass hysteria amounting almost to paranoia.

However, these psychiatrists might have taken comfort and sought succour in the statement of the New York psychiatrist who preferred to attain his immortality through anonymity:

> We are all of us a little paranoid; if we were not we would be mentally ill.

Of much more pungent interest and more apposite in describing the three etiological factors leading to the crisis of the X Factor, is Karl

Kraus's strikingly forceful aphorism, which surely cries out for a hundred doctoral theses to be written upon:

> Western society may yet destroy itself through the lies of its newspapers.

Substitute the word "culture" for the word "society," and making allowances for the onrush of Western technology in the twentieth century, add to the word "newspapers" the words "radio and television," those parts of the media, as it is called today, then unknown to Karl Kraus, and the indictment proffered by Karl Kraus, is damning alone without conviction.

To return to that slice of real American life promised by television, under the guise of fun, frolic, and hilarity, television accomplished in a few short years that which a thousand years of West-European, and of late American Culture had never envisaged, and which, when any signs of such had ever risen, had been extirpated with vigour and ruthlessness. This was the utter denigration of the male in the household and the final emasculation of the father figure. Emasculation firstly as a husband, and then as the father. Day after day and evening after evening, as with a Pavlovian reaction, the repetition of the situation comedies did its insidious job.

To name some, "My Little Margie," "Father Knows Best," "I Love Lucy," "I Married Joan," "The Honeymooners," "The Flintstones," "Our Miss Brooks," "Blondie," and others too numerous to mention. In each of these situation comedies, what was portrayed was not comedy at all, but almost with a manic and persistent force, a relentless attack on everything that smacked of male competence and authority. The father, or the male figure, was portrayed as a bumbling fool with an IQ just barely above the idiot level. In program after program, the American family was subjected to a brutal onslaught on the father, or the male figurehead. The male, who in the dynamism of world cultures, had been granted the authority as head of the household, as head of the tribe, as head of every nation and empire, was now relegated to being the pawn and moved from square to square with all the compliance of an automaton, all this accomplished by the genetically enabled "little woman," be she wife or associate.

These so-called comedies joined together with the intense interest in all forms of sport and other recreational activity tended to propel the competence of the American male out of the home into macho land. No more Kiplings:

> The flanneled fool at the wicket—the muddied oaf at the goal.

The World Series, football and hockey, golf on Saturdays and Sundays, moving from green to green from coast to coast, tennis as it follows the sunbelts of the world; and Grand Prix auto racing with its grease-stained heroes catering to the American male's great love affair with his automobile, all combine to rivet the attention of the family to television. So father again is displayed as an impotent, bumbling, Monday-morning quarterback, not the head of a neat, cosy, tightly knit interdependent family group, as in the past—a victim of Spengler's *panem et circenses.*

For the woman at home, there were in profusion what at first were called soap-operas, reduced in nomenclature to "soaps." Name some of them if you will: "Mary Hartman," "All My Children," "One Life to Live," "Edge of Night," "As the World Turns," "Guiding Light," and now latterly "Dynasty" and "Dallas."

Are these shows watched? (Editor's interjection. Does Dolly Parton sleep on her back?) If so, who are attracted to them and why? The many years that these productions have survived, as attested to by the results of the Neilsen polls and others, have confirmed their constant and abiding popularity. Who are the viewers? Of course these attractions are placed commencing at or about the noon hour and for most of the afternoons. The main person thus caught on the sticky paper of our times is the "little wife" at home. What is it that so attracts a goodly and great percentage of the female population of America? In a negative sense, she tarries little over the wiles and machinations of the villainesses; she worries about the schemes and seductiveness of the "other woman"; she knows that these things are happening to her neighbour and not to her. But in a positive sense, that with which she identifies is the suffering of the "good" woman with whom she has total empathy. She sits as if mesmerized and accepts the ultimate triumph of the "good" woman in the redemption through love. Whose love? Why, of course, the love of the good woman—herself. To whom does she now turn to share her feeling of unredeemed love? To her daughter (or daughters) naturally. The cultural pattern has ordained that the young impressionable daughter should return home after school, to be the helpmate of the mother in the home. What better for the mother to seek solace and comfort in a binding of her to the daughter, only too ready to absorb from her own mother a slice of "real life" in her own family, a soap opera not of strangers but of those nearest and dearest to her.

Daddy has already, by the situation comedies, been relegated to the role of the buffoon, and now by the even more pervasive "soaps" to the person who denies "love" to mother, and by his very position in this seemingly tightly knit family, to the daughter herself.

Slowly, but surely, Daddy has vicariously now abandoned his daughter. Certainly, this is not the case of every American family, this would amount to an absurdity, but it is true in an increasingly significant percentage. This transference of abandonment has now enveloped through the sixties and seventies and now in the eighties, the second generation of daughters. In the minds of a significant portion of the homes of this country, what commenced by a persistent stimulation to the imagination, has now in that receptive mind become a reality. Paranoia, and mental illness? No. The X Factor to which this introduction leads. *To the Finland Station,* if you will. Edmond Wilson, that giant of American letters, writes of Lenin, in Switzerland as an exile from his native Russia, and having in 1909 written his revolutionary tract *Cho Delat—What Is to Be Done?"* and how? The beleaguered forces of the Central Powers that were Germany and Austria; they and their allies had brought Lenin from Switzerland across the continent in a sealed train and there willingly, as the author of their own destruction, had deposited Lenin at the Finland Station in St. Petersburg, with what incalculable results only history has been able to show.

## THE AMERICAN DILEMMA DELINEATED

In the foregoing there have been shown three factors that could be said to lead to the confrontation of American culture amounting to, in fact, a cultural dilemma. There are no doubt many other contributing factors and of which any social scientist will pick his or her favourite to add to the list. When we deal with the first of these factors, that is, the assassination of President Kennedy in November of 1963, America has this dilemma. By the Constitution it is believed and been held that every American is entitled to bear arms, and every American does so. Perhaps this is an overstatement, but is in a great sense true. To avoid each citizen's right to carry arms would mean a Constitutional amendment; not only is America chary of doing this, but in fact present political trends obviate any possibility of success. The assassination following of Robert Kennedy, of Martin Luther King, the attempted assassination of President Ford, and again of President Reagan, all point to an uncontrollable factor in American life. If such violence is to be controlled in the United States of America, then, say the proponents of gun control, the Constitution must be amended to prevent weapons falling into the average citizen's hands. And of course the proponents of gun control say in their way that guns kill, people don't, and would leave this up to the untrammelled American spirit to decide. Again, for the first instance, a truly American cultural dilemma.

The dilemma presented by the second of the etiological factors mentioned above once again becomes an internecine struggle in the scene of the American Culture. American Culture has held, throughout its history, that the male is the head of the household without any mistake. The struggle now to amend the Constitution to include the Equal Rights Amendment and the striving of women for equality, let alone superiority, now places the dilemma four square before the American people. America represents a free and open society in which any man may compete with his neighbour for his right to exist and now, increasingly so, men and women are placed on an equal footing to compete in the marketplace for employment, greatly strictured through the advent of technology and leaving men and women . . .

America, being a free and open society, has this dilemma to face; therefore it is this culture to throw its enormous weight of government and organized society against the onrush of the expectations of womanhood for equality or superiority and thus attempt to return to the *status quo ante,* a truly American dilemma.

With respect to the third of the etiological factors developed above, the cultural dilemma is even more and most pointed. Once again it must be stressed that America is a free and open society, its newspapers are protected by the Constitution of the land, the right to self-expression can be abridged only in the most drastic cases, and of course the media as a whole has an almost unchallenged right to exert its own influence as it sees fit in a free and open society. The dilemma is here, even if it can be shown conclusively that the results of absolute liberty in publication and in the operation of the media as a whole are affecting adversely American society and American culture; will America attempt to take a stand in this free and open society to do that which is tending to draw that same society into a state of decay? On the contrary, present political trends in the United States lean to deregulation, even of the media, and the allowing of the free-enterprise media to conduct itself with complete liberty, or as some might say, licence. Truly an American dilemma.

It should here be noted that these onslaughts on western culture in recent history, and these three major American social phenomena—the assassination of national father figures, the development of women's liberation movements, and the media denigration of the role of father—are all part of the multifactorial etiology of the rising divorce rate in America. They have provided the setting for the operation of a newly here-described "X Factor"—the psychopathic wife in the marital holocaust. However, they are all significant factors leading to the destruction of marriage and family life, the foundation of western culture since its inception, and contribute to the ultimate tragedy, the dissolution of the nuclear family.

## SCENARIO NUMBER ONE

Father and daughter, sitting in the den viewing television, father obviously harried by the recurring thoughts of the day's struggle for existence, daughter hyped up by what she has just seen on the tube. Phone rings, daughter answers:

> "Hi, kiddo, what you been doing? Watching the Mary Tyler Moore show. Me too. Hey great, huh? That's one smart gal. Yeah. She really

put those stupid clowns in their place. She really showed them which end was up. Who's here? My father? What does he think about that cute MTM? Oh, him? Who pays any attention to what he thinks?"

Father, feeling goaded beyond restraint, pummels daughter about the face: "Who cares what I think? What I do around here isn't good enough? I'll teach you."

Mother, nursing her own grievances, real or imagined, reports father to the police. Provocation no defense to assault. Cruelty to child, equally cruelty to mother. End of nuclear family. End of family.

## SCENARIO NUMBER TWO

Divorce lawyer and female client in his office.

"Madam, for over an hour, I have been trying to get from you what was the cause of the break-up of your marriage. All I can get from you is a long list of nebulous dissatisfactions. In fact, you sound to me precisely like a scenario of any one of a dozen soap operas on TV. You talk to me like running soap opera dialogue."

"Sir, I don't even know what soap operas are. I never watch television during the daytime."

"Madam, in all the years I have been sitting here, I have never yet heard one woman admit to watching daytime television. Surely, if this is true, then the advertisers are seriously misled. But never mind that, what about your kids, and especially the girls in the home?"

"Sir, they hate him so much that they wish he would just go away. They don't even think that he is their father. They ignore him like a stranger."

"Madam, what about the girls? How are they doing?"

"Sir, I am having a little trouble with them. I know they are bringing home things they don't pay for. But they are only small things, so it really doesn't matter, does it?"

If indeed it can be accepted that the three etiological factors discussed are in fact operating as a cancer in the body politic, feeding on itself and growing as if it were a nuclear reaction, then how is America to resolve this American cultural dilemma to at any stage limit the growth of the destabilization of the American family? It is instructive to look backward to the times when the West-European Culture was in its infancy, to the Middle Ages to be specific, where we can see the reaction of society to any menace to its cultural balance.

In the blind passion with which people followed their Lord or their party, the unshakeable sentiment of right, characteristic of the Middle Ages, is trying to find expression. Man at that time was convinced that right is absolutely fixed and certain. Justice prosecutes the unjust everywhere and to the end. . . . The chronic insecurity made the possible severity on the part of the public authorities desirable; crime to be

> regarded as a menace to order in society, as well as an insult to divine majesty. . . . The popular sense of justice always sanctioned the most rigorous penalties. (J. Huizinga, *The Waning of the Middle Ages* [New York: Doubleday & Company, 1924; Anchor Books Edition, 1954.])

To protect any inroads to the culture as it was conceived at that time, society was prepared to go the ultimate limit.

In this regard it would be most instructive to have a fresh look at what has been considered the rigors of Victorian morality. The determination that attended the prosecution of Oscar Wilde can be viewed in a new light as a successful effort to bring to an end the defiance of a settled cultural pattern, the genius of Oscar Wilde notwithstanding. Homosexuality, once exposed to public scrutiny, was not a form of conduct to be tolerated by this culture, steeped in the biblical concept of such conduct and carried over into the West-European Culture as an abomination.

So too may be viewed the outcome of the Charles Parnell-Kitty O'Shea "scandal." Such conduct as the master-mistress relationship was tolerated behind the locked doors of the Victorian scene, but not so when exposed to public scrutiny, and when such conduct was employed by those such as Parnell, sworn to uphold all those tenets of that culture.

This however, cannot be the way of the late twentieth century. This is not the American way. This then, to recapitulate, is the dilemma of the West-European-American Culture, of which America is, in the world today, the most prominent and influential member. How can this country cope with the onslaught of the X Factor, which is doing so much to destabilize the American nuclear family, the bulwark of this, our present culture?

## THE X FACTOR DELINEATED

In the early part of the decade of the seventies, there began to appear on the divorce scene something quite new, quite startling and quite alien from the hitherto accepted rationale of divorce. For the first time, a significant number of spouses, having experienced extremely short marriages, i.e., one to five years, began clamouring for relief from, as they felt, the shackles of matrimony. With the wives, the initial and glibly facile approach was the time honoured, "I just don't love him anymore"; however, underneath this flippant statement, there is a new phenomenon, first described here as the main theme of this book: the emergence of the female psychopath onto the modern marital scene.

## SCENARIO NUMBER THREE

> "Look, young lady, you have been married for just over a year and you want a divorce. Tell me why. You know, in some many years in

dealing with these problems, I have never yet heard of any bride dragged kicking and screaming to the altar. Were you any different?"

"Well, I thought I liked the guy and my mother kept telling me I should get out of our home and the only answer seemed to be to get married. I let him get into my pants before the big day, if you know what I mean. He thought that was the greatest thing since the Green Bay Packers won the championship. I told him I had a couple of different guys already. You are kind of muttering under your breath at me, aren't you? You want to know why I had to leave home. Well, I'll tell you that that place was no bed of roses, believe me. It was a hell hole. All I can really remember was my mother and father screaming bloody blue murder at one another from early morning to late at night. Almost always my mother doing the honours. What did my father do? He would mostly just sit there time after time, saying over and over, "Jesus Christ, Jesus Christ, Jesus Christ, what do you want of me, what do you want?" Well, you asked, did I ever find out what she wanted? No, I never did. I never could figure out what went on between them in the bedroom. You know, I kinda liked him a lot, and he always tried to steer this uproar away from me. I never had much time with him. I know he really cared for me. What's that you say, love me? Yeah, I guess he did. He used to buy me everything I wanted, I guess to make up for what I really wanted. What did I really want? I wanted him to love me so I knew it, so when I married this guy I figured he would hold me and cuddle me and be like my father should have been. All this guy wanted to do was roll me into bed. The whole thing left me cold. Sometimes I would let him and sometimes I wouldn't. He'd go ape. Sure, I shouted at him a lot. Well, my mother did to my Daddy. That would get him so upset he wouldn't try to screw me. He kept telling that I was making his life one hell on earth. Well, my father put up with it, so what was the big deal? I see you are putting your head in your hands. Don't you believe me? What do you mean?

With the husband, the victim of this type of marriage, the approach and the reaction was much different. Inarticulate, completely shorn of all those traits one commonly expects in a man's figure, stripped of any self-confidence, and seemingly emasculated.

## SCENARIO NUMBER FOUR

Excerpted from original, raw and unedited.

After granted a divorce from my first wife, somewhere around 1969—with whom I had six children—the divorce was granted on the basis of alcoholism and fooling around on her part. I was alone for about six to seven years. In 1971 I took a trip to Europe, going from one country I landed in Finland where I met my second wife. We wrote to each other for three years or so. She wanted to come over, so I sent her the ticket. Five and a half months later, we were married. December 1975, I believe. Now most of my kids had left home except the youngest daughter, Paulie—her observation—I did not know the girl (would you believe on our honeymoon in Hawaii she went on a moonlight cruise by herself), the day before we left (before the wedding) the boys had a stag for me. I had little sleep for days. After the third day in that sun, I had to get some sleep. I cut the trip short, was going to try and get the wedding annulled, but I can't stand a crying woman so after two weeks of that I agreed to try it again. Assets in 1975 were about one million to one and a half million dollars. We did extensive travelling to Arizona every winter. Florida, Mexico, Hawaii. She took two boys by herself to Finland. By the way, when my wife, Eila, first came from Finland she could not speak English, she could not drive a car, she could not even boil water. Now she can do all that stuff 'cause I taught her. My daughter Paulie told me, when she was about fourteen years old, "Don't marry that woman, all she wants is your money" (out of the mouths of babes—should've listened). Bought her a used car first, then a new Chrysler. I found out from her she was a painter. I took back two loads of picture frames for her from Mexico. I encouraged her as much as possible and spoiled her ass off. Gave her everything she wanted. She never wanted anything to do with my kids. The two years Paulie was home she wanted to board her out. One thing for the very first time we talked serious. She was told I drank a little (I met her in a bar where there was dancing), how many kids I had and so on, that I did not want any more kids. Her answer, "I don't either." I was honest with her right from the start, but she could somehow make a mistake and blame me for it. I would let it go because of the language barrier. Maybe it doesn't matter, but I never did cheat on her once until after the agreement was made out. Yeah, she put me on rations several times. She would always be away all day and so would I. I would ask her how her day was for conversation sake, she would say, "None of your business." First time she cut me off for over two weeks, so when I'd ask her and tried every which way, no dice. I didn't think it would work but tried it anyway, I said, "How about if I give you two hundred dollars if we go to bed right now?"—Okay—she had her hand out. I paid her and very serious about it. She was in bed before me. She did help a boyfriend just before I met her, through seven years of law—as soon as he got his ticket he dumped her. I got her on the rebound. There is no doubt in my mind she is a fantasy dreamer, a split personality. She would like to be single and have all the security of married life. This isn't a compliment to myself, but at a party friends would say, "Where in the hell did you get her?" I must have been hard up. Back to business here in 1975. We were living in about a seventeen-room home in Walnut Gove (I built for my first wife, worth about $250,000). One and a half years after, she made me sell it in a hurry for $98,000 on two and a half acres of land, landscaped. Sold too soon, I did not want to sell at all. She did have a slick way of intimidating me, she can in fact make me do things I did not want to do, for instance, she wanted to go someplace special and wanted me to drive, she would map out the day with a carrot on the end or put words in my mouth. You might say she had seven years of law and had me buffaloed. The last time she went to Finland by herself was three years ago on the 14th of June and arrived back on the 1st of July. She seemed changed even more so. We had a little trip up the coast by land, back by sea. We fought and scrapped all the way. Then she moved out across the highway into a little shack owned by another couple. She stayed there one year approximately, then came crying to me, the stove doesn't work, there's not enough water, it's too cold. By that time I was going nuts so to save what little sanity I had left, I thought I had better get to work, so I bought that big turkey upstate, that motor inn, put a down payment on a house up there and moved up.

Back to Walnut Grove now, where the wife was bitching and crying so yours truly can't stand a woman to cry too—"Would you like to move back in the house?" I asked her, so she did, so it has been on again, off again. So the next thing she says to me when we were getting back together again, when I told her I am sure I am going to lose everything, so she said to me, "You better help me get my money out of this house, and then we'll take whatever money is left and we'll go and buy a nice smaller house and I'll be the best wife you have ever seen." (I though, why wasn't she this good a wife before?) Then I said, "Okay, so I help you get whatever money we can and buy the house you want, tell me, will my name go on half of it?" "Oh no," she says, "no way." "Well," I said, "I guess that's it, isn't it? You son-of-a-witch, go and take a flying fuck at yourself!" and I grabbed my bags and walked out.

Not only did I lose one million since I married Eila, I lost at least a million more since because I was a 75 to 100 year man. I am not saying it was all her fault because I did go down the aisle and said "I do." You know the funny part is, I asked her if she would sign an agreement to read that I promised to leave her the house and $50,000 before we married. She said in broken English, "I will not sign anything," and old loverboy says its okay. "Darling, we will marry anyway" (Shit). I don't think I could do it again or would want to. Despite her hostile position, I have been taking her groceries this last winter and spring, up to a few days ago. I still have the key to the house which she gave me back last November. When she wasn't home I checked inside the house, not a thing in the fridge so I'd load her up with groceries and I would have to put them through the window because she would give me shit for bringing them. She would say, "Don't bring me any more groceries, I want the money," screaming. At the same time she wouldn't have enough for a church mouse in the fridge.

To the people she liked she was nice to. Butter wouldn't melt in her mouth and I love this woman very much, enough for allowing things to such a state where I went broke, hoping she would change. She always treated me like I didn't know how to tie my own shoelaces. She brought a total of $1,800 cash into the marriage, I helped it grow to about $10,000. I didn't keep any of her money.

## THE END OF SCENARIO NUMBER FOUR: LOVE'S LABOUR LOST OR THE TYRANNY OF SEX

"Look, you wretched man, you tell me that you got yourself a legal separation in December of 1980. I know that you are not telling me the whole story. Now, just what has been going on?"

"Lawyer, I'll tell you. I have been seeing her, all right. I can't stay away from her. What do I mean seeing her? Well, every time I go over there, she tells me how she needs me and grabs me into bed. How often? Well, I've figured it out like—1981 February two times,

March four times
April three times
May four times
August through October steady
December three times

1982— January two times
February two times
March four times
April four times
May through September steady
September three times
October four times

"Lawyer, you think I'm crazy, eh?"

## SCENARIO FIVE

The following scenario was reviewed with Dr. Reid and so excited his interest that he made a copy to present to his Symposium of Psychiatrics held at Cambridge University at England at the end of August 1983 and elicit from Dr. Reid the comment "A True Psychopath."

A. He went up there a week or two before I went.
Q. Ma'am, are you trying to tell this jury that you just happened on him in some town in Michigan?
A. No, I did not go with him. Your question was, did I go with him.
Q. All right. Let me rephrase it for you. Did you and old Tom have some specific discussions with each other as to where he would be and where you would be and where you all would meet?
A. Yes.
Q. Okay. Now, let's get back to your suggestion concerning role-modeling for a minute. Do you think it is a good role model for someone who is married to be having sexual relations with someone else prior to the time that they are divorced?
A. I would like you to restate that, please.
Q. All right. Do you think it is good role modeling for a married woman to have sexual relations with someone who is not her husband?
A. I am not married.
Q. You are not?
A. No.
Q. We are all wasting our time down here in Lincoln, I guess?
A. Uh-huh.
Q. I thought there was a pending divorce action here.

A. We are only married on paper. We have not been married many months.
Q. Oh. I see. In your mind, you are not married?
A. That is correct.
Q. Oh. Okay. Well, have you had an opportunity to discuss with your lawyer the fact that you are in fact married?
A. Only on paper.
Q. Only on paper, I see. Okay. Well, when did the marriage end in your mind?
A. It ended when he left for Saudi in October.
Q. Okay. So, in your mind, you were divorced in October?
A. For all practical purposes, yes.
Q. Okay. Now, do you believe that the institution of marriage is important in this country?
A. Yes.
Q. And there are certain vows and other things you do when you get married, is that right?
A. Yes.
Q. And you agree that you are not going to go out and have sexual relations with folks who aren't your husband or wife or what have you, don't you?
A. Yes.
Q. And children at the age of nine, ten, around that age, are fairly impressionable, aren't they? Have you learned that at your school?
A. Yes.
Q. And do you think it is a good modeling role for a mother of a nine-year-old little girl to be out having sexual intercourse with folks she is not married to?
A. Rephrase the question, please.

Mr. Long: Read it back, please.

Court Reporter: Question:

"and do you think it is a good modeling role for a mother of a nine-year-old little girl to be out having sexual intercourse with folks she is not married to?"

The Witness: That depends.

Q. On what?
A. On presence or absence of the child.
Q. Okay. I take it then from your statement it is all right to have sexual relations with anybody as long as the children are not present?
A. Well, qualify "anybody." That doesn't belong in the question.
Q. All right. I take it then from your statement that it is all right in your opinion for a woman to have sexual intercourse with a man who she is not married to so long as her nine-year-old girl is not present?
A. Yes.
Q. And is that the way that you intend to counsel and guide these folks that you are going to counsel and guide up there in Montana?
A. I can't answer that with a yes or a no.
Q. Is that the way you are going to counsel and guide your little girl, Norma?
A. I have separated my needs from her needs. Okay?

Q. But the question is—
A. No, I can't answer it with a yes or no. My needs have been separated from her needs. I do not have Norma present when my boyfriend comes to see me.
Q. I am going to ask you one more time. Do you intend to counsel and guide Norma that it is all right for a woman to have sexual intercourse with a man to whom she is not married so long as her children are not present?
A. No, I am no going to counsel Norma that way.
Q. Okay. And do you still maintain that your values are better than Doctor Johnson's?
A. Definitely.
Q. Okay. Thank you. Where were you on Mother's Day?
A. I can't remember.
Q. You weren't here, were you?
A. I can't remember.
Q. Well, did you have a fun, enjoyable sort of day with your child or children on Mother's Day?
A. John had the children, as I recall.
Q. Do you know when Mother's Day was?
A. Yes, it was sometime in May, and I recall that John had the children.
Q. And--
A. I am sure that he did.
Q. And do you recall a discussion that he had with you where he asked you if you would like them or if you would give him a telephone number or anything so that they could talk to you and be with you on Mother's Day?
A. I was at the apartment, as a matter of fact, and I phoned the children, because I talked with Norma that afternoon.
Q. Are you sure about that?
A. And in fact, I called my son long distance—or my son called me long distance that same afternoon from Omaha, up north.
Q. Well, were you with Tom on Mother's Day?
A. No, I was at home at my apartment.
Q. By youself?
A. Pardon?
Q. By youself just sitting there?
A. I can't really remember, but I was at the apartment because I remember my son calling from Omaha, and I remember calling Norma.
Q. Have you and old Tom discussed whether or not you intend to get married when this case is over?
A. Yes, we have discussed it.
Q. What did you say to him?
A. Yes, I want to marry him.
Q. Okay. How long has Tom been a geologist?
A. He has worked in geology for a good ten years up in Michigan.
Q. Has he ever been arrested for anything?
A. No.
Q. You know that yourself?
A. We are certainly open enough in our communication that he would have told me.

Q. Okay. Are there a lot of opportunities for geologists in Helena, Montana?
A. I really don't know.
Q. Does Tom pretty much agree that he is going to go to Helena with you?
A. Yes.
Q. Live in your house?
A. Probably.
Q. Well, what kind of activities has Tom been involved in with the children?
A. He has been involved on with Norma.
Q. What has he and Norma—
A. And specifically—
Q. Excuse me. What have he and Norma done together?
A. Norma, Tom, and I have gone out for dinner on a few occasions.
Q. How many?
A. Three, that I can remember.
Q. Where did you all go?
A. Within Lincoln.
Q. Whereabouts?
A. At the Peking Chinese restaurant, the Italian restaurant over on Central Boulevard, and we have gone to the Dubrille Playhouse.
Q. The three of you all?
A. Yes.
Q. And what kind of relationship does old Tom have with Norman?
A. Norman doesn't know about him.
Q. Are you at all concerned about what kind of relationship they might have if this jury appoints you the managing conservator of the child?
A. Yes.
Q. Or is he just going to be at boarding school and it doesn't matter?
Q. Why hasn't old Tom met Norman?
A. I didn't think this was the time to introduce him.
Q. How come?
A. Because I have been keeping a low profile. I didn't really want to go advertising around town that I am going out with someone at this time.
Q. Okay. Did you in fact write Doctor Johnson's name on a check and cash it for payments made out to him?
A. Yes, I did.
Q. And did you give the money to Doctor Johnson that you cashed?
A. No, I did not.
Q. And you feel it is just all right to write somebody's name on a check that is not your name and cash the check?
A. I forgot to endorse it with my name as well.
Q. Just forget to?
A. I just forgot to, because on some of the checks, I did as well write my name on the checks to cash it. He left me with no money. What else could I do?
Q. Now, Ma'am, you know he paid the mortgage, didn't he?
A. He paid the mortgage.
Q. And he paid the utilities, didn't he?

A. Not adequately.
Q. Not adequately and he made the repairs.

## THE MANOR

*Isaac Bashevis Singer*

*Clara walked on. Whenever she had fallen in love, bad luck had always followed, bringing vexation, complications, and misunderstandings.*

*There are people who must hurt themselves. It's hard to understand why they do it.*

## WHAT IS THE X FACTOR?

The X Factor is that which is destroying a considerable portion of Western nuclear families—a previously largely unrecognized phenomenon, THE FEMALE PSYCHOPATH.

It should again be noted that these onslaughts on western culture in recent history, and these three major American social phenomena—the assassination of national father figures, the development of women's liberation movements, and the media denigration of the role of father—are all part of the multi-factorial etiology of the rising divorce rate in America. They have provided the setting for the operation of a newly here-described "X Factor"—the psychopathic wife in the marital holocaust. However, they are all significant factors leading to the destruction of marriage and family life, the foundation of western culture since its inception, and contribute to the ultimate tragedy, the dissolution of the nuclear family.

The remainder of this book will address itself to the problem of the female psychopath as she wreaks her havoc on the American family, destroying her chief victim, the husband and effectively crippling the children. This is the first definitive study of the female psychopath in her natural milieu, the American family.

# II

# THE PSYCHOPATH: CHARACTERISTICS AND DISCUSSION

No discussion can be given to the psychopath nor can the subject be dealt with in any depth at all without first referring to the true pioneer in the study of psychopathy, Dr. Hervey Cleckley. Dr. Cleckley's monument is *The Mask of Sanity,* first published in 1941 and the fifth edition published in 1976. It is fair to say that with the publication of the first edition in 1941, there was felt a tremendous impact coast to coast in the United States because for the first time Dr. Cleckley had presented a detailed study of the workings of the psychopath in modern American society. Not only that, he defined and illustrated and characterized the psychopath so that there could be no doubt that this almost separate class of individual did exist, and does exist, in American society. The question abides, what is a psychopath, and how does one tell a psychopath? Perhaps the most succinct and obviously too simplistic definition of a psychopath is purely and simply "rebel without a cause." Dr. Cleckley himself accepts, it would seem, this almost aphorism as a suitable guidemark for the singling out of the psychopath. (See Hervey Cleckley, M.D., *The Mask of Sanity,* Fifth Edition, St. Louis: The C. V. Mosby Company, 1976, p. 405.) This succinct definition, although not totally pertinent to the work in *The Mask of Sanity,* which deals almost in its entirety with the male psychopath, will be seen to be of much greater force and validity when dealing with the female psychopath. From world literature perhaps there is one paragraph more than any other that seems to hold husbands caught in an almost hopeless web of the psychopathic wife, from *The Manor,* by Isaac Bashevis Singer, at page 243,

> Although Calman worked hard (expenses had increased exorbitantly), he slept fitfully. Who would have imagined they could spend so much? Clara lived like an empress, flinging money about, ordering people around. Before the marriage, she had bought a queenly trousseau, and her closets were filled with clothes and accessories, but as soon as the wedding was over she complained she had nothing to wear. She screamed at the maids and constantly criticized the kosher cook Calman had brought from Warsaw. When she wanted the smallest

> thing, she yanked the bellpull. All her whims and her passions for luxury were indulged, yet she never stopped complaining. The meat was either too tough or too tender, the soup too fat or too watery, the compote too sweet or too sour. Although the floors shone so brightly that Calman thanked God each day that he didn't slip, Clara insisted they were dirty. She lied so much and made so many accusations that Calman could hardly believe his ears. He knew wicked people existed; where else did wars come from, or the calamities that had befallen the Jews? But for a Jewish daughter to know so much about sin! Her words of endearment were mixed with derision. She mocked Calman's beard, his long copote, his prayer shawl, his praying, and his habitual "God Willing." She would speak to him affectionately and then address him as a stranger.

Many men, reading that one page from Singer's work, would without hesitation remark almost unanimously, "My God, that's my wife." However, it can be said now that psychopathy does not concern itself with mental illness, but rather with a character defect. The psychopath is not within the purview of the psychiatrist in general. The psychiatrist, of course, is a medical doctor and being a medical doctor a psychiatrist is interested only in that of which there can be a cause and is only interested in that which he can cure. The problem vis-à-vis the psychiatrist and the psychopath is that there is no known cause of the psychopath and there is of a certainty no cure for the psychopath. The psychiatrist washes his hands of the psychopath if in fact the psychiatrist does recognize a psychopath and will have little or nothing to do with him. The few psychiatrists who have dealt in depth with the problem of psychopaths, such as Dr. Cleckley and others who have followed in his footsteps, have devoted their careers and their lives to the study of the male psychopath. Why only the male? The male psychopath takes his animus out on organized society. This is the role given to the male, that is his relationship with organized society. As such, therefore, he is the subject of study by prison officials, by psychiatrists, by psychologists, by reformers, by everybody connected with crime and its prevention in society. However, it is well to remember that society itself is a fairly resilient organization and can take the blows that a male psychopath wreaks upon this organism called society. It is almost like a featherbed and can absorb a punch or a blow from the psychopath, regroup, and reform to its original constitution.

When dealing with the female psychopath, however, the great problem arises, where to observe and identify the female psychopath. Those studies that have been made to date of the female psychopath concern those when subject to enprisonment or those women who spend extremely short time in mental hospitals, where they are immediately diagnosed not mentally ill and released without further ado. The thesis here is that the female psychopath exerts her animus against the family unit, which is the role given to her to play in society and in this culture. In fact, traditionally, her only role. It is postulated here that the family unit is a fragile one, and its unity at the best of times hangs by a silken thread. It does not take much to break this thread and destroy the family as an organism. Thus, the depredations of the female psychopath serve to destabilize the family unit more than any other factor. Before leaving this subject, it is perhaps well to point out that the male psychopath, when found and defined, by and large, makes a good and satisfactory husband and father, astoundingly so.

If all avenues to explore the nature of the female psychopath seem to be closed, then it should be pointed out now that there is one last resort towards the study in depth of the female psychopath and that is where the splitting up of a family, a euphemism for divorce, is centred on the fault complex, that is, unlike the majority of the states in the Union, where irreconcilable differences have now become the sole grounds for divorce. In those lessening jurisdictions where fault is at issue, then the reason for the break-up of the marriage can be gone into and pursued. This is an ever-narrowing field with very few jurisdictions in the world left to adhere to the fault system.

To answer the question of a definition, "What is a psychopath?" Dr. Richard L. Jenkins, M.D., writes in a journal of nervous and mental diseases, volume 131, 1960, in an article entitled, "Psychopathic or Antisocial Personality":

> A psychopathic personality shows not a disorder of personality but rather a defect of personality, together with a set of defences evolved around that defect. The defect relates to the most central element of the human personality; its social nature. The psychopath is simply a basically asocial or anti-social individual who has never achieved the developed nature of *homo domesticus.*

Dr. Cleckley significantly has accepted this definition as given by Dr. Jenkins and relates it thus in his *Mask of Sanity,* Fifth Edition, page 370.

Dr. William McCord, writing with his wife, Joan McCord, as authors of *Psychopathy and Delinquency,* published in 1956, give their definition of a psychopath as follows:

> The psychopath is an asocial, aggressive, highly impulsive person, who feels little or no guilt and is unable to form lasting bonds of affection with other human beings.

## HOW TO RECOGNIZE A PSYCHOPATH WHEN ONE SETS EYES UPON HIM OR HER

Dr. Cleckley, in his monumental work *The Mask of Sanity,* has set out sixteen characteristics of a psychopath and has discussed them each in turn, commencing on page 337 of *The Mask of Sanity.* Therein he, male, or she, female, is interchangeable in the discussions concerning Dr. Cleckley's characteristics with, the exception of No. 16, the life plan, which must be dealt with without complete acceptance.

Before relating Dr. Cleckley's classic sixteen-point clinical profile of the psychopath, a great cautionary note must be sounded here. Firstly, it will be seen that the victim in this psychopathic Dance of Death will rarely ever be able to place himself in proper perspective. The cold, bald fact is that that victim is in the eye of the hurricane and, of course, is unable to see those immense forces swirling about him. Secondly, perhaps to the casual observer of the psychopathic scene, the greatest caution must be extended that this type of observer does not fall within Dr. Leo Kanner's centerization of the definition of a psychopath:

> A psychopath is somebody you don't like.

The need for caution in assessing such statements is vital because we will see in this volume how the psychopath can be, and often is, a likeable, in fact, utterly charming individual to those outside the cauldrons of the marriage.

## DR. CLECKLEY'S CLASSIC SIXTEEN-POINT CLINICAL PROFILE OF THE PSYCHOPATH

1. **SUPERFICIAL CHARM AND GOOD "INTELLIGENCE"**

   More often than not, the typical psychopath will seem particularly agreeable and make a distinctly positive impression when he is first encountered. Alert and friendly in his attitude, he is easy to talk with and seems to have a good many genuine interests. There is nothing at all odd or queer about him, and in every respect he tends to embody the concept of a well adjusted, happy person . . . He looks like the real thing. Very often indications of good sense and sound reasoning will emerge and one is likely to feel soon after meeting him that this normal and pleasant person is also one with high abilities . . . Everything about him is likely to suggest desirable and superior human qualities, a robust mental health.

2. **ABSENCE OF DELUSIONS AND OTHER SIGNS OF IRRATIONAL THINKING**

   Not only is a psychopath rational and his thinking free of delusions, but he also appears to react with normal emotions. His ambitions are discussed with what appears to be healthy enthusiasm. His convictions impress even the skeptical observer as firm and binding. He seems to respond with adequate feelings to another's interest in him and, as he discusses his wife, his children, or his parents, he is likely to be judged a man of warm human responses, capable of full devotion and loyalty.

**3. ABSENCE OF "NERVOUSNESS" OR PSYCHONEUROTIC MANIFESTATIONS**

Regularly we find in him extraordinary poise rather than jitteriness or worry, a smooth sense of physical well-being instead of uneasy preoccupation with bodily functions. It is true he may become vexed and restless when held in jails or psychiatric hospitals. This impatience seems related to his inability to realize the need or justification for his being restrained. What tension or uneasiness of this sort he may show seems provoked entirely by external circumstances, never by feelings of guilt, remorse, or intrapersonal insecurity. Within himself he appears almost incapable of anxiety as of profound remorse.

**4. UNRELIABILITY**

Although the psychopath is likely to give an early impression of being a thoroughly reliable person, it will soon be found that on many occasions he shows no sense of responsibility whatsoever. No matter how binding the obligation, how urgent the circumstances, or how important the matter, this holds true. Furthermore, the question of whether or not he is to be confronted with his failure or his disloyalty or called to account for it, appears to have little effect on his attitude.

Furthermore, it cannot be predicted how long effective and socially acceptable conduct will prevail or precisely (or in what manner) dishonest, outlandish, or disastrously irresponsible acts or failures to act will occur.

**5. UNTRUTHFULNESS AND INSINCERITY**

The psychopath shows a remarkable disregard for truth and is to be trusted no more in his accounts of the past than his promises for the future or a statement of present intentions. He gives the impression that he is incapable of ever attaining realistic comprehension of an attitude in other people which causes them to value truth and cherish truthfulness in themselves.

After being caught in shameful and gross falsehood, after repeatedly violating his most earnest pledges, he finds it easy, when another occasion arises, to speak of his word of honour, his honour as a gentle man, and he shows surprise and vexation when commitments on such a basis do not immediately settle the issue.

**6. LACK OF REMORSE OR SHAME**

The psychopath apparently cannot accept substantial blame for the various misfortunes which befall him and which he brings down upon others. Usually he denies emphatically all responsibility and directly accuses others as responsible, but often he will go through an idle ritual of saying that much of his trouble is his own fault.

Whether judged in the light of his conduct, or his attitude, or material elicited in psychiatric examination, he shows almost no sense of shame. His career is always full of exploits, any one of which would wither even the most callous representatives of the ordinary person. Yet he does not, despite his able protestations, show the slightest evidence of major humiliation or regret.

**7. INADEQUATELY MOTIVATED ANTISOCIAL BEHAVIOUR**

Not only is a psychopath undependable, but also in more active ways he cheats, deserts, annoys, brawls, fails, and lies without apparent compunction. He will commit theft, forgery, adultery, fraud, and other deeds for astonishingly small stakes and under much greater risks of being discovered than will the ordinary scoundrel. He will, in fact, commit such deeds in the absence of any apparent goal at all.

**8. POOR JUDGMENT AND FAILURE TO LEARN BY EXPERIENCE**

Despite his excellent rational powers, the psychopath continues to show the most execrable judgment about obtaining what one might presume to be his ends. He throws away excellent opportunities to make money, to achieve a rapprochement with his wife, to be dismissed from the hospital, or to gain other ends that he has sometimes spent considerable effort toward gaining.

Despite the extraordinary poor judgment demonstrated in behaviour, in the actual living of his life, the psychopath characteristically demonstrates unimpaired (sometimes excellent) judgment in appraising theoretical situations. In complex matters of judgment involving ethical, emotional, and other evaluational factors, in contract with matters requiring only (or chiefly) intellectual reasoning ability, he also shows no evidence of a defect. So long as the test is verbal or otherwise abstract, so long as he is not a direct participant, he shows that he knows his way about. He can offer wise decisions not only for others in life situations but also for himself, so long as he is asked what he would do (or should do, or is going to do). When the test of action comes to him we soon find ample evidence of his deficiency.

**9. PATHOLOGIC EGOCENTRICITY AND INCAPACITY OF LOVE**

The psychopath is always distinguished by egocentricity. This is usually of a degree not seen in ordinary people and often is little short of astonishing. How obviously this quality will be expressed in vanity or self-esteem will vary with the shrewdness of the subject and with his other complexities. Deeper probing will always reveal a self-centredness that is apparently unmodifiable and all but complete. This can perhaps be best expressed by stating that it is an incapacity for object love and that this incapacity (in my experience as well marked psychopaths) appears to be absolute.

He is plainly capable of casual fondness, of likes and dislikes, and of reactions that, one might say, cause others to matter to him. These effective reactions are, however, always strictly limited in degree. In durability they also vary greatly from what is normal in mankind. The term "absolute" is, I believe, appropriate if we apply it to any effective attitude strong and meaningful enough to be called love, that is, anything that prevails in sufficient degree and over sufficient periods to exert a major influence on behaviour.

The psychopath seldom shows anything that, if the chief facts were known, would pass even in the eyes of lay observers as object love. His absolute indifference to the financial, social, emotional, physical, and other hardships which he brings upon those for whom he professes love, confirms the appraisal during psychiatric studies of his true attitude. We must, let it never be forgotten, "judge a man by his actions rather than by his words." This old saying is especially significant when it is a man's motivations and real feelings that we are to judge. This lack in the psychopath makes it all but impossible for an adequate emotional rapport to arise in his treatment and may be an important factor in the therapeutic failure that, in my experience, has been universal.

**10. GENERAL POVERTY IN MAJOR EFFECTIVE REACTIONS**

Vexation, spite, quick and labile flashes of quasi-affection, peevish resentment, shallow moods of self-pity, puerile attitudes of vanity, and absurd and showy poses of indignation are all within his emotional scale and are frequently sounded as the circumstances of life play upon him. But mature, whole-hearted anger, true or consistent indignation, honest, solid grief, sustaining pride, deep joy, and genuine despair are reactions not likely to be found within his scale.

**11. SPECIFIC LOSS OF INSIGHT**

He has absolutely no capacity to see himself as others see him. It is perhaps more accurate to say that he has no ability to know how others feel when they see him or to experience subjectively anything comparable about the situation. All of the values, all of the major effect concerning his status, are unappreciated by him.

Let us consider a man whose wife, after many years of struggle equal to that of others discussed in some detail here, had left him and was seriously considering divorce. It is difficult to imagine a situation in which the necessity of permanent separation could be more clear or imperative. Nor is it likely that any patient described here has given a marital partner more reason to feel this need or has more fully demonstrated that, no matter what he said, he would continue to behave, towards her and in general, just as he had since their marriage. A few excerpts from his letters to the wife are illuminating:

> . . . you will never be happy either by yourself or with some other man . . . we have too much in common . . . I have no reason to lie or to misrepresent things to you now, even though I did try to explain it to you before . . . There will be another day, so I am told and believe, and even though I don't expect to get proper judgement here on earth from you and yours I will up there and if I am wrong I am willing to suffer for eternity. . . .
>
> I do love you. I have never loved anyone else since childhood. . . . If I kill myself my blood will be on your hands . . . it will be heavy on your heart and soul. . . . All wrongs will be righted on Judgement Day . . . you should have stuck by me, should never have left me. . . . I have suffered now really more than I can stand. . . . You think it will bring you happiness to be rid of me. . . . I sincerely hope and pray that it does if you do such a thing. I wish I could feel likewise . . . and believe everyone is at fault but me.

There is more in all this than simple false promises and fraudulent efforts to persuade the wife not to get a divorce. There is also indication of inability in his fundamental reactions to size up normally what he has done, what he is, and what he has been.

**12. UNRESPONSIVENESS IN GENERAL INTERPERSONAL RELATIONS**

The psychopath cannot be depended upon to show the ordinary responsiveness to special consideration or kindness or trust. No matter how well he is treated, no matter how long-suffering his family, his friends, the police, hospital attendants, and others may be, he shows no consistent reaction of appreciation except superficial and transparent protestations. Such gestures are exhibited most frequently when he feels they will facilitate some personal aim. The ordinary axiom of human existence that one good turn deserves another, a principle sometimes honoured by cannibals and uncommonly callous assassins, has only superficial validity for him, although he can cite it with eloquent casuistry when trying to obtain parole, discharge from the hospital, or some other end.

**13. FANTASTIC AND UNINVITING BEHAVIOUR WITH DRINK AND SOMETIMES WITHOUT**

A major point about the psychopath and his relation to alcohol can be found in the shocking, fantastic, uninviting or relatively inexplicable behaviour which emerges when he drinks—sometimes when he drinks only a little. It is very likely that the effects of alcohol facilitate such acts and other manifestations of the disorder.

Most of this asocial, unacceptable, and self-defeating behaviour associated with a psychopath's drinking seems to occur without the benefit of extreme inebriation.

For whatever reason the psychopath may drink, it is true that, in contrast with others who use alcohol to excess, he hits upon conduct and creates situations so bizarre, so untimely, and so preposterous that their motivation appears inscrutable. Many of his exploits seem directly calculated to place him in a disgraceful or ignominious position. He often chooses pranks and seeks out situations that would have no appeal for the ordinary person, whether the ordinary person be drunk or sober.

**14. SUICIDE RARELY CARRIED OUT**

Instead of a predilection for ending their own lives, psychopaths, on the contrary, show much more evidence of a specific and characteristic immunity from such an act. This immunity, it must be granted, is, like most other immunities, relative.

Also worth noting is the fact that most real psychopaths, not once or a few times but habitually, work themselves into situations that might strongly prompt the normal man to end his own life. Since suicide threats, like promises and well-formulated plans to adopt a new course, are so frequently offered by these patients, there is good reason to keep in mind the fact that they are nearly always empty. Many bogus attempts are made, sometimes with remarkable cleverness, premeditation, and histrionics.

**15. SEX LIFE IMPERSONAL, TRIVIAL AND POORLY INTEGRATED**

As might be expected, in view of their incapacity for object love, the sexual aims of psychopaths do not seem to include any important personality relations or any recognizable desire or ability to explore or possess or significantly ravish the partner in a shared experience. Their positive activities are consistently and parsimoniously limited to literal physical contact and relatively free of the enormous emotional concomitants and the complex potentialities that make adult love relations an experience so thrilling and indescribable. Consequently they seem to regard sexual activities very casually, sometimes apparently finding it less shocking and enthralling than a sensitive normal man would find even a glance of his beloved.

Entanglements which go out of their way to mock ordinary human sensibility or what might be called basic decency are prevalent in their sexual careers. To casually "make" or "lay" the best friend's wife and to involve the husband's uncle or one of his business associates in a particularly messy triangular or quadrilateral situation are typical acts. Such opportunities, when available, seem not to repel but specifically to attract the psychopath. Neither distinct appeal of the sex object nor any formulated serious malignity towards those cuckolded or otherwise outraged seems to be a major factor in such choices. There is more to suggest a mildly prankish impulse such as lead the ordinary mind to violate small pedantic technicalities or dead and preposterous bits of formality as demonstration of their triviality.

**16. FAILURE TO FOLLOW ANY LIFE PLAN**

The psychopath shows a striking inability to follow any sort of life plan consistently, whether it be one regarded as good or evil. He does not maintain an effort toward any far goal at all. This is entirely applicable to the full psychopath. On the contrary, he seems to go out of his way to make a failure of life. By some incomprehensible and untempting piece of folly or buffoonery, he eventually cuts short any activity in which he is succeeding, no matter whether it is crime or honest endeavour.

## CRITIQUE

*The proper study of mankind is man.*

—Alexander Pope

No assessment of Dr. Cleckley's monumental work can minimize the thoroughness with which he has pursued his subject nor the importance of his conclusions. No study of the psychopath can be made without an in-depth analysis of Dr. Cleckley's "Sixteen Characteristics." However, it is well to remember that in the overall study of the problem contained in Dr. Cleckley's *The Mask of Sanity,* that his primary concern is in dealing with the male psychopath. The reason for this is obvious, that the male psychopath vents his animus against organized society and is to be found in the mental hospitals (where he is soon discharged) or in the prisons. This is the laboratory available to Dr. Cleckley and his successors, in general.

However, the scene of depredations of the female psychopath is the family home, the family circle, if you will. This is the institution into which she pours all her venom. This is the institution that suffers by virtue of this. Not the mental hospitals, for it is rare that a female psychopath is ever observed for long in a mental institution. She is much too convincing, much too clever, much too able to nullify her own "guilt" in the family destruction, and much too plausible, in that she is able to convey and transfer any disruption or discord in the family onto the husband or the children. And as far as prison institutions are concerned, statistics purport to show the ratio of the male to female psychopath is roughly five to one, and even with this minimal amount of the female psychopath available for observation in the prisons, it can be readily seen that this type has exerted her animus not against the family but against organized society and purportedly that this female psychopath has "liberated" herself from the family. True, Dr. Cleckley deals with the female psychopath and gives us an instance, Mildred, one of the protagonists in Somerset Maugham's novel, *Of Human Bondage*.

This, however, is not given as a direct observation of female psychopath operating within a family, but as one given from already described literature. In the same way Dr. Cleckley deals with Scarlet O'Hara, almost superfluous to say, the heroine of *Gone with the Wind*. A true laboratory for the testing of the female psychopath and her depredations is, and must be, the family. Unfortunately, the family unit is one that is largely denied to the observations of Dr. Cleckley, his associates and successors. But the family becomes a main concern of two groups of professionals in American life, i.e., the lawyer dealing in matrimonial matters and the G.P. or the general practitioner of the medical profession. To each of these is given the family *in extremis*. To each of these professions is brought home daily the stark effectiveness of that magnificent epigram of Dr. Samuel Johnson:

> "Depend upon it, Sir, when a man knows he is to be hanged in a fortnight, it concentrates his mind wonderfully." (Boswell's *Life of Johnson*, Volume 2, p.167.)

This dictum of Dr. Johnson's is particularly applicable where the lawyer dealing in matrimonial causes practices where the fault system in divorce is still in effect. Unfortunately, this is denied to most American lawyers now where the main concern is that irreconcilable differences shall be the sole test for the divorce and the breaking up of the families. However, if it is given to this matrimonial lawyer to enquire into the true causes of the breakup of a marriage, in the instances where the psychopathic wife is revealed, the husband's mind is forced to be concentrated by the fact that the fate of his children is about to be decided, that his fortune or pocketbook are about to be assaulted, and his reputation is about to be dragged into the muck and the mire, enough to concentrate any husband's mind.

As far as a general practitioner in the medical profession is concerned, he observes also the husband of the female psychopath under terms of dire stress, where in fact the danger to life and limb may hang upon the general practitioner's ability to serve the needs of the victim of the female psychopath. Dr. Cleckley is disturbed, and rightly so, at the instances where he has seen the psychopath coming from out of what he feels to be a normal home with normal parentage. What the worker in the field of the matrimonial home begins to learn after many years of observation, is that there is really no such entity as a "normal" home. In truth, the only way that the quality of a home can be tested is by going behind the locked front door of the house itself and to go behind the bedroom door to find out really what goes on there between two people. The integral members of a home under enquiry will, to the researcher, dissemble, hide, evade and do all those things to show the whole family unit in a light utterly divorced from reality. It is only where the blade of the guillotine is about to drop that any facts vaguely resembling the true state of affairs of a family will become available, for it is given to the members of the two professions last mentioned to see that behind these matrimonial hells called "home" in America are the true origins of one class of psychopath presented in this work, i.e., the female psychopath.

Dr. Cleckley, in placing forward his sixteen characteristics of the psychopath, and more particularly in characteristic #16, "Failure to Follow Any Life Plan," deals, as one might expect given the circumstances of the research available to Dr. Cleckley, with this characteristic, as it affects the male. Those working in the field observing the female psychopath at work at her worst should see that the female psychopath does indeed have a life plan. The female, much more deadly than the male, when she has sprung her trap and enmeshed her victim, indeed has a life plan. That life plan is to destroy her victim completely, stripping her victim of those things that enable a male to exist and survive in his culture, that is, the love given to his children and the love expected in return from the children, his fortune, his fame, anything that smacks of male integrity; those are the things that the female proceeds to destroy and strip from her victim, usually of course, her husband.

The female psychopath is totally egocentric and able to carry out her depredations with what is observed to be diabolical cleverness and ability to manipulate everyone and everything to make sure that this life plan is carried out. Relationships are formed and events orchestrated carefully to further her domestic female life plan and thereby concentrate her psychopathy in the family. The basic life of the female psychopath, orchestrated to destroy her victim, more often than not encompasses the abuse of the role of motherhood to gain her social stature that she can attain to make absolutely certain that her life plan may continue and succeed. If her life plan should go awry, if her life plan should be challenged in any respect, then the female psychopath begins an organized recruitment of forces against her husband, the victim. Children, relatives, friends, employers, social workers, psychiatrists, police, and any other member of society will be recruited to join in her campaign to destroy her victim. Since the female psychopath is so plausible, she has little difficulty in rallying all of the foregoing people about her to provide for her ability to follow a consistent life plan, the destruction of her victim, the husband, and in the end her greatest desire, as noted by Chaucer in "The Wife of Bath's Tale," is her dominion over man.

When we turn to the work previously discussed, *Psychopathy and Delinquency* by William McCord, Ph.D., and his wife Joan McCord, Ed.M., published by Grune & Stratton, New York and London, 1956, we see that they have dealt with the characteristics of the psychopath in the fashion as their mentor, Dr. Cleckley, but have condensed the characteristics as they see them of the psychopath as six in number.

1. **THE PSYCHOPATH IS ASOCIAL**

   In almost every culture, the psychopath can be found. What he does will differ; what his society condemns will vary—but the purposeless rebel, the unsocialized misfit, the person who feels no guilt in breaking social mores can be found everywhere. Consequently, any adequate study of the psychopath must look beyond asociality.

2. **THE PSYCHOPATH IS DRIVEN BY PRIMITIVE DESIRES**

   His satisfactions have always been fleeting and highly changeable from childhood through maturity. Consequently, he seems to know no greater pleasure than constant change, and a search for excitement at any cost becomes an important motive.

3. **THE PSYCHOPATH IS HIGHLY IMPULSIVE**

   The psychopath has no stable goals. His life is dominated by fleeting desires which leave no space for farsighted planning.

4. **THE PSYCHOPATH IS AGGRESSIVE**

   The psychopath is highly aggressive because he has never learned more socialized ways of dealing with frustration. The normal man has learned to control aggression. He reacts to frustration with sublimination, with constructive action, with withdrawal—less often with aggression. The psychopath, on the other hand, characteristically reacts to frustration with fury.

5. **THE PSYCHOPATH FEELS LITTLE GUILT**

   When the normal man violates the moral strictures of his culture, a gnawing uneasiness grips him: his conscious hurts. But the psychopath—and this is a crucial trait—have few internalized feelings of guilt. In the usual sense, a psychopath has no conscience. He can commit any act with hardly a twinge of remorse.

6. **THE PSYCHOPATH HAS A WARPED CAPACITY FOR LOVE**

   The psychopath has often been characterized as a "lone wolf." He seems cold and compassionless. He treats people as he does objects: as means for his own pleasure. Though he may form fleeting attachments, these lack emotional depth and tenderness, and frequently end abruptly in aggressive explosions.

The McCords, on page 17 of their work, place a heavy onus on the observer of a psychopathic state in the concluding words of the chapter, and they state:

> Unless an individual exhibits the two critical psychopathic traits—guiltlessness and lovelessness—he should not be categorized as psychopathic.

Here follows a quote from *Pay Any Price* by Ted Allbeury, Panther Books, Granada Publishing Ltd., 8 Grafton Street, London, W1X3LA 1983, page 62.

> A psychopath is someone with a defective conscience, with aggressive and irresponsible conduct and a complete lack of regard for others. They seldom respond to medical treatment. They frequently pretend to regret what they have done, but in fact, they are incapable of regret for their own behaviour.

## THE PSYCHIATRIST AND THE PSYCHOTIC PSYCHOPATH

Study in Interpersonal Relations
Renard A. Cruvant, M.D., and Leon Yochelson, M.D.

*The American Journal of Psychiatry*
Baltimore
1949–1950

*Discussion*

Dr. Hervey Cleckley (Augusta, GA), "I am glad the authors have devoted their attention to the 'blind spot' that psychiatrists often show in their attitude toward the psychopath (so called). It has handicapped our profession in its efforts to evaluate the psychopath and contribute something useful to social and legal agencies which are still without facilities to handle these obviously disordered and sometimes very dangerous people."

> It seems doubtful that substantial progress can be made with this urgent problem until psychiatry can bring itself to admit clearly and unequivically that psychopaths are unquestionably ill. Such an attitude should not lead to more laxity in protecting so-called society against felonies and other damaging acts. It should, on the contrary, open the way for adequate protection against disordered persons who cannot now be controlled by any means until after serious, and sometimes tragic, antisocial acts have been committed.

Once again here is underscored in Dr. Cleckley's discussion the seriousness of the effects of the workings of the psychopath on society. But even more deeply noted is the lack of realization firstly, that the female psychopath apparently at all exists, and secondly, the lack of some means or suggestion for controlling the depredations of the female psychopath.

## THE PSYCHOPATHIC OR ANTISOCIAL PERSONALITY

Richard L. Jenkins, M.D.

*The Journal of Nervous and Mental Disease, 1960*

Since we will undoubtedly have the problem of the psychopath with us long after our theories have been modified, it is worthwhile to take a careful look at these facts. Unfortunately they are not readily available to most psychiatrists in private office practice because the well developed psychopath does not feel the need for psychiatric treatment, nor does he seek it unless with tongue in cheek as an alternative to receiving punishment.

The typical psychopath and the typical psychoneurotic are, in some important regards, on opposite sides of the normal. Where the psychoneurotic suffers from excessive inner conflict, the psychopath makes others suffer from his lack of inner conflict.

Dr. Leo Kanner satyrized this practice when he offered the definition: "A psychopath is someone you don't like." Often this simple definition seems to be distressingly accurate.

Just as the layman has been reluctant to assign responsibility for the psychopath to the psychopathic profession, the psychiatric profession has been very reluctant to assume any responsibility for the true psychopath. And such unpopularity is not undeserved.

If one attempts to treat a classical psychopath, one quickly realizes that he has evolved a set of inner defences to protect him from any insight or discomfort in his antisocial adaptation to life. One suspects it is not simply that other people have little emotional meaning for him. It is necessary to his inner balance and way of life that they should have little meaning for him and that such rudimentary truly social impulses as he may have developed be repressed or stifled to maintain his inner balance. His comfort and the stability of his way of life are protected by a kind of morbid homeostasis. It is not simply that he fails to learn truly social responses. He definitely refuses to learn truly social responses for they would destroy his stabilized maladjustment and his way of life. It is for this reason that he rationalizes that everyone is trying to do him dirt—he is no worse than others, but only quicker or smarter.

# THE MYTH OF THE PSYCHOPATHIC PERSONALITY

Ben Karpman, M.D.
St. Elizabeth's Hospital, Washington, D.C.

*The American Journal of Psychiatry*

Baltimore
1947–1948

Perversions such as exhibitionism belong to the neuroses not psychopathes. The psychopath has no conflict.

*Lying*—The lying of a true psychopath is purely defensive; he is always in so much trouble, and not knowing where punishment may come from, that to protect himself from any adverse or unnatural consequences, he lies as a matter of course.

*Inability to postpone pleasure; impulsiveness*—In fact, and paradoxical as it may seem, the true psychopath is in a sense the least impulsive of them all. In the psychopath, no conscience is interposed between desire and realization; for conscience in him is minimal or nonexistent.

*Inability to profit by experience*—There is, however, a different reason why the psychopath vs. the neurotic and psychotic cannot profit by experience; and it is this, in reaching out for particular results, the psychopath is not guided by any positive social considerations nor the need to resolve special conflicts, but only by the pressure of his immediate purely instinctive needs.

*Antisocial behaviour*—It is maintained that while an occasional lapse in conduct from accepted social standards may be found in many normal people, chronic antisocial activities are characteristic of psychopaths. It is entirely true that a life-long trend in antisocial conduct ischaracteristic of psychopaths.

The true psychopath, however, is all antisocial with no redeeming positive social traits. The psychopathic child may well have been over-indulged, as many other children are. But, because of his otherwise impossible and unbending nature, he often so antagonizes his family that in sheer defence they try to use repressive measure on him; every possible effort is made to cultivate repression in him, but to no avail! The true psychopath lacks completely the basic capacity to acquire repression and thus grows up with a total inability to defer pleasure and sacrifice immediate gains; whereas the over-indulged neurotic maybe over-impulsive in some instances, but entirely well repressed and well controlled in other instances.

On the other hand, the true psychopath, as a child, often creates so much tension at home that eventually the family gives up taking care of him as a hopeless proposition and ceases to be interested in the child. This is not to deny some psychopathic children are actually rejected, but such rejection is in no wise responsible for their behaviour, since their psychopathic behaviour antedates the rejection by a considerable period.

The true psychopath is not reachable or amenable to deep psychotherapeutic approach, though, if put in a controlled situation, he can be handled with greater ease. Conventional punishment has no effect on him.

## THE BRITISH JOURNAL OF PSYCHIATRY

*The Journal of Mental Science*

Published by Authority of
The Royal College of Psychiatrists
Index to Volumes 126 and 127
Ashford, Kent

Heedley Bros. Ltd. 1975

*The Multifactorial Model of Disease Transmissions*

## SEX DIFFERENCES IN THE FAMILIAL TRANSMISSION OF SOCIOPATHY
(Antisocial personality)

by C. Robert Cloninger, Theodore Reich
and Samuel B. Guze

The greater deviance of the parental home experiences of sociopathic women compared to sociopathic men is further evidence of the importance of familial environment.

These data are consistent with an interaction between genetic and environmental factors, which is further supported by Lee Robbins's finding that strict and consistent discipline diminishes the proportion of severely antisocial children who go on to develop sociopathy, as adults (33). The relevant importance of genetic and environmental factors is still uncertain, however, and any description of the mode of transmission of sociopathy must take this into account.

One of the most striking features about sociopathy is the unvarying preponderance of men. Ratios are from four to eight men to one woman have consistently been found in different countries, socio-economic conditions and age groups (1, 14, 15, 23, 27, 28). A variety of explanations for this sex difference have been offered. Wurter hypothesized that boys are more susceptible than girls to intrafamilial disharmony and biological stress, because he could show a correlation between parental discord and antisocial behaviour in boys but not in girls (37).

And now carrying on the work of Dr. Hervey Cleckley, who is now retired and residing in his home in Augusta, Georgia, is Dr. William H. Reid, M.D., M.P.H., of the Nebraska Psychiatric Institute and Department of Psychiatry, University of Nebraska, College of Medicine (Omaha), and the work now being carried forward by Dr. Reid is contained in his book entitled, *The Psychopath.*

## COMPREHENSIVE STUDY OF ANTISOCIAL DISORDERS AND BEHAVIOURS

Published by Bruner/Mazel Publishers,
New York, 1978

This work is a collection of authoritative articles by various people engaged in the field of the study of the psychopath, including Dr. William H. Reid himself.

## A JUDICIAL DEFINITION OF THE PSYCHOPATH

*Black's Law Dictionary,* by Henry Campbell Black, M.A., Revised Fourth Edition, West Publishing Co., St. Paul, Minn. 1968, page 385.

> **Constitutional Psychopathic Inferiority.** Individuals who show a life-long and constitutional tendency not to conform to the customs of the group, and who habitually misbehave, and have no sense of responsibility to their fellowmen or to society as a whole. These individuals fail to learn by experience and are inadequate, incompatible, and in efficient (Page 385).

From the same publication, page 1392:

> **Psychopath.** Person having mental disorder. More commonly, mental disorder not amounting to insanity or taking the specific form of a psychoneurosis, but characterized by a defect of character or personality, eccentricity, emotional instability, inadequacy or perversity of conduct, under conceit and suspicousness, or lack of common sense, social feeling, self-control, truthfulness, energy, or persistence.

# III

# THE FEMALE PSYCHOPATH IN MARRIAGE AND DIVORCE

The assessment of the depredations of the X Factor, that is, of the psychopathic wife, in marriage and divorce cannot be separated from the effects of the X Factor on the victims of the psychopathic wife in marriage, that is, the husbands and the children. It must be borne in mind that the effects of the X Factor do not die with the divorce but are carried forward in the working out of the life plan of the psychopathic wife, that is, a plan of destruction that will continue into the second marriage, second divorce, and third marriage, and so on until the Circes of the victims is finally found in the grave of psychopath. If current psychopathic thought has a basis for validity, then there is certainly no known cause of the psychopath and with even more certainty, if such can be held, there is no known cure for the psychopath. This is truly the Gordian Knot untied.

To discuss the appearance of the psychopath on the scene, the approach can be made from five different viewpoints:

(a) the social;
(b) behavioural;
(c) economic;
(d) cultural;
(e) genetic.

To discuss the problem from a social standpoint, it is well to adopt the geometrician's ploy, "When in doubt, drop a perpendicular." If you turn to the dictionary, you find the definition of the word "social" is given:

1. All having to do with human beings living together in a group in a situation requiring that they have dealings with one another.

It can be readily seen that the social approach does not give the answer to the psychopath or the problems arising from the psychopath.

The definition of the word "social" merely sets the stage, that is, human beings living together as a group, and required to have dealings with one another, such dealings being dealings within the family.

The approach may now be considered from a behavioural standpoint and behaviour, dictionarywise, can be defined as:

> 2. An organism's muscular or glandular responses to stimulation, especially those that can be observed.

And to continue further in the dictionary definition of the word "behaviourism," again quoted:

> 3. Coined by John B. Watson, American psychologist, in 1913, the doctrine that observed behaviour provides the only valid data from that property: it rejects the concept of mind.

Once again, if adopted, the behavioural approach does not even skim the surface of the problem. The behaviour of the psychopath and the victim being simply observed provides no clue whatsoever as to the cause of the psychopath's actions, nor of the victim's responses to the onslaught of the psychopath.

To approach the problem from the economic standard, again a Webster's Dictionary definition of the word economic can be applied:

> Of the satisfaction of the material needs of people.

In addition to the Webster's definition, a quote from *Black's Law Dictionary*, Revised Fourth Edition, at page 603, might be pertinent:

> Includes that which pertains to the satisfaction of man's needs.

Again, these definitions of economic reduce to almost hopelessness an attempt to unravel the problem of the psychopath and the victim from the economic standpoint. Purely and simply, the psychopathic problem does not relate to the needs of either sex. On the contrary, the actions of the psychopath and the reactions of the victim are totally over and above the needs of either the male or the female. They are in a sense a "luxury" superimposed upon mankind's needs.

From a standpoint of a cultural approach, it is again well to define "culture" by dictionary definition:

> The concepts, habits, skills, arts, instruments, institutions, etc., of a given people in a given period; civilization.

The incongruity of attempting to tie in a psychopath with a cultural concept has never been better presented than by Dr. Cleckley himself in his Fifth Edition of *The Mask of Sanity*, at page 327, when he discusses at length the figure of Alcibiades, set in a Greek cultural background:

> This man led me to ponder at a very early age on many questions, for which I have not yet found satisfactory answer.

In numerous quotes from Plutarch, Dr. Cleckley recites the attractive background of Alcibiades himself, and the personal attraction of this man who had access to all that was great in Greek culture. Yet there was some fatal flaw in Alcibiades. He was in truth a blatant psychopath, and the harm that he did in Greek culture itself has been shown by Dr. Cleckley in his analysis of the character of Alcibiades.

## THE PSYCHOPATH AND THE GENETIC PROBLEM

In discussing and reaching out for the causes of the psychopath and the consequences of the onslaught of the psychopath on its victims, be it society or the individual, there must be a consideration of whether or not genetic factors play some part. Dr. Cleckley, in *The Mask of Sanity* at page 413, alludes in a cursory fashion to the possibilities of relating the cause of the psychopath to a malfunctioning chromosonal pattern. And while not making this distinctly a genetic reference, Dr. Cleckley does allude to a chromosonal disorder as being a defect possibly contributing to the formation of the psychopath.

In the article entitled, "Genetic Correlates of Antisocial Syndromes," written by Dr. William H. Reid and contained in his valuable work already referred to, *The Psychopath*, at page 252, Dr. Reid gives the following:

> Eysenck and Eysenck have studied character disorders for many years, often approaching the subject in ways different from the usual clinical and social conceptualizations. Their recent chapter and a summary of the 1975 NATO Advance Study Institute, attempts to place these concepts in a genetic framework. After carefully explaining their diagnostic criteria, which involve a three dimensional continuum of extra-version, neuroticism, and psychoticism, the Eysencks' critically review the pertinent literature and conclude that at least fifty percent of total variance between psychopathy and controls is due to genetic factors. Using complex statistical measures for calculating hereditability, they cite fairly good evidence that . . . individual differences in the personality variables which have been shown to be associated with psychopathic behaviour are determined to a large extent by genetic causes.

Towards the end of this article on the genetic correlates of antisocial syndromes, Dr. Reid is constrained to say:

> As a friend has said, "If you can find a better study, let's hear it."

It is apparent that observation in the laboratory of humankind reveals the female psychopathic wife wreaks her destruction in the marital holocaust best when she attracts, enslaves, or entraps a suitable victim, the husband. Of necessity, by definition, and by observation, for every psychopathic wife, there is the husband as a victim.

The facility with which the male becomes the victim is brought about by uncertain factors. The one triggering mechanism that seems to transcend all others arises through the stress of the matrimonial scene, which stress is constant and remitting. This will be shown in the next chapter in a discussion of those relationships formed in the cauldron of matrimonial strife and hatred.

But the question arises, is there any other factor that induces the male to become a victim of this psychopathic attack? Could it be that the great Dr. Samuel Johnson, the Great Cham himself, was right when quoted by Boswell:

> *Boswell:* How hard is it that man can never be at rest.
> *Johnson:* It is not in his nature to be at rest. When he is at rest, he is in the worst state that he can be in; for he has nothing to agitate him. He is then like the man in the Irish song,
> There liv'd a young man in Ballinacrazy,
> who wanted a wife for to make him unaisy.

Is there indeed something in the makeup of men that denies them the right to leave well enough alone things that work? Perhaps this story that may be apocryphal does apply. It related at the time of the troubles in Cyprus in the late 1950s that a British major walked up to an old gnarled Cypriot peasant who addressed the major in the following words, "Sir, you should have been in Cyprus before the troubles, it was a veritable paradise." The major's succinct reply, "Well, my good man, why didn't you leave it that way?"

To try and throw a rope around the problem of the female psychopath, what numbers can be counted on to provide, can it be said, "this class" of psychopath? It is informative to refer to the statistics supplied by the Department of Health, Education & Welfare:

National Center for Health Statistics,
Health Resources Administration,
Division of Vital Statistics, in reference to
Population—Marriages—Divorces, U.S.A.
1972–1976

In these statistics we find child population, U.S.A. 1975, . . . 70,522,000.

Children—divorced parents
ten year period, 1965–1974 . . . 8,609,000,
which includes children 0–18 years of age.

Mathematically therefore, we have the number of total children, we have female children of divorced parents alone in the ten-year period of 1965 to 1974 in the figure of 4,304,000. It is more than a good guess, but by observation in the laboratory of human beings in the cauldron of the matrimonial holocaust, it can be given with a great certainty that a certain important percentage of these females will be triggered into becoming the female psychopath in the matrimonial holocaust that ensues upon her marriage. The difficulty arises when the researcher attempts to ascertain what is it that is the triggering mechanism for the development of the female psychopath. Whether or not the psychopathy is a latent problem arising through the inheritance and genetics is an interesting question. Can it be that the latent psychopath is affected genetically, as the diabetic who with complete certainty has a background of a latent genetic problem that may latent and be triggered by various environmental mechanics. A good example may be the triggering of the latent diabetic through the use of cortisone or cortisone compounds for other medical purposes.

In any event, what of the research through the observation of the destruction of many thousands of marriages and of which a goodly portion consists of the actions of the female psychopath can be said to be brought about by the desertion of the female child, or children, by the father, either voluntarily or involuntarily through the operation of law. Divorce, with its enormous increase in the last twenty years, is an operation of law and the separating of the father from the girl children of the family, by the granting of the divorce decree, and in almost all instances the granting of the custody of the children to the mother, has amounted to an effective separation of the father from the children. The female child deserted by the father, either voluntarily or involuntarily by the operation of law, suffers from what might be called, "the father/daughter syndrome." This syndrome arises from the trauma of desertion of the daughter/child by the father, with the result that the female child engages in an eternal quest for a father-substitute. Valid is the concept or not, Dr. Cleckley himself, the grand old man of the study of the psychopath, had this to say:

> Well, Mr. Fleishman, your theory is just as good as the next person's.

And to quote again what Dr. Reid has to say about the problem. Requoting from page 255 from his own article already given, "Genetic Correlates of Antisocial Syndromes," in the book which he so ably edits, *The Psychopath*, at page 255, "as a friend has said, 'If you can find a better study, let's hear it.' "

# THE FEMALE PSYCHOPATH IN THE MARITAL HOLOCAUST

An attempt to outline and give a well-rounded view to the female psychopath, the creation of her family, and the ultimate disaster of the inevitable divorce in the psychopathic female's family, can best be given under six major headings:

1. The Early Years.
2. The Determative Years.
3. The Trap is Set.
4. The Trap Springs.
5. The Male Awakens.
6. Divorce Action, or subtitled, The Collection.

## THE EARLY YEARS

An extensive perusal of the literature relating to the psychopaths, which incidentally is not voluminous, shows that there really is not one acceptable theory, let alone a presentation of fact, as to the cause of psychopathy be it male or female, but having due regard to those who have had an extensive experience in the field of matrimonial law coupled with a vast reading in the field of the psychopath and by correlating the vivid experiences, the extensive reading with analytical discussion with members of the medical profession, it is possible to put forward a possible scenario for the early years of the female psychopath. Whether or not there is a genetic predisposition towards the creation of the psychopath is a long-alluded-to possibility, whether primary in the causation of the psychopath in that she (referring to the female) may be made rather than born. There are secondary factors that could trigger the active psychopath from underlying genetic predisposition. Conjoining the primary and secondary factors would then show the psychopath as being both born and made. The factor of early post-birth phenomenon of "bonding" is worthy of discussion in some detail. In order to appreciate the discussion of the six-fold problem of the female psychopath, it is a practical must that Dr. Cleckley's clinical profile of the psychopath, that is the sixteen characteristics given by Dr. Cleckley in *The Mask of Sanity* be set forth again here to guide the reader.

1. Superficial charm and good "intelligence."
2. Absence of delusions and other signs of irrational thinking.
3. Absence of "nervousness" of psychoneurotic manifestations.
4. Unreliability.
5. Untruthfulness and insincerity.
6. Lack of remorse or shame.

7. Inadequately motivated antisocial behaviour.
8. Poor judgement and failure to learn by experience.
9. Pathologic egocentricity and incapacity for love.
10. General poverty in major affective reactions.
11. Specific loss of insight, i.e., the absolute incapacity of the psychopath to see himself or herself as others see them.

And here it is noteworthy to further note from Cleckley at page 350, "It is perhaps more accurate to say that he has no ability to know how others feel when they see him or experience subjectively anything comparable about the situation. All of the values, all of the major affect concerning his status, are unappreciated by him."

12. Unresponsiveness in general interpersonal relations.
13. Fantastic and uninviting behaviour with drink and sometimes without.
14. Suicide rarely carried out.
15. Sex life impersonal, trivial, and poorly integrated.
16. Failure to follow any life plan.

All of these characteristics may well be based upon the innocent and young child (and we are discussing the female) finding an inability to trust any responsible individual in her early environment.

This lack of trust thus leaves the child with an inability to take risks in loving or to form limits as to the existence of a conscience, in fact to be so crippled as to have really no appreciation whatsoever as to how a "normal" feeling and conscientious human being should act or react in a given situation. It is possible and must be considered that the concept of "bonding," in which the young infant is psychologically and physically bonded to one important individual, most notably the mother, in the very early hours and days of the post-natal period, could well be one factor in the setting up of the psychopath. It is noteworthy that it's found by many social workers and family physicians, and even by some lawyers who have been instrumental in handling the legal problems of adoption, that many psychopaths appear to come from adoptive homes. There can well be here, as felt by many primal psychiatrists, a possible appreciation by the unborn child in the womb of a hostile, uncaring, confused, and bitter mother, caught in the situation of being forced to have this child and give it up, or in the alternative, committing her life to the bringing up of this unwanted child. Neither solution is satisfactory and often confusing and leads to the feelings of bitterness and nastiness, not only in the mother with the child in her womb, but to the child itself upon being adopted out. This last is at this stage in development only a theory, but certainly is one embraced by such primal psychiatrists as Arthur Janov, author of *The Primal Scream*, and many other books on "primal psychiatry."

Perhaps a more easily understood reason for the so-called bonding failure occurs in the early hours of a newborn child's life situation, either by separation from the natural mother in preparation for adoption, or the reception of the newborn child by this mother of a youthful nature, barely old enough in many, many cases, to conceive of child and who approaches the birth of this child with uncertainty and undoubtedly mixed feelings about the motherhood situation. Whether such bonding failure is an important element in the creation of the psychopath, only time and further research will tell.

Another factor that looms large in the development of the female psychopath is the father rejection, which can occur either where the father stays in the physical home and opts out of any significant relationship with the child, or because the father is driven out of the home, either emotionally by the mother or physically by the mother through the courts. The maternal hostility must have a great deal to do with the development of any sense of security and social organization in a child in its very early years. Whether this maternal hostility is of importance to the pregnancy itself and whether it is of importance in the early years of psycho-social development in the child remains a definitively unanswered question, but it most certainly must be a very strong source of upheaval to the growing child.

But of a certainty is my observation, "Those who have never known love as a child cannot give love as an adult."

## THE DETERMINATIVE YEARS

The determinative years are the teen years. These years cannot be called the formative years, as the psychopath has already been formed in the early years. The formative years can be said with some certainty to be those up to and including the age of six. As the Jesuits have often been heard to say, "Give me a child up to the age of six and I will make of him what I will." The teen years are the years in which the psychopath begins to act out and put forward what seems to be the psychopath's major view of life, that is, "I'll get what I want, and to hell with the rest."

In the teens, confused and difficult years for any developing adolescent female, it can certainly be seen that a child crippled by a lack of social conscience, by a lack of responsible social interaction with two apparently healthy parents, and by the lack of a sound, stable, natural-parented home situation, almost "naturally" develops the psychopathic characteristics of the young female. It is at this period of life that the young psychopathic female decides that in fact her role will be that of the most socially acceptable over the many centuries of this culture, that is motherhood. Not for the normal biological and psychological reasons of most mothers, but more as a role in which she knows she can get what she wants because, as it has often been said, "Who can argue against motherhood?" It may well be said that this is ascribing too much wit and deviousness to the average adolescent female, but by observation the average adolescent female has, in fact, just such wit and deviousness if she has been brought up in a home catering to her psychopathic tendency.

When she falls into the teenage years, she realizes that she has really not been brought up in a close social and moral structure, she lacks the sense of the strong nuclear family and in our society, of course, lacks the extended family as well because this society is one of movers. In most family situations nowadays, there are few grandparents, uncles, or aunts in the geographical surroundings to offer a developmental alternative pattern for the child. In addition, in the late part of the twentieth century, there no longer exists the peripheral extended family present in the small towns in what has been referred to as "the good old days," in which the child was also exposed to the village blacksmith, the village seamstress, the other caring members of a village society who could also help form the personality of the individual child. In this, our present American society, it is basically the nuclear family that either succeeds or fails, setting the moral and social frameworth in which the developing child can develop a sense of right and wrong, a sense of responsibility.

## THE TRAP IS SET

The trap may be set very early in the teenage years, as many psychopathic females begin their "amorous" digging for a potential victim in their teens. One major factor in the setting of the trap is the psychopathic female's search for the "caring father," whom she failed to have in her early years. As she sets the trap for this young gentleman and future father, there is the usual scenario of the irrational, romantic notion that, "We will have the most wonderful family, we two will be three, then four, five and six, with you as daddy and me as the protective mommy." It becomes a disturbing problem that frequently in the psychopathic female's quest for early marriage, the marital trap is sprung by a premarital pregnancy, with the understood expectation that the male will do the "honourable thing" and marry this beautiful young wife "in child."

Once this trap is set, the marriage is under way and supplies a setting for the female psychopath in that this scenario is a beginning of the "Pot of Gold at the end of the rainbow." This young woman now, feeling secure in her marriage, is on her way to achieving the ultimate female identity as mother and, as is so typical of the psychopath, maybe doing the right thing for all the wrong reasons. But in the end this will lead to a number of hostages, i.e., children, to be used in the manipulation of the father in the marriage and to be used against him in his destruction when the psychopathic female finds this to be opportune and in the end as cannon fodder in the courts for the ultimate victory of motherhood, that is, *dominion over man.*

## THE TRAP SPRINGS

Here, as discussed in the last paragraph, the psychopathic female has now graduated into her role of motherhood. The child is born, often surrounded by wild, hysterical protestations akin to the "second coming," that we two are now three and will forever endure for the sake of our children. Tantamount to the finding of the Holy Grail. In reality, this is often just the scenario calculated to confuse the adult male into endless servitude. There is no way that he can argue with the concept of motherhood; there is no way that he can argue with a plausible psychopath, who convinces him that he must work more, earn more, provide more, do more, suffer more, and sacrifice more, all for the sake of his lovely wife and children.

The marriage itself will go on for a variable period of time, depending on how successful the psychopathic female is in "running her man." Should he continue to do as he is told and should she continue to be able to change her scenario of life as it occurs to whatever she thinks should occur, the marriage may carry on with a remarkably happy aspect to external observers. In fact, in many of these cases divorce comes as a complete surprise to friends and relatives with the statement, "Oh, but weren't they such a happy couple and such a loving family."

As the marriage unfolds and should it go the way of the psychopath, then all appears to be externally well in most situations. In other situations, even if the male is properly servile, properly attentive, properly a provider, the female psychopath can have no emotional interaction in this situation. As we have seen in Chapter Two of this work, she has the pathological egocentricity and incapacity for love that characterizes the psychopath, she has general poverty in major effective reactions, and she has specific loss of insight. These factors, amongst the others in a clinical profile of the psychopath, eventually lead either to her reaching outside the marriage for lovers, or such other support as is required for "her case," or results in the male eventually awakening to his position. However, because of these secondary factors of her destructive behaviour outside the marriage and because of her destructive behaviour inside the marriage, in which she begins to belittle him first in her eyes, then in his own eyes, then in his children's eyes, and then in society's eyes, her control mechanism may founder; it backfires and may, in fact, "awaken him."

## THE MAN AWAKENS

Suddenly in this kind of marital situation, the male may, if he is fortunate, have the realization that "I'm not important here, I am only an employee of supermother and the childrens' farm." Any attempt on his part to discuss in a rational fashion his plans for life with his wife, his own feelings, his own plans for his professional career or otherwise, are all subjugated by the wife and twisted around to be eminently plausible and presented to him in a fashion that his responsibilities to his wife and children are paramount, his feelings are really of no significance! In addition, if anything has been going wrong in the marriage, undoubtedly it is his fault. Unfortunately, her clever plausibility may in fact so intimidate the male that he becomes the husband victim who will be discussed in a number of case histories arising from out the case history laboratory and cauldron that will follow.

He then, for a variable period of time, fulfills the unfortunate social victim role—the victim needs his psychopath like a martyr needs his tormenter. Should she continue on her destructive path without the male seeing the light and getting out of the marital situation, she will continue to perpetrate endless acts of emotional and physical violence on the luckless husband. But most notably, as will be delineated in the following chapter, these acts are in fact projected out onto the other marital partner; they in fact all become his fault. As can be seen in the actions ascribed to the psychopathic females, very often allegations of violence, alcoholism, emotional and physical abuse, incest, child beating, etc., all are attributed to the poor husband. Of course, to say that this is nonsense is not to prove to the contrary. But as can be seen from the scenarios presented in this work, from many of the assertions by the husbands (often supported by medical and psychiatric assistance), these allegations are by and large not the case and are a projection of the female psychopath's powers of transference. The female psychopath widens her nefarious sea of influence as necessary to build up ammunition in her war on her feckless husband in that he soon becomes demeaned in the eyes of his children; he may suffer loss of face amongst his fellow workers at the hands of the psychopathic wife; he may in fact find that his own family has been drawn into the war and plausibly convinced that it is all his fault; the psychopathic female will enlist the forces of society on her side; the police, the social workers, the psychiatrist, and inadvertently and most unfortunately, very often the court itself.

Should this scenario reach a boiling point, the husband has really very few alternatives as his raging anger builds at his inability to handle the situation. Either he must become the husband victim or he must attempt to break through this holy motherhood/child complex, perpetrated on him by the female psychopath. The end result of his unholy hegira leads to suicide, to homicide, to wife and child beating, and to desertion and divorce. The last two effects mentioned, notably desertion and divorce, are the only salvation for the psychopathic female's husband. If he is unable to see that the only solution to a psychopathic marriage is to give up, get out, give her what she wants, and get on with his own life, starting anew, then he is in fact trapped into the husband-victim syndrome, even should he not wish to be there. The endless legal battles, the endless court appearances, may in effect keep him still struggling on as victim; rather than becoming a victor, albeit he may feel a "vanquished victor" if he can cut and start his life anew. This latter course is very difficult to take in our society, as all the social pressures are against the desertion of the family, and champion the holiness of motherhood, the supremacy of children's needs, etc., but it must be the *only* salvation of the husband victim of a marauding psychopath.

## DIVORCE ACTION

### *The Collection*

As far as the divorce situation is concerned, by now the psychopathic wife has decided that she must drive this man out of the house and then proceed to crucify him emotionally, financially, and otherwise. She will enlist all members of society in her quest for just such a victory. She is unfortunately, as "wife and mother," very often highly successful in doing just that in our current legal system. It should be noted that the plausibility of the psychopath leaves the court stunned at the "injustice" to her and the children by the husband, missing completely her absolute egocentricity, her untruthfulness and insincerity, specific loss of insight, and all the other characteristics of the psychopath as discussed by Dr. Cleckley in his clinical profile of the psychopath. It can be offered with certainty that the officers of the court are never provided with social work or psychiatric assistance to sort out the psychopathic characteristics of the female on the rampage, and therefore are often misled by the appearance of the wife and the children in court and all the accusations thrown in by the wife's lawyers, psychiatrists, social workers, etc., calculated to crucify the male. By this time, if he is in fact awakened, then his only solution is to desert the home; the poor male is portrayed as a vile, vicious, irresponsible, deserting husband and father, and the court may soon hasten to marshall the full forces of society to redress the wrongs perpetrated upon this unfortunate woman and her children.

# IV

# CASE HISTORIES

## GENERAL INTRODUCTION

A consideration of individual case histories: eight cases from family law practice over the last thirty-six years, cases that show very clearly illustrations of the female psychopath at work in the marital situation.

It is the intent to provide some ease in the consideration of these complicated legal cases, to present them each under a format as follows:

1. An introduction. This introduction will be a brief discussion of what the case will show the reader, the Cleckleyian characteristics in the clinical profile (discussed in Chapters 2 and 3) in these individual cases.
2. Next will be presented the documentation. This consists of the legal, psychiatric, social work, and other documentation quoted directly from the court documents, which are public documents, but in which of course, the names and locale have been changed to protect the "guilty."
3. The third and final consideration of each case will be a discussion and summary of the documentation as it reveals the Cleckleyian profiles in the cases in question.

### THE JANNSEN STORY

*Documentation and History of the Marriage*

By the way of background, this is a story of a marital breakdown process in a couple in their late forties. Notably, she was married to this gentlemen in her second marriage, he in his first. It is to be noted that this gentleman became involved with this woman during the break-up of her first marriage. Obviously he was very carefully selected, as psychopaths are wont to do, for his sterling qualities of honesty, integrity, desiring a happy family, and willing to do damn near everything and anything to insure that he had a happy family. It is amazing how often the psychopath is so diabolically clever at picking out just such an individual, interestingly these individuals picked out by the psychopath are exactly the mirror image of the psychopath in the fact that they have all of the or appear to have all the essential moral fibre for the construction and caring on of a good marital relationship, but alas none of these abilities or traits are in anyway protective in the destructive marital relationship created and perpetrated by the female psychopath.

The second relationship with the current husband began in 1954 during, as we have said, the break-up initiated by the wife, with the usual psychopath complaints that the first husband was a dimwit, a traitor, totally incapable of loving, etc., etc. This gentleman was very quickly seduced into a relationship and subsequent marriage to this woman, and immediately upon consummation of the marriage you will see from the testimony that this woman felt that all was well because she had a marriage license, which was a guarantee of her future. It should be noted that immediately upon the marriage began the destructive activity to attempt to break the marriage up and that this destructive activity continued for some twenty years before the husband finally, with the help of outside professionals, saw that this was an irrecoverable marriage. This, too, is so characteristic of the psychopath marriage in that they seem to be able to pick the men who hang in there and are brainwashed and abused to the point where they somehow feel that they begin to believe that the psychopath female is correct in that everything happening wrong in the marriage is due to the husband; and everything happening right is due to the wife and, of course, the mother, since here too motherhood is the be-all and end-all of the psychopathic female and really gives her the ultimate power to destroy the husband, marriage, and unfortunately in the process, the children, as they become hostages in the marital wars. This case very clearly points out the total inability of the female psychopath to undertake any meaningful sexual relationship and also the ability of the psychopath to use the sexual desires of the other mate as a weapon with which to constantly abuse him and undermine his manhood. Here too is shown the fact that the sexual relationship is so ultimately trivial and impersonal and is really a tool relation in that any sexual activity is only used as part of her psychopathic life plan, in that any sexual activity allowed is only to create children, as was the case in this situation.

The delivery of the first child was effected by Caesarean section. It is very interesting to ponder the necessity of a Caesarean section in a labour that was not apparently, according to the notes of the doctors, a complicated one, which should have ended in a section for any mechanical reason or any reason that could have been predicted, but it in any event wound up in a section. The husband points out that he was present during much of this, and he felt that it was mainly the emotional difficulties that necessitated the section. We don't have a medical opinion on this, but it is very interesting to wonder whether this was not just a further extension of the woman's psychopathy, either as an extension of her martyrdom of motherhood (and this being another of the typical miracle births that occur to psychopathic females) or whether this was just another example of her personality defect in that she was unable to maintain a steady plan in the management of the labour and became histrionic and hysterical and necessitated the termination by Caesarean section.

It would be interesting to know what the incidence of psychopathy is in women undergoing Caesarian section for non-progressive labour. These statistics are not available to our knowledge, but it is certainly an interesting point to ponder and one I don't think has been attended to in the past.

So the consideration of this scenario begins with a letter from the obstetrician in attendance on the family from 1964 to 1971, in which it is pointed out that the wife and husband were first seen in 1964 before starting a family regarding difficulties with their sexuality, and it was pointed out by the wife, according to the doctor's letter, that "the basic problem here was memory of rather rough treatment from the first husband who was a homosexual. Also history of treated familial syphilis with a positive Kahn." Obviously, here too it was not the woman's fault; it was the man's fault, and his sexuality was at fault in the first marriage. As we will soon see, she proceeded to use the same excuses of homosexuality, etc., etc., regarding the failure of sexuality in this current marriage. They were seen again in 1971 with complaints of painful intercourse, and psychological factors were discussed at length. The wife wanted a hysterectomy and an operation to enlarge the vagina, and this operation was carried out in 1971 and, of course, despite fully adequate healing and full physical abilities for easy intercourse, as the obstetrician notes in his letter, we will see that no such thing was to take place in this psychopathic marriage.

There are a number of documents that should be mentioned here to show that the husband had a great number of character references, the first being one from the Salvation Army, which pointed out the real leadership qualities of the husband; Cub Pack, which he led, "to be a very compassionate and determined gentleman. He has co-operated in all areas of his involvement with us. I would say his personal character is above reproach. From my many discussions with Mark, I know that as a father he is a very loving and caring man and that he only wishes the opportunity he should be given to raise his boys as God directs him." As we will see, that was not to be.

*Dr. ———, M.D.*
*Obstetrics and Gynaecology*

March 31, 1978

Mr. Luke and Mrs. Alana Jannsen

Dear Mr. and Mrs. Jannsen:
I am submitting the following information as requested from my records, when you attended me in North Beach (Mrs. Jannsen accompanied by her husband). The following is the basic summary of events:

1. Seen first September 1964, with strong psycho-inhibitory problems before starting a family. The basic problem here was memory of rather rough treatment from the first husband, who was a homosexual. Also history of treated familial syphilis with a positive Kahn.
2. Attended and performed two Caesarean sections for the two children, July 17 1965 and June 21 1967.
3. In June 1971, questioning a sterilization procedure, and complaining of painful intercourse with difficulty at entry. Full discussion as to the psychological significance of painful intercourse, the need to relax, have good cooperation between husband and wife with a basic need for love and understanding on the part of both. Suggestions that adequate time should be taken to iron this out with considerable care.
4. Wanting a hysterectomy in view of heavy periods, and wishing an enlarging operation to the vaginal entrance, as discussed as a possibility in June. The latter operation was agreed to be done by the writer, however, it was pointed out to both of you that an operation alone does not guarantee easy intercourse. Muscles will still over-react with sensitivity, if there is not willingness on the part of the wife and there is not a good love-making technique on the part of the husband. This was clearly understood by both of you. Several long discussions in regard to technique and understanding was provided by the writer to both of you over the course of these interviews.
5. 25th October, 1971—vaginal hysterectomy and Fenton's vaginoplasty were performed. The latter being the opening operation described above.
6. December 15th, 1971—follow-up examination indicated all to be healed well, and the vagina admitted two fingers easily, which in my experience would allow easy intercourse, both of you bearing in mind the psychological and mutual consent and attempt factors.

I am sorry to hear that your marriage is possibly breaking up. I hope there may still be a possibility of reservation of your problems for both your sakes, and for that of the children. There is nothing more that I can add to this testimony, and all the above is a true summary of my medical records, and in view of the many hours I have spent with both of you to help you with this problem, my memory is also clear as to the veracity of these statements, and the attempt to advise you both to overcome your mutual problems including that of achieving a satisfactory sexual relationship. I have nothing further to add.

North Beach Citadel Corps

March 15, 1979

To Whom it May Concern:

*Reference: Mr. Mark Jannsen*
Please allow me to go on record by saying that Mark has displayed here at the Salvation Army real leadership qualities which we have come to appreciate greatly.

We have recently opened a Cub Pack under his capable leadership. In order to open a Cub Pack and become its leader he had to be accepted by our head office and was well able to do so. I have found Mark to be a very compassionate and determined gentleman. He has cooperated in all areas in his involvement with us.

I would say his personal character is above reproach. From my many discussions with Mark, I know that as a father he is a very loving and caring man and that he only wishes the opportunity he should be given to raise his boys as God directs him.

If you require any further information, please contact me at the above numbers.

Sincerely,

K. J. Chappell
(Lieut.)

Further, there is a note from the Boy Scouts noting the appreciation of the group during a presentation to him as a token of appreciation for his many years of untiring effort and leadership.

In addition, there are other documents here noting the extremely extensive counselling that was undertaken by this beleaguered husband in attempting to salvage his marriage from numerous psychiatrists, and it is noted from his family physician, "I did not find him to be suffering from any active psychiatric illness," this, despite his wife's constant accusations. In addition, a letter from a group of marriage counsellors in which they note that the prognosis for the marriage would not appear to be good, and I quote, "However, it also seemed apparent to me that the gentleman in question was strongly motivated to do everything in his power to maintain and improve the relationship." Quite glaringly, there is no mention of the same motivation on the part of the female involved. In addition, there is a letter from a very good friend of the husband pointing out a great number of positive qualities in the husband, and I quote, "I have known and seen him take undue criticism and much deliberate abuse, and yet in those circumstances he did not become bitter or resentful, and did not retaliate or revile. He has a remarkable forgiving nature, never holds a grudge, and searches his own heart in times of being slighted." It is peculiar how often the psychopath manages to pick out a devoted husband who is constantly searching his own heart for the problems in the marriage when in effect the marriage is doomed by the woman's psychopathy.

Boy Scouts of America

Mr. Mark Jannsen,<br>3054 Baird Road,<br>North Beach, CA.

Wolf Cubs

Dear Mark:

Be Prepared

Ventures

R S

On behalf of the 18th North Beach Group Committee, Cubs and Cubs parents, I would like to make this presentation to you as a token of our appreciation for your many years of untiring effort and leadership. We were very sorry that you and Charles Frame could not be present at the recent Father and Son Banquet when we also honoured Al Johnson and Frank Seidel for their work within the Scouting Movement.

It is our sincere hope that you may one day be in the position to return to the Cub Group. I know that you are really missed by the boys in the Sioux Pack and by us all.

Our best wishes go with you.

A. M. Warren, M.D.<br>Family Physician

December 3, 1978

*Re: Mr. Mark Jannsen*

I thought it may help to clarify matters regarding the circumstances surrounding Mr. Jannsen's visit to psychiatrist, Dr. T. Balcom.

I quote the following extracts from a letter Dr. Balcom wrote to me following the patient's first visit to see him on the 29th August 1978.

> "He presented with a request for psychiatric assessment for the purpose of child custody and other Family Court related matters."
>
> "I did not find him to be suffering from any active psychiatric illness."

Yours sincerely,

"A. M. Warren"
Family Physician

March 22, 1978

To Whom It May Concern:

Mark and Alana Jannsen presented themselves to me for marriage counselling on April 4th, 1975. I saw them in both individual and conjoint interviews over a number of weeks, terminating June 20th, 1975.

During that period of time it appeared evident to me that the prognosis for the marriage was not good, basically because of lack of motivation on the part of one of the partners involved.

However, it also seemed apparent to me that Mr. Mark Jannsen was strongly motivated to do everything within his power to maintain and improve the relationship.

To Whom It May Concern:

Mark Jannsen is my friend, and for the past 5 or 6 years we have confided in each other as brothers. I know him to be kindly, patient, outgoing and compassionate. He has a quiet and humble nature. I have known and seen him take undue criticism and much deliberate abuse, and yet in those circumstances he did not become bitter or resentful, and did not retaliate or revile. Mark has a remarkable forgiving nature, never holds a grudge, and searches his own heart in times of being slighted. My friend also has a keen sense of justice and mercy. He works hard to correct wrongs done by others. He is concerned about the welfare of all, has a great deal of love for children and has sacrificed many hours for the sake of unfortunates. Mark has been very deeply hurt by meddlers in his family affairs and still has not turned to alcohol, drugs, or violence, as many persons might have done under similar stress. I have talked at length with Mark's wife, Alana, and believe her to be suffering from a persecution complex as well as having medical and spiritual problems. (This is my opinion only.) Mark is a conscientious worker and a good provider, and has given his wife a home and luxuries far surpassing what the average person receives. My friend hopes and prays always for a reconciliation despite what has gone before; because he has faith in the future.

I admire his courage when things have been so badly distorted. His optimism that circumstances will change, and his desire to use the love that God gave him, to unite him once more in a peaceful home are certainly admirable.

Mark is not a destroyer, but a builder, and type of citizen which we need more of. There would be very few broken homes and no need for a Welfare State if everyone were like my friend Mark.

I'm convinced because I know his creator and mine.

April 3rd 1979

In addition, this friend notes, "I have talked at length with Mark's wife, Alana, and believe her to be suffering from a persecution complex as well as having medical and spiritual problems. This is my opinion only."

*Summary and Discussion*

Now the meat of this marital disaster is delineated clearly and cogently by the husband in a document some thirty-seven pages in length, which is entitled "Reasons Why I Claim Custody of Both My Children," a hope that in our court system certainly seems rather irrational despite the extensive pathology that will be pointed out throughout this disposition.

Here again, it begins with a discussion of the five official child and family counsellors with whom they have worked. And I quote here that the husband states, "It must be noticed here that five official child and family counsellors have been told by my wife that she is not prepared to work constructively at her marriage with me." And he goes on to list these people: two psychiatrists; family counsellor; family pastor; school psychologist, and goes into some length into the deliberations with these different professionals over his attempts to save this obviously doomed marriage.

"My wife has proven to me too often that her attitude towards even the closest people leads to conflicts. Conflicts with parents, neighbors, relatives, friends, myself and even the children."

Here the psychopath is showing her inability to form or maintain close relationships of any kind with anyone.

> The children need to grow into maturity and self-reliance and become willing to look after responsibilities. But, as they have been spoiled to some degree, they were never given any task or responsibility such as making their own beds, tidying up their rooms, putting away their clothes and shoes, helping in cleaning the yard, etc. In fact, they have grown quite careless and unaccustomed to normal routine and discipline.

Here again, is shown the psychopath's treatment of her children as My Miracle Children who are perfect in every way, and it also shows clearly the wife's inability to teach responsible loving-caring-living because she herself is totally unable even to understand these concepts, much less pass them on to her children.

> The smallness of mind in regard to others, her display of hatred and disgust for my parents, her over-emphasized affection for her own mother and lack of good words for her father, her insulting and emasculating attitude towards me are only devastating results of her poor spiritual being and were, as she probably could not see the severity of these, fully displayed to the children. Her antagonism regarding my religious convictions and ridicule of the Christian faith have already done their destructive work in the minds of our boys.

Here is shown very clearly the widespread destructive behaviour that the psychopath is capable of in the marital disaster. She cannot, again, form any lasting relationship nor can she be ordinarily civil with those who are involved in a family relationship with her. Anything that the husband believes in is automatically relegated to the garbage heap. Here, interestingly enough, she becomes very anti-Christian because her husband is Christian and, as you may remember from Case Two, since the husband was not religious, the first wife became a religious maniac, quoting extensively from religious poetry and stating that it was God who allowed her to be healed and to do all of the depraved things that she did to her husband. Here one sees very clearly how the psychopath acts in a given situation in any marriage, and that is just as the movie editor in which any parts that are not in keeping with the main story (as only she sees it, and this is very far from reality) are cut out and left on the cutting floor; all the rest is patched into a continuous and often unfortunately terribly plausible and convincing movie of life as it is according to her, this being extremely far from reality.

This is an extremely common characteristic of female psychopaths in that they not only can appear to be very plausible people, and as Dr. Cleckley says in his characteristic Number One of the psychopath, that they have a superficial charm and good intelligence. In fact they have a diabolically clever streak that enables them to twist everything that happens in a marital situation and, in fact, without it if they need that support for creation of long-term life plans. They are able to twist anything and everything around to create life as they see it and this often has nothing to do with life as it really is.

> The unrelenting expressions of hatred in regard to some individuals, including my parents and myself, will not cease, in my opinion, if the children were under the custody of their mother. The fearful result will be that the children will develop, because of the continuing demonstrations of husband rejection, an inferiority complex for being male and their future chance of becoming good family men will be small. Also, a severe risk exists that they become aware of the unfairness of their mother's attitude and therefore develop a subconscious rejection and suspicion of women in general and wives in particular.

A very perceptive comment by the husband, in that this is so often true, as we see in this office all the time; the children of currently divorcing mothers will be in the office within ten or fifteen years to get their own divorce because they too have been crippled by the psychopathic female. Here is the best example of the crippling of the children, *folie a deux,* as they say in psychiatry, the illness created in the child by the illness of the parent.

> As already mentioned, a number of counsellors who had attended on our marriage, evaluated the "marriage" as destructive on all family members, advised dissolvement of the marriage for the benefit of the children and recognized the fact that it was the wife who did not wish to work constructively on the matrimonial relationship.

It is interesting that here too the psychopathic wife never sees that it is her unwillingness to work on the marital relationship (possibly because she can't conceive of what a matrimonial relationship should be, or could be), and usually the relationship evolves into a slanging match in which everything good that happens in the marriage is her responsibility and everything had that is happening in the marriage is "all his fault." Therefore the husband is in a no-win situation with a psychopathic wife and can only hang in there, as they so often do for ten, fifteen, or twenty years, to try to preserve some form of family life for their children, but all the time realizing in the back of their minds certainly that this cannot work. However, again one sees the fact that the man who really could see the writing on the wall still hung in there in an attempt to carry on a marital relationship and provide a home for the children.

I will love you if you will love me and hate your father. Real love is unconditional, but my wife's love is conditional. She goes into hateful actions if the children show affection to their father and co-operate with him.

Here again we see the wife recruiting the children into her campaign against the husband and continuing to promote just absolute emotional and spiritual disaster in a matrimonial and family relationship. And here again, it is so well pointed out how crippling the psychopathic mother can be on the development of the children who may well become psychopathic themselves.

My wife encourages the children to use profane language.

He gives many examples of this, in which she allows the children to go on and on using profane language, doesn't stop them, and enjoys seeing her husband's discomfort over allowing this to happen. This extremely irrational behaviour again shows total irresponsibility and amorality, and also further use of the children in recruitment against the father's feelings, undoubtedly his religious feelings and his Christianity. He further points out the things his wife did in front of the children to further her aims at alienating them and confusing their sexuality, since her own sexuality is trivial and superficial, if not totally absent.

My wife started to yell at me. Knockhead. Don't listen to that dirty old man—God damn—I will cut his balls from his body. Your old man is dangerous. I will call the police. He is just stupid. He was a rotten kid at home, so his Dad kicked him out of the house when he was sixteen. All the neighbors know he is a bastard. . . . And there was much more than that.

Here again, one sees the psychopathic female's undermining of the male presence in the household. Here, for the first time, we also see her mention of the police. She has extended her recruitment in her battle against the husband. And here too has she not only recruited the police and the neighbours, but is also now recruiting his parents as allies in her cause because she states that he was a rotten kid and kicked out at home, so obviously the parents are on her side too.

Next we go on to the statement of the husband's feelings of what the expected behaviour of his wife would be if she were given custody of the boys as he has determined from his twenty years of observing her behaviour.

Poor attitude and contempt of relatives and acquaintances will involve the children.

Here again is her inability to form any relationship of any lasting importance.

> "Fluctuates severely from being extremely tolerant to extremely harsh."

Here is the "marvellous" inconsistency of the psychopath because she really has no ability to set up moral limits or standards, or even behaviour limits or standards for the children, therefore fluctuates wildly and again poisons the minds of the children.

> Raising pity for herself. Dramatizing hospital treatments she had. Excessive complaining and crying.

Here again is the martyrdom and the miracle-birth syndrome, etc.

> No leadership in designating tasks at home. No building up feelings of responsibility. Frustrates religious thinking. Ridicules religious beliefs. Boycotts religious training and participation.

Well, here again, it goes without saying that the psychopath is totally unable to determine what is moral or amoral or what is responsible or irresponsible and is actively involved in tearing down any of the creations of the husband in the marital situation, such as his religion.

> Must have a "victim" to discharge evil and hostile feelings on. The "victim" with certainty will be the children as I, the original victim, will not be there if my wife has custody.

Here again, one sees an interesting statement: that the victim needs his persecutor as the martyr needs his tormentor. This, of course, can very well be transposed into the psychopath's needs. Here too one sees that the courts are not apparently able to deal with the appreciation of the situation that carries on after the dissolution of a marriage when a psychopathic wife is given custody of the children and is thus able to continue to create and perpetuate her bizarre parental style, thereby crippling the children; crippling so that they too are doomed in any marital situation in which they will become involved in the future.

A statement typed by the husband and headed "History of Sexual Relationship, Mental Cruelty, Insults and Verbal Violence":

> Six years prior to our legal wedding, my wife (at that time married to Mr. X) approached me with a plea for helping her with problems she had in her marriage. I believed her accusations of adultery, brutality and negligence against her husband.

Here again, we see the utter plausibility of the psychopath's creations and a psychopathic female's ability to convince others that it is all the husband's fault. She lies, twists reality, anything to fit the script of life as she sees it. He points out in his petition that before the court actions of her first divorce procedures, his current wife and he had become lovers.

> I felt committed to her and as I believed strongly that she was within her rights I personally moved her from her matrimonial home to the home of her parents, and on her behalf I handled all her legal activities and became a main instrument in that matter.

Here again, the plausibility, the convincing of the husband with an almost religious zeal with which the psychopathic female recruits her intended mate and transforms him into her shining knight and savior.

> Looking back I cannot see why I allowed myself to be led into a situation not acceptable by my own standards. I know now that Mrs. X merely exchanged husbands for the sake of material improvements. Her false pretences to achieve this have bothered me very much and must be considered mentally cruel.

Interesting to note that this statement, which he is now making, is twenty years after the fact of the marriage that culminated the seduction by the wife as she got out of the first marriage, directly into a relationship with her current husband. Here again, the wife appeared to be plausible and of good character and had gotten the husband fully recruited in her campaign against the original husband. Here again we see the marvellous ability of these people to recruit others in their marital disaster wars against the current husband.

> Approximately six months before the divorce actions had started, Mrs. X had moved into my quarters on the request of her mother as Mrs. X could not live in peace with her younger sister in their parent's home.

Here again a marvellous example of even the psychopath's mother noting that this woman was unable to maintain any normal relationship within the family (quite possibly the mother in this case was also a psychopath, but that is only an assumption).

Next he goes on at great length to discuss the sexual disaster present in the marriage and states:

> During that period of living together it would have been, naturally speaking, inevitable that we lived fully a married life. But I soon found that my partner could not perform or did not want to perform the complete act.
>
> Mrs. X claimed that her sexual inability was, as her doctor had advised, a physical matter and could be helped with a minor operation as soon as desired. To me, she mentioned that she felt fortunate that this was not done during her marriage with Mr. X, the original husband,

> as children would have resulted from that marriage. Now, after the experiences reported in here further, I see that this thing was not merely a physical problem, but a problem of the mind and that her first marriage could not last and that my own "marriage" with her had to run to an end despite the 20 years of frustrations and 20 years of patience in anticipation of an improving relationship.

Here one sees many things. First, the inability of a psychopath to form a sexual relationship; secondly, the extreme cleverness with which the psychopath can use sex as an excuse and as a weapon, and also how she can dangle the hope of a good sexual relationship in front of the man. It was amazing that she could dangle this for twenty years; however, that she did. And as so often happens in a psychopathic marriage, he was still hoping. Hope seems to be a great characteristic of the husband of the psychopathic female, in that she has carefully chosen him, as we have said before, for his marvellous ability to hang in there and try his damnedest to promote a healthy family life. Here the husband puts in his own words: *"20 years of patience in anticipation of an improving relationship."*

It is amazing that the psychopathic female can select her victims so well. They seem to pick very cleverly a male partner who is exactly the opposite of the psychopath in that he has all the qualities that the psychopath lacks; is able to formulate long-term plans, to endure frustrations, to attempt to provide a happy home for the family, etc., etc.

He goes on to state:

> I entered marriage with my wife on the assurance given by her that indeed the sexual handicap could be resolved, but this proved to be false . . .
>
> I now feel that I must have been infatuated in the beginning as my wife's emotional disorder and sexual inability did not seem to shake me very much and also it was probable that the outward symptoms of emotional disorder at that time were only very mild as naturally she could not afford to jeopardize the intended legal wedding with me.

Here one sees pointed out very clearly Dr. Cleckley's point Number Three, which is the absence of nervousness or psychoneurotic manifestations in the psychopathic female. The husband feels here, obviously, that this was a planned thing by the female, whereas we would feel this is part of her psychopathy: That she really did not have a plan. She just lacked any nervousness or psychoneurotic manifestation and at the same time certainly lacked any sense of remorse or shame over her inability to carry on a sexual relationship. It also points out her extreme untruthfulness and insincerity in her discussions of her sexual problem. Her promises for the future, etc., are hollow as we will see all down the line in further discussion of this case. Again, it must be emphasized these women are so plausible and so clever that they are able to talk anybody into anything.

I recall some occasions on which she revealed some of the darker aspects of her inner self which I used to classify as common with any individual and not worthwhile remembering.

Here we note again the husband excusing the psychopathic female and really not paying attention to the darker aspects until some twenty years subsequent when he is writing this anguished account. He can see things a bit more clearly after extensive counselling and after having been relieved of the presence of the psychopathic female (who, by her very presence, seems to cloud any husband's thinking and his ability to see clearly what is happening in the marital situation).

When she started to side with my landlady in regard to the landlady's marital problems, she could no longer hide her feelings concerning me and called me a dictator, a slave-driver, a dirty egotist, accused me of taking advantage of her, etc.

We had agreed that during our wedding ceremony no other people would be present other than both our parents, yet she permitted all her brothers and sisters and cousins to attend but my own brothers and sisters did not come in accordance with the agreement.

Here we see the inconsistency and the ability of the psychopathic female to do whatever she feels she wants to do in the relationship and her demand that the husband or suitor accept her feelings, and carry on with the original agreements, even though she herself is unable to appreciate the importance of the agreement.

Also a heavy shocker and an early indication that her reason for the relationship was only a materialistic one was that after the wedding had taken place she told an acquaintance of our how glad *she was that she now had the marriage license which gave her the assurance that she would be looked after in the future.*

Here is shown the total amorality of the psychopath. Her feelings, now that she had a marriage license, this was a license to really let loose on her psychopathy without having to worry about the future because she would be looked after. Because she is unable to see into the future and because she feels that she, her marriage, and her motherhood are miraculous, she cannot conceive of the fact that the marriage will not function in the future and only sees it as a comfortable pew from which she can now carry on with her previously designed life plan.

After our wedding had taken place, the promise to see a doctor as early as possible was not adhered to. In the summer of 1964, the doctor put her in hospital for examination. After this the doctor explained to both of us that she was physically a normal woman and that intercourse *had to be possible.* As a result of the doctor's instructions, we had intercourse twice, but actual penetration did not take place. We were fortunate, however, and conceived Stanley.

Here again is described what is almost a miraculous birth, but most importantly we see the sex life is totally trivial and impersonal and only indulged to complete her life plan—to gain the child. Nothing of an inter-personal relationship whatsoever as far as sexuality is concerned.

> The Cesarean Delivery. I feel now that the problem in the delivery room was caused by the same emotional disorders that are incapacitating her of having sex. In this light, of course, it is a rare hope that she will ever have a normal sex life if she cannot even co-operate in delivering her baby.

This was discussed in the introduction. It is interesting to note that her inability to carry on normal sexuality extended into her delivery-room deliberations. The second child was delivered by Caesarean section as well.

> After the birth of the second child the inability of having sex remained as it was, and with the responsibility of having a family, I did not see any other alternative than to live with the very difficult situation.

Here again it is pointed out the remarkable ability of a psychopath to pick a devoted family man, as she obviously did in that he was willing to put up with anything and everything to maintain a normal family.

> October, 1972, the doctor recommended a hysterectomy for my wife and a second operation which would make normal sex possible.

Here is an indication that the doctor was confident that normal sex at that time was still not the case and that he was determined to do anything within his power to improve the situation.

> Both operations were carried out. For over two months my wife had been laying or sitting on the chesterfield day and night doing nothing but drinking coffee, smoking and staring at some fixed point. She claimed not to be *capable of doing anything* because the surgery had to heal.

Here again is the inconsistency and the failure to carry through on promises that the psychopathic female is famous for. Also, again, the martyrdom of the psychopath. She had given up her uterus and was therefore martyred on the couch, unable to do anything. Again, the long-suffering husband hanging in there.

> It was about at the third month after the hospital release that we tried to have intercourse. It did not work. *I could not help noticing my wife's satisfaction in that she still was incapable of the normal sex act.* As this occurrence was not only a demonstration of physical inability but what is more, proof of willful mental and emotional alienation, there has been from 1972 to the present, 1980, no further physical contact.

Again, it shows another characteristic of the psychopath in that she was in total control and although totally incapable of participating in a sexual relationship as a healthy part of a marital relationship, she was only able to use sex in furthering her own diabolical wishes. First she had used it to very miraculously become pregnant for the delivery of two children and was now using it to totally undermine the man's manhood. Here is the "dance away, lover" routine. She managed to pull the old trick of suck the guy in, promise him everything, and enjoy the fact that, "sorry, fella, heh, heh."

> It must be emphasized that after 20 years of frustration and of excusing my wife all that time for not being responsible for the way she was, it is a despairing thought to find that there is not the slightest goodwill on her side and that her attitude evidently is chronic.

Here again, the supreme tolerance of the mate who was so carefully chosen and also the peculiar inability of the mate to see the fact that the relationship is totally finished, but he just can't get out of it. Only after a great deal of professional intervention from the outside is the male in the psychopathic female marriage able to bail out and save himself. Unfortunately, the courts tend to award custody to the mother and therefore the psychopathic generations carry on; the father is out alone and only further demeaned for abandoning his family, etc., etc., since the very plausible wife is so often believed by society to be the pure and holy Mother, and who can argue against Motherhood?

Furthering his quote:

> This means she has not only rejected me physically in a permanent way, but has also very consciously rejected me as a person. It also means that she has not only robbed me from a good marriage and a happy family for the future, but that she has robbed me of that in the past 20 years in a deliberate and willfull way. Also, last but not least, it must be emphasized that besides me she has robbed our children of much happiness and given them frustration, anxiety and a future life of many emotional problems and personal conflicts. I have been working and aiming for a healthy marital relationship which was to form the basis for a healthy atmosphere for the children to grow up in. This was my purpose but she has destroyed it.

This is a very cogent description of the marital destruction reaped by the psychopath; it is very well described in his own words, with very little to add.

> Even after the last attempt at intercourse *I still did not give up trying* to keep the atmosphere sufficiently unstrained for the sake of all of us. I have shown her affection and concern, I have asked her to forgive the things I have done wrong. I have offered to forgive her and forget everything. Nothing has helped. I received arrogance, greed and hostility in return but I only failed to see that this situation would never

> change. It was only as a result of the advice received from two of the various counsellors we had that I finally had to admit that the situation was severely destructive on all of us and that at least the children had to be protected.

Here again the wonder of the long-suffering husband asking for forgiveness. Lord knows what he apparently did in a major way to try and destroy this marriage compared to the psychopathic female, but here again we have him wanting to forgive, forget, and start all over again. It is the old victim's approach to the psychopath. Her again the final realization that the marriage is doomed only comes from outside professional pressure, which finally enabled the victim to end this pathological marriage. It does not allow the pathological effects on the children to end since the psychopathic mother is usually awarded custody, as she was in this case.

> I am in no way wanting to take revenge on my wife but my purpose is (and this is all that is left for me as a last resort) to confront my wife with this petition and all the possible consequences of it. I sincerely hope that by means of this court action she will come to understand that the present situation cannot be maintained and that she therefore runs the risk of becoming deprived of her family and of a meaningful life. Hopefully that as a result she may come to see her rebellious attitude towards her husband and all the damage that was caused by it and that as a result she may then agree on a *RECONCILIATION*

Here again it is almost becoming pathological on his part, his wishes for a reconciliation and the endless hope that the psychopath can be taught something. The psychopath is totally unable to learn from experience, and therefore any maneouvres to teach her anything are doomed to failure.

Further quote:

> Further, she must agree that we both will receive counselling regarding normal family life, rearing children, managing finances and a normal sex life. If satisfactory results are not achieved within a six month period, it must then be assumed that the reconciliation was not based on genuine intentions. In that event the claim for divorce and custody of both children would be reinstated.

Here again the desperation of this husband to try and create a happy life out of the marital wreckage; he is "plea bargaining," trying to threaten her into changing and maintaining a home by the threat of divorce and a custody fight for the children. It is unfortunate his use of the words "genuine intentions," since psychopaths are incapable of "genuine intentions." They wouldn't know what a genuine intention was.

It was on New Year's Eve, 1965/66, that she erupted in a kind of psychotic discharge which must have been boiling within her from the beginning. She called me names and used curses and vulgar language. When I tried to comfort her, she tried to kick and punch and she clawed me in the face. There was no apparent cause for this. The thing I had hoped for was a quiet and intimate New Year's Eve for the first time as a family (we had our six month old Stanley). I went out for a walk in order to let her come to herself and to avoid becoming abusive myself.

Here the violent irrational behaviour of the psychopath precipitated by alcohol on New Year's Eve; even though the violent and totally irrational behaviour was seen early in the marriage, he is still wishfully thinking that she will, and I quote, "come to herself." *What a hope.*

When the baby was born she told people and myself that I hurt her feelings badly because I took the duties of a Mother out of her hands. But when the baby had to be fed during the night she slammed doors and made enough other noise to keep me awake deliberately. This forced me to look after the baby in order to keep the night quiet, the interruptions short and my wife at peace. Hence, her complaint was not rational.

Here we are with the Martyrdom of Motherhood again.

In 1967 we bought our house. For nearly a year she hardly did anything to the interior of the house because she said the house was not what she wanted. For about three years she kept nagging and arguing about the house (which was new and a palace compared with what we used to have).

Here the never satisfied egocentricity of the psychopathic, which so very often revolved around houses, cars, trips to Hawaii, the trappings of a good life, so-called.

Her demands were always opposing what I did or what I had done or what I intended to do. The final result of that attitude is that, like the matter of the house, nothing could be done except to keep things as they were at the sacrifice of progress and activity.

Here again the husband cannot win, and this requires untold sacrifice.

When the children had become little boys and both had become aware of their surroundings, my wife started to use them as a shield for her protection when assailing me with all kinds of unreasonable demands.

Here she has really reached the Martyrdom of Motherhood. She has real weapons to employ in the marital destruction and the assault on her husband; she has *hostages* in the marital warfare.

> She uses abusive language, humiliating statements and assumes an overbearing and domineering attitude, attempting to emasculate me in the eyes and the minds of the children. On many occasions up until this time, when the children showed any sympathy for me she would hurl abusive words and humiliating remarks at the children.

Here is a sign of the peculiar "morality" of the psychopath as far as loyalty is concerned. The children should be loyal to her (even though as a female psychopath she wouldn't even know what loyalty is); to her it is a word, not a concept.

Further evidence of her use of the children as a shield:

> In the nights she would yell for our boys when she thought I made sexual advances. In the night she often called me the most filthy things and used to say I was just like a "rabbit" and that I should see a doctor as wanting sex "every" night (there never was any for the last many years) was a sickness. Also to protect herself from any sexual action from my side and to fully pacify me she very often would take the youngest one (the oldest one would take up too much space) and put him in her bed.

Here again the children used as a shield, the use of sexuality as a weapon in the marriage, and the psychopath's great song that "I'm okay, you're the one who is depraved."

> My wife has done a lot of brainwashing in this fashion to instill in them an antipathy against their father. She achieved this to quite an extent. In this respect she follows the attitude of her mother who all too often openly "accused" or ran down my wife's father. As a result, none of my wife's brothers and sisters had much regard for their father. Attending the funeral of her mother my wife displayed a stubborn hostility against her father, who at that time was dying in the hospital. I believe that children who have a chronic hate against parents will be guilt-ridden and unhappy for their entire life.

Here is a brilliant statement on the origins of psychopathy. Like mother, like daughter. The female psychopath implants in the children a crippling attitude towards sexuality, towards motherhood, fatherhood, towards family life, towards in effect any relationship of any kind, either with people, with religion, etc.

> On many occasions in the presence of the children my wife tried to provoke my anger to such a degree that I felt the tendency to physically harm her. Although I have never done such a thing, she tried to instruct the boys to testify that they indeed had seen me hurting her.

Here we see her lying and recruiting the children in the war.

While the children, together with their friend, Jay, arrived on the scene she hung on to the door, kicked it, pushed me and dropped herself partly to the floor, while yelling and screaming. She kicked the door of my study hard and flung it open, she took my bicycle and threw it in the door opening, she ripped a tapestry from the basement wall and then ran outside where the children were, yelling: "He hurt me, call the police, call the neighbours, stay away, kids, he is dangerous. Now you have seen what an animal he is. Now we will make him leave the house." Twenty minutes later I overheard the conversation between my child and Jay.

"Can I sleep in your house tonight?" asks Jay. "No, not tonight, Mom says we may have to sleep in another place."

*Jay:* Why?

*Leslie:* You know, my Dad is dangerous.

*Jay:* Can you come and sleep in my house?

*Leslie:* I'd like to, but I'd better not. Where would my Mom sleep?

*Jay:* She'll stay in her own home.

*Leslie:* No, I'd better not. We always sleep with Mom. Dad will not do anything when people are around.

*Jay:* Why?

*Leslie:* Mom says he is really dangerous.

Here, very clearly, her attempts to intimidate the husband, to undermine his relationship with the children, to make him out as the great ogre in the marital situation, creating scenes to justify her anti-husband activities, her histrionics, her screaming, her recruitment of the people, the neighbours, and even, sadly, of little Jay at age eight, into this conspiracy against the husband and the marriage as a whole.

On another occasion—reversed situation. The children were in bed trying to sleep. My wife was playing records loudly. My children asked me to tell Mom to turn the noise down. When I did she became hostile. A little later when I was in the basement I heard her turn the sound up and fling the bedroom doors open, giving the sound the opportunity to enter the boys' rooms full strength.

Here the psychopath's absolute need for total control. "I'll show you who is in control of this household."

Evidently to re-inforce her strength against me, in August 1973 she invited her sister (loud-mouthed woman of terrible morals and a terrible temper) over, even though it was against my will. During her stay in our home she continuously tried to antagonize me with insinuations and interfered with our marriage problems and instilled further discontent in my wife's mind.

Here again is the wife in total control, inviting this terrible sister into the situation; obviously, she a psychopath in her own right, having come from the same family disaster as the psychopathic female in this marriage; she has recruited her also in the marital destruction.

> After four weeks with us, my wife's sister returned to Holland where she phoned my parents and upset these 78 year old people with slanderous and defamatory information regarding my personal behaviour.

Here again, just the total amorality of the psychopathic female. She's lying, she's recruiting steadily to her cause, even recruiting aged parents of the husband across the Atlantic Ocean into her relentless assault on the husband and the marriage.

> For years my wife has threatened to blackmail me by "disclosing" my "real personality" to my supervisors at work. She has recently done this. This particular person advised me of what he had heard from my wife. The details covered my sexual behaviour and complaints about lack of money.

Here again the psychopath's inability to see the consequences of her actions. Again an extension of her recruiting now of his employers—another attempt to undermine the husband out in the workplace when her efforts to destroy him in the home are insufficient. Interesting that the accusation that she made to his superiors covered sexual behaviour and lack of money, two common battlegrounds for psychopathic females. It seems that the male caught in this situation can never earn enough dollars to satisfy the needs of the psychopathic female who is devoted to the trappings of the better life, Hawaii, furs, huge homes, etc., etc.

> When a friend visited us she openly claimed that I had for some time been associating with public women.

Here again lying, vilification of the husband, and the recruiting of the friend on to her side.

> In regard to her inability/unwillingness to have a normal married life, she repeatedly says it is not she, but it is me who is sexually unfit and she says that this is obvious for if I was normal, I would go out with other women.

Here again one sees the total amorality of the psychopathic female. She is just totally unable to recognize that this is an amoral statement. It is also a furtherance of her campaign that, "It is not me, buddy, it is you who is crazy and crippled in this world."

> It is obvious, however, that she hopes that I at some time will become accuseable of adultery so that, I suspect, she will then be able to use that against me and claim custody of the children and demand a high alimony.

Here the poor husband attributes to her a "normal degree of foresight," one that she cannot really form because she is totally unable to plan that far ahead and one would suspect her statements about going out with other women are just another sign of her total amorality.

Further statements in entrenchment of "I'm right and you're wrong" in the marital fight are these quotes from the husband's record on her statements to him and other people about him. And to quote:

> No wonder you have no friends, you are just rotten to everybody.
>
> "Touch me if you dare, I will call the police on you. You're a homosexual. (Interesting that her first husband was also repeatedly a homosexual.) You're repulsive, no wonder other women don't want you."
>
> "You're an imbecile."
>
> "You need psychiatric care."
>
> "You're not a man."

She certainly worked hard to impress this on him.

> "There are much better men for me than you are."
>
> "I will bring your clothes to the doctor so he will know how you stink."

Here again she is working as hard as she can on his sense of right and wrong, his manhood, his sexuality, his sense of cleanliness, his intelligence.

Here again the violence after no apparent cause, an incident on whether the boys should watch later TV or whether they shouldn't, so he turned it off and away she went on a totally irrational and violent attack upon him.

> (The following paragraphs 2.29 and on were written on the dates shown.)
>
> 2.29. The following is another record of how my wife tried to provoke fights in order to agitate the children against me and perhaps to make them witness against me. It was Saturday evening, December 20 1975, 7.30 P.M. I was studying Scout requirements with Stanley and Leslie. The boys expressed enjoyment. Wife showed intolerance by interfering with us. 8.05 P.M. "Million Dollar Man" on TV. The boys started to watch that and I went down to my study for reading.
>
> 9.35 P.M. One of the boys banged on the floor, calling me up. Stanley asked for continuation of the Danny Kaye show, Leslie was asking for same. Both had gone to bed. Wife was lamenting that the boys had gone to bed because of me. She had promised them the TV show but they knew I was against it.
>
> Wife had deliberately changed the channels from 9 to 12 at 9 o'clock to introduce the Danny Kaye show to the boys. She knows I do not

concur with TV shows right before bedtime. (Regular bedtime is 8 for Leslie and 8.30 for Stanley. But often they go much later without my OK.) The Danny Kaye show would have lasted till 11.30 P.M., much too late to my opinion and therefore, I insisted that they stayed in bed and went to sleep.

9.40 P.M. Wife went on with arguing and insulting me in her usual manner, also challenging me to hit her so she could call the police. She obstructed me when I wanted to move into the kitchen to get myself something to drink before going to bed. I wanted to leave her by herself and retire early. She started to yell for the boys. None of the boys came immediately. When I moved back she took a broom and hit me a few times with it. The mop flew off and the metal end hit me on the head leaving a boil. At the instant of the beating, Leslie had come out of his room, saw what was going on and went back into his room screaming of fear.

In the previous chapters of this document, I described the destructive mentality of my wife and expressed the damage that was already done and above all I expressed my concern of damage that was being incurred on our two children in regard of emotions, mentality, education, etc.

I believe that my concern would be accepted as genuine and the threat to my children likely. However, not much could I show as evidence.

Here he shows that there is offered no hope in our court system for such a man to get custody of his children since he himself states, "not much could I show as evidence." In the psychopathic home, so much of the violence, emotional, physical and spiritual goes on behind closed doors and such a good front is so often put on outside that the husband in this situation in truth really has no evidence to show on the outside in support of his declarations of this marital disaster. In fact, even the long devotion these husbands usually becomes involved in (some twenty years) would appear to prejudice the case because certainly most rational people cannot understand how an individual could put up with such vilification, abuse, and disaster just to maintain a happy home. However, it again points out the extreme cleverness of the psychopath picking a mate who is devoted to building a happy family and, just like a dog at the end of a rag, won't give up.

Stanley and Leslie have to my feeling, been fully pressurized by their mother not further to be active in Cub Scouts. I am very certain about my wife's motives; as I was the leader of the Cub pack Stanley and Leslie were a member of, I had great influence on their growth in skill of all sorts, physical, moral and spiritual. This was the only fellowship I had with my children and was severely resented by my wife.

Here again the psychopathic wife's inability to tolerate "disloyalty" by her children, and the outlook of the psychopathic female that any show of loyalty, which would be accepted as normal, to the male in the situation is looked on as a terrible threat to her Motherhood creation and therefore must be disposed of—so she furthers her interference in the father/child relationship.

> Approximately November, 1977. My wife uses every opportunity to ridicule Christian beliefs and scoffs religious practises. She knows I am anxious to see my children grow in knowledge of the hidden but much more important aspects of life, but she wishes to make this a point of controversy and in lieu deceives the children with blasphemy and imposing the fantasy world of TV on them.

Here again the psychopath's maintaining her total control by ridiculing her husband's beliefs. And, of course, here the modern world of North American TV certainly becomes an accomplice to the psychopath wife in that so much of the TV world of family life shows the father as a doddering, sweet but incompetent fool. Interesting here because the husband is religious, the wife becomes anti-religious, where in Case Two where the husband was not religious, the wife became a fanatical religious nut. It appears that any course of action that is anti-establishment of normal relationships in a marital situation is to be applauded, and therefore the psychopathic wife sets out to destroy any shred of spiritual life in the home situation.

Further alienation of the father from family life is very clearly pointed out in this common occurrence in psychopathic households, that of alienating the father from family councils. The only family council most fathers manage to get being mealtime. And I quote:

> She either eats early, before I get home from work or she does not set a place for me. On one occasion she claimed she had kept my supper warm in the oven. I repeated what I always insisted on, that as I am mostly home early, I want my meals with my family. Now she is practically not cooking for me.

Here again she is using her tremendous power to interfere with the father having any part whatsoever in the counselling of the children.

The following episode is an example of further recruitment in her war against the husband, now of the "authorities."

> On a Sunday morning in February 1977, I asked Stanley and Leslie to clean up the front yard. My wife started to yell using many curses, that the boys did not have to listen to that dictator (me) and that she was going to call the police if I said a further word to the children. I told her I was not impressed with her actions including her mentioning police help. Then I left for some business in the meeting place of the Cub Scouts.
>
> In the evening, 9 o'clock, the wife returned with two police officers, one male and one female. The wife called me as there was "someone"

> to see me. So I came. The male officer asked me if "everything was quiet" and on my affirmation they immediately left again. The wife still managed to ask the lady officer if she (wife) could call again if he (me) did it again. She did not get an answer, and I wonder what she meant by "do it again" as she was the only one out of line.

Here again the psychopath's recruitment of outside authorities to maintain her control. Also her feeling of, "I'll show you, you bastard, I mean business," and in addition we see her conspiratorial abilities and her inability to see reality. Really the police wanted no part of this dispute, which they didn't see as anything of any importance, and yet she still attempted to carry on by asking the lady officer (most notably rather than the male) if she could call again if he did whatever he did again.

In summary of this case, *Jannsen v. Jannsen,* there is really provided the best all-round documentation and opportunity for interspersed commentary on the classical psychopathic female and her marriage. There can, therefore, be no hesitation in stating that this documentation is a classical chronicle of flagrant female psychopathy.

## MOLDERS

This is a perfect classic example of amorality bordering on immorality of the typical female psychopath. The two letters to follow in the documentation were written eleven short months apart, and they illustrate very clearly the psychopath's tendency to be like the movie editor—whatever in life doesn't fit their particular plan for the movie, they cut out and leave on the cutting room floor, patch up the rest of it, and come out with their own version of *"reality."* It also very clearly shows the remarkable ability of the female psychopath to make everything that happens in life that is wrong be the fault of the mate and everything in life that is right to be the wonderful work of she, the loving devoted wife and mother.

The two letters speak for themselves, but note that the first letter was accompanied by five pages of typed prayers, which were sent obviously as a learning experience, to the husband by the psychopathic female who had done as is so commonly the case, placed her destiny outside of her own hands so that it was not only the fault of the hopeless husband, but was also now in the lap of the gods—she has no responsibility whatsoever.

*Documentation*

November 23, 1978

My dearest darling husband:

I cannot bear being away from you for so long. I have suffered enough for my pride, I cannot take any more. I am moving this weekend into a two-bedroomed condominium at the Montecito house complex. My new phone there will be 299–4077 and will be in service on Monday the 27th. I am taking such an expensive place as I want to give Luke a home from Christmas and pray to God and all the saints in heaven that my husband and Baby Luke's father will come home for Christmas. I told Joyce that it was my intention to spend Christmas in Walnut Grove but this is not so. I intend to spend Christmas at my new home unit #7—7313 Montecito Drive and to watch the door and hover over the phone praying that my husband will knock on the door or telephone saying that all was forgiven and that he wanted the two of us, the three of us together again.

Dylan, my husband, please forgive me and take me back, I cannot bear any more the pain and anguish of being away from you. Joyce told me that you intend to leave America if you do not obtain a divorce from me. Dylan, if you do that I shall wait until my tenant's lease is up, sell up the house, pack my bags, put Baby Luke, your son, on my hip and follow you where ever you go. Even if I am not with you I want to be near you and I shall wait a million years for you to look around and see me loving you and waiting for you. The past is past, my darling, and it has only served to prove to me just how valuable and dearly beloved you are to me. Please return to me and your son and I shall worship and honour you all the days of my life and shall not want any more. My new home has been chosen with you in mind, for you have always loved a beautiful home and even though I will find it financially crippling I shall maintain it as long as possible, hoping and praying that you will come in. I shall be spending Christmas alone with Baby Luke in my/our home and shall live in hope that you will come. Please come, my darling. Do not be too proud to reach out for me and your son, we have a lot of making up to do and a lot to live for.

I now truly appreciate what a wonderful husband you have been and will be and how truly, and how desperately I love you. I have been praying to St. Jude, the saint of the church we were married in, to bring us together again; and if it takes the rest of my life, I shall continue to pray and wait for you.

With my life and spirit I love you and want you back.

*Devotion to St. Jude Thaddeus*

Sign of the cross
Rosary

O glorious apostle, St. Jude Thaddeus, patron of hopeless cases who was chosen by God to give testimony of the true faith, suffered all kinds of tortures and in the end gave your life and blood rather than deny it, obtain for us a similar faith and like you to be ever ready and glad to confess it at any time and on every occasion and to be ready to die rather than deny it. Encourage us, dear saint, to mortify our rebellious flesh by penance so that dying to the world and to ourselves we may live in God alone and gain merits for eternity.

(Our Father, hail Mary and glory be)

Pay for us, blessed Jude Thaddeus, that we may be worthy of the promises of Christ

Let Us Pray

O God, who through thy blessed apostle Jude Thaddeus has brought us into the knowledge of thy name, grant us both to celebrate his eternal glory by making progress in virtue and by celebrating his glory to advance in virtue through our lord, Jesus Christ.

Amen

## Hymn to St. Jude

Thou the hope of all the hopeless
None who seeks thine aid's bereft
None who turns to thee in anguish
In the wilderness is left
So to thee I turn for comfort
In mine hour of dark despair
All my path is strewn with sorrow
Great St. Jude, O hear my prayer
In this vale of tears so lonely
I have seen but dark and pain
Friendless, broken, poor, forsaken
I have sought the stars in vain

## Litany of St. Jude

Lord, have mercy on us
Christ, have mercy on us
Lord, have mercy on us
Christ, hear us
Christ, graciously hear us
God, the Father of Heaven, have mercy on us
God, the Son, Redeemer of the world, have mercy on us
God, the Holy Spirit, have mercy on us
Holy Trinity, One God, Have Mercy on us

Holy Mary, pray for us
Holy Mother of God, Pray for us
Holy Virgin of Virgins, pray for us
St. Jude Thaddeus, Pray for us
Kinsman of Jesus, Mary and Joseph, pray for us
Worthy and glorious apostle, pray for us
Apt student of the divine master, pray for us
Faithful follower of Jesus, pray for us
Pilgrim under divine providence, pray for us
Witness of the faith, pray for us
Lover of Poverty, pray for us
Model of humility and patience, pray for us
Lily of purity, pray for us
Flame of divine love, pray for us
Star of holiness, pray for us
Vessel of divine grace, pray for us
Terror of hell, pray for us
Pillar of the Holy Church, pray for us
Consoler of the afflicted, pray for us
Advocate of sinners, pray for us

Light of the perplexed, pray for us
Support of the timid, pray for us
Staff of the despairing, pray for us
Great wonder worker, pray for us
Gracious intercessor of divine grace, pray for us
Speedy advocate of those who invoke thee, pray for us
Faithful assistant of those who trust in thee, pray for us
Willing helper of the needy, pray for us
Ready supporter in the most difficult circumstances, pray for us
Powerful advocate in desperate cases, pray for us
Loving protector of all who honour thee, pray for us
Lamb of God, you take away the sins of the world
Spare us, O Lord
Lamb of God, you take away the sins of the world
Graciously hear Us, O Lord
Lamb of God, you take away the sins of the world
Have mercy on us, O Lord

Pray for us, blessed Jude Thaddeus, that we may be made worthy of the Promises of Christ.

*Let Us Pray*

Holy apostle, Jude Thaddeus, faithful servant and friend of Jesus Christ, who on account of the similarity of your name to that of the traitor fail to obtain from many the devotion which is your due by reason of your apostolic and holy life and yet in every corner of the universe are revered by devout Catholics as the special patron of the unfortunate and despairing, obtain from God for me by Your Intentions, Comfort in my sorrow and distress, help in my present urgent emergency and peace in my last hours so that with you and all the elect I may sing the praises of God for ever.

AMEN

St. Jude, glorious apostle, faithful servant, and friend of Jesus, too often have we passed thee over in our devotions. But all those who attentive to the honour the holy church pays thee have recourse to thy intercession have abundant proof of thy power to help as especially when things seem desperate (here mention your request). Pray for me who am so miserable. Make use, I implore thee of that particular privilege accorded to thee to bring visible and speedy help where help is most despaired of. Come to my assistance in this great need that I may receive the consolation and succour of heaven in all my necessities, tribulations and sufferings and that I may bless GOD with thee and all the elect throughout eternity. I promise thee, O Blessed Jude, to be ever mindful of this great favour and I will never cease to honour thee as my special and powerful patron and do all in my power to encourage devotion to thee. Amen

Our Father, hail Mary and Gloria
Most sacred heart of Jesus—have mercy on us
Immaculate heard of Mary—pray for us
St. Joseph—pray for us
St. Jude—pray for us—sign of the cross
Sweet saviour, bless us ere we go
Thy word into our minds instill
And make our lukewarm hearts to glow
With lowly love and fervent will
Through life's long day
And death's dark night
O gentle Jesus, be our light
O gentle Jesus, be our light

Grant us, dear Lord, from evil ways
True absolution and release
And bless us more than in past days
With purity and inward peace

Do more than pardon
Give us sweet sweet fear and sober liberty
And simple hearts without alloy
That only long to be like thee

9281 Gold Coast Ad
Peninsula

Personal and Confidential

Mr. Jan Molders
c/o Janice Kahlen,
3546 Wellington Avenue,
Walnut Grove

To all whom this may concern as copies at the end of this letter.
I shall be putting this letter (and copies) into the mail to you *on my* way to the airport for my very much needed and overdue vacation. Some couple of months ago I indicated to you that I would be taking Baby Mark my two year old son on a vacation overseas and hoped to be able to afford to be away for 3–6 months. You replied that if I was away for over 3 months you would be damned if you would continue to pay maintenance for a child that was not yours, and that you had no access to, and that you would "mud rake" if I failed to return in three months. This blackmail has been held over my head as a threat for too long, i.e., ever since you decided that it was a powerful blackmail threat to use over me to get your own way and this past year or so it has worked very

well. Recently however I have been turning in prayer to the Infant Jesus of Prague and a few days ago I sent a letter to the Reverend Father there making a full written confession and asking forgiveness for my mortal sin and my adultery. Shortly after posting the letter the idea of this letter making a written declaration and full confession occurred to me, and after initial hesitation I am now convinced that it is the best thing to do. "The Truth Shall Set You Free" and I feel that what I did was with your implied consent, and my intent was to add to the marriage. Also I am very proud of my son and not sorry or ashamed of his parentage at all, for after all Jesus Christ Himself, was born out of the marriage of Joseph and Mary.

This letter is therefore to avoid the need for "mud raking" and needless legal fees and courtroom charges. After 3 years of marriage, and wanting a child very much, I got off the birth control pill unofficially hoping that when I conceived I would be able to announce that the event had happened by accident. A year later I was "off" the pill officially and each month I got physically sick with disappointment. You urged me to go and see my family doctor when you realized how important it was for me to have a baby. My family doctor advised that before he proceeded to take any tests on me he would have to carry out some tests on you. Apparently tests on the male were relatively simple compared to complicated and long tests on females.

After your first test you phoned me in the office completely terrified that I would leave you as the doctor had informed you that your chances of fathering a child were nil. Later on at home you begged me not to leave you and promised that we would have a child "somehow or the other—you did not care how. Just as long as I did not leave you." However Dr. Rodney Andress had asked you to come in another week's time for a further test and after this test Dr. Andress informed you that your sperm count had improved considerably and if it continued to improve your chances of fatherhood would too. However at this time the monthly disappointment was too much for me and on a pretext of having the flu I went and saw my doctor alone and asked him to be quite frank with me. I told him that I wanted a child terribly, to the point where I was getting physically sick every month. I told him that knowing the truth would be a relief and that I could not continue to live on unfounded hope like I was doing. Dr. Andress was very sympathetic and suggested that we should consider artificial insemination or adopting children. I went home and never mentioned that Dr. Andress had informed me that your sperm count would have to improve not 10%, or a 100% for you to have children, but well over 100%—which to me at the time seemed improbable. I discussed artificial insemination with you and you were not in favour of this. You phoned your father in Boston with the query as to whether he had the same problem as you did and he said he had not. (However on a further occasion your mother informed me that she had tried hard to conceive a second time by your father and it did not occur. She also pointed out that Sabine happened along late in your father's second marriage.) At this time, no doubt you suspected the truth, you suggested that you would be in favour of artificial insemination by your father's sperm, and I said this sounded immoral to me and that I would not consider it. Anyway on repeated occasions you begged me not to leave you for another man and said we would have the child we wanted somehow or the other.

I decided to take matters into my own hands and give myself the miracle I wanted more than life itself. I knew for a certainty that parenthood by you was impossible, and yet found it impossible to leave you. I began to look around for a suitable donor. The donor would have to be single and unattached to any one, and would also have to be someone I found physically attractive and would also have to be well educated and intelligent. A tall order! The miracle happened and my prayers were answered for soon after my search began I met just the right person to father my child. I gave him the strongest "come on" he had ever received and he was quite flattered and interested. Initially after our first meeting I impressed on him that I was violently attracted to him and took his telephone number. On numerous occasions I telephoned him and finally one day I went Christmas Eve shopping with him and had lunch. I made a date for a rendezvous for January 3, 1977 for we had been keeping a chart of my monthly cycle and I figured that I would be at my ovulation time just then. Any earlier appointment would be impossible to keep as you would be at home till the 2nd (and would be returning to work on the 3rd) and any date past the 3rd would be too late. Even as I made the "date" I prayed that I would not miss my ovulation cycle. However on the 3rd morning you took my temperature and I was right there, at the right time for conception. Even so I almost failed to keep the appointment but "Mark's father" phoned saying he was on his way to pick me up. That day for the first time in my married life I commited adultery and for the first time in my left slept with a man other than my husband. Mark was conceived between the hours of 11 A.M. and 3 P.M. on January 3, 1977 and that was the greatest and best thing I ever did. It wasn't at all difficult to tell "Mark's father" that I was "in love." He was very attractive, very thoughtful, kind and considerate and from a good social and family background. He was quite musical too, for in his apartment was very expensive stereo equipment, an expensive guitar, a flute and an accordion. He took me home and let me off at the corner block after making me promise I would call him soon.

Six weeks later the doctor confirmed what I knew for a certainty and you were so very happy. You phoned me from out of town to the office before I went to the doctor's for my pregnancy test and after I returned from the doctor's for the results. You were not due in town for another couple of days but that evening you flew back into town, to be with me on that day of splendid news. You were so delighted, so happy, such a different person.

On many occasions during the pregnancy you jokingly asked me who the father was, etc., etc., and I in turn replied that you were the father. You told me that I had indeed been incredibly discreet for you had absolutely no idea who it could be and only hoped that I had done a good job of matching the person to you so that the child would be like you. I knew that you knew the truth, but did not want to hear it and at the time I never thought I would ever need to confess the truth. After Mark was born you on many occasions complimented me on the fact that he looked like you. I worked hard on statements that he looked like you and more so like Janice, your mother. (Each month that passes Mark terrifies me by looking more like his natural father and my greatest fear is that one day they will be together and the resemblance will be too startling for anyone to miss. I am hoping that this fear is just in my head, but the nose and eyes are surprisingly similar and Mark has his father's manner of dropping his eyes and looking out from under them. The chin is also similar and the Eurasian heredity is unmistakeable.)

It is my intention never to divulge Mark's father's name by spoken or written word. I do not want any more claims on the child and any requests that I marry the father and give him a legal father. His natural father also has parents who no doubt would pressure me for their "grandchild." I absolutely refuse to complicate my life any further or have any shadow of further legal hassles if I can help it. Mark's natural father is only 29 years old and although, fortunately I was attracted to him, complicating my life with marriage to him and legal hassles is totally unwelcome.

I almost lost Mark during delivery as he had managed to wrap his umbilical cord around his neck. Being the mother of the unborn child I wanted so much I refused to push down and kept absorbing all the pain of restraining the contractions until I persuaded my family doctor that something was terribly wrong. Mark had made history at St. Paul's by wrapping his umbilical cord four times around his neck (something that my obstetrician Dr. Schonberg had never encountered before—maybe once around the neck, or twice or three times, but never ever four times). Mark was saved within 10 to 20 minutes of losing his life and I was made poignantly aware that what God had given God could so very easily take away. I was really shaken up at the near tragic and unsupportable loss.

Two weeks after returning home, I received for the first time, after my "date" with him on the 3rd of January, a call from Mark's natural father. He talked to me quite naturally and asked me how I was. Then to my distress and fear baby cried. He immediately asked me who that was and I said just a baby. He quietly told me "You mean it's my baby, don't you. That was the reason you saw me, wasn't it? You were not in love or even very attracted to me. You just wanted a baby. I could not understand why you dropped me the way you did and then a month or so later on I learnt that you were pregnant and I realized why you had seen me." (You see, Jan, being a woman I too knew how to use the words "I love you, and cannot be without you" to my advantage. It's a time honoured term of seduction). He asked me what I had named his son and I told him. He told me that he still cared for me and would give me three months to leave my husband and come to him with his son. I told him this was impossible. He told me that I had no need to ever fear him and up to now he has kept his word.

This letter is in no way to construe that I deny Mark his right to maintenance which I put into the bank for his future financial requirements. Mark was born for the marriage, into the marriage by your implied and ardent request and by my very urgent and great need to have a child. This letter is only to free myself and my son from the need for "mud raking" and is a statement of a fact of which I am very glad and so very thankful that I did. I am almost sure that God has now forgiven me but if there is any more punishment due I shall gladly take it with the fervent prayer that He absolves my son Mark from any, now and for always.

This letter in no way is to construe that I have made any implied suggestions as to the illegitimacy of any children since born or as yet unborn to you, Jan Molders. Since Helene Bandaramka got pregnant after being apart from you in England for a month, and since she has had a history of unwed pregnancies (one to our knowledge which was documented as an "unwanted pregnancy and illegal abortion" in our efforts to "adopt" her and give her an opportunity for a better life—and two by written statements by her mother to me informing me that Helene had been pregnant twice and that she did not want her back in Goa) and casual abortions, I reserve the right to have my own convictions on the matter. As they say, a Jan Molders is born every day! Helene Banderanika's fertility is a documented fact and frankly at this time am keenly aware that this indeed is "Not my problem or concern."

Frankly, if anyone told me last year that I would reach this stage of healing I would not have believed it, but thank God, He is also merciful, and although I did commit a mortal sin, He has also touched me and helped me heal. I also feel that I have been at certain places at certain times when I have been of very real help to persons. I have also felt pain and need for help and have understood the same need in others and found time to extend it. Something that I did not understand a few years ago and something I may not have fully responded to.

By copy of this letter to my brother Harold Jonathan Saiera and to my sister Felice Joy Banderamka, both of Walnut Grove, I charge them both to treat this statement in extreme confidence. This copy of this statement to them is to confirm my Last Will and Testament wherein I have given custody of Mark Molders to my sister Christine and appointed my Brother Harold (Johnny) as his trustee. The purpose of copying you on this statement is to give you my written consent, in the event of my untimely death, to use this written statement in any way desirable and necessary to ensure that the custody of Mark Molders (failing my subsequent marriage) remains in my family's hands. If it is necessary, this is also your authorization to obtain from Dr. Rodney Andress all copies of test reports on sperm tests taken on Jan which will positively prove that at that time his chances of fatherhood were remote. The truth revealed by this statement and authority to use it is only active and legal in the event that I am no longer alive or by some remote chance am incapacitated, mentally unstable, sick or incapable of acting on my behalf. Any action taken to be solely in the interests of, and for the benefit of my son Mark Molders. My dying wish is that his upbringing is in the hands of my sister and also my brother. I have since realized that although we may not necessarily compulsively attend church every Sunday, our morals, character and ideals and sincerity, charitability is outstandingly good and commendably high and my wish is that Mark be brought up with it and in it, sincerity, decency and high moral attitude no matter what, i.e., that if any act, statement or action of his should cause harm, pain or grief to another it is wrong and should not be done, no matter how difficult it would be not to do it. In other words Mark should be brought up to love his fellow man and his God and work at it every day.

I am taking this holiday at great expense but I cannot bear to go to work any more and spend the day away from my only child. I did not postpone my child for so many years so that I would leave him with a babysitter. By my vacation I will be able to spend every day with him and watch him grow in my love and protection. He has been well taken care of in love and care by Janice and Pat but I feel that mine is more powerful, deeper and more necessary and being able to afford it I shall give it to him. I have worked hard this past year, paid off my debts, taken a loan for my tickets and have a substantial amount to spend and with careful budgeting and "freeloading" with relatives should be able to manage very well.

Jan, I wish you well with your new family and trust that our paths have parted for good by now. You have Mark's Saving Account number and you have indicated that all maintenance payments will be deposited into it, i.e., my earlier letter to you. I eventually have to return, i.e., maximum of 6 months and pay off my debts and get a new job. I have quit my job but feel the time with Mark will be worth every dollar.

Alma Molders

I swear the above regarding
Mark's conception is the truth

Copy to: Janice Kahlen
Pat Kahlen
Harold Jonathan Seiera
Felice Banderamka

*Summary and Discussion*

In these two letters, the total amorality of the psychopath is clearly noted. I am sure the reader is aghast at the amorality of the individual who is writing the second letter, which chronicles the careful arrangements that she made to become pregnant and "present" the husband with a child. It points out clearly, in the second paragraph of the letter and the third paragraph of the letter, another common characteristic of the female psychopath, and that is that she is absolutely manic about having a child to justify her existence. This woman shows the inordinately vile depths to which the female psychopath can sink in order to fulfill this mania. It will be noted in the fourth paragraph of this second letter that she manages one of the most amoral statements yet seen in print, that being that the conception was between 11:00 A.M. and 3:00 P.M. and followed confirmation of the day as being the propitious date for conception since *her husband* had taken her temperature to determine her fertility on that very morning, prior to her leaving to meet *her lover.*

She goes on to say, "That was the greatest and best thing I ever did." It is just mind-boggling to think that any human being can consider such an amoral act as the greatest and best thing that they have ever done. She also continues in the best psychopathic fashion to pat herself on the back, pointing out how clever she was in using her feminine wiles to select and seduce the appropriate donor, and goes on at great length pointing out how brilliant she was in this selection, thereby confirming another common characteristic of the psychopathic female—a diabolical cleverness at manipulating the facts and arranging anything and everything she feels is important in the marriage by whatever amoral or immoral means is necessary for her to attain her own ends. That is, pregnancy, motherhood, and dominion over man.

This woman, using the term loosely, goes on to reveal how she can further twist reality by placing the burden for selection of the suitable donor on the poor ex-husband and again, magically, "I knew that you knew the truth, but did not want to hear it. . . . You told me that I had indeed been incredibly discreet for you and have absolutely no idea who it could be and only hope that I had done a good job of matching the person to you so that the child would be like you." Such madness one rarely, thank goodness, ever sees written down as this husband had no idea whatsoever of these ghastly arrangements to present the marriage with a child.

Here it might be noted that the psychopath shows another characteristic in that there is a peculiar magic and sense of wonder associated with anything created by her through her diabolical cleverness; she creates a great story about how this is a magical birth to the point that this was the single most wonderful birth since the birth of Jesus—in short a true miracle.

She notes further down that "Luke (one wonders if this is of the sainthood variety) the son was born for the marriage, into the marriage by your Implied and Ardent Request, and by my very urgent and great need to have a child." The only place where she comes anywhere near the truth in this whole sordid affair is where she notes that she has a very urgent and great need to have a child, again showing the psychopath's abuse of the role of motherhood. Here too, we see that it's the husband's fault in that she points out that he was the main conspirator and she was just doing something that was best for the marriage and under the eyes of God, as she goes on to point out. She also points out that she is very able to lie to herself as to everyone else in that this letter is now a "stage of healing." Not only does she feel that everything she has done is being excused by God, but that He has helped her to become a healer. Another sign of the religious mania, so often adopted by the psychopath when the chips are down to show that she is always on the side of Right, and God is always on her side.

This dismal woman goes on in the third from last paragraph to point out that she has sent a copy of this letter to both her brother and sister, again confirming the total immorality of the psychopath—nothing is sacred. If it doesn't fit the story line, change it, and then send it to *everyone* so you can get them marshalled on your side in the coming battle. She further goes on in the same paragraph to point out how wonderfully religious she is and how she will bring Luke up with "sincerity, decency and high moral attitude no matter what." This coming from a woman who obviously has no idea of what morality even is, much less what is involved in a moral attitude to bringing up a child.

Here, we end this case with a most appropriate quotation from the meagre literature on the female psychopath as it relates to her "sexual life."

> Like male sociopaths, the females often function sexually very well. Their ploys may generate an excitement that is quite stimulating, especially when they are operating successfully. Since a victorious manoeuver often first involves first giving and then denying sex to the victim, such ladies generally have a few lovers to whom they turn for satisfaction and to complain about their current marital hardships. It's an active life.
>
> The sexual strategies that these women most often use, whether consciously or not, are designed to reduce the swash and machismo of their plunder. The simplest deceptions work like bear traps on a friendly large monkey. One of the easiest is to deny ever being satisfied, no matter how excellent a lover the man is. Some mysterious quality is missing; the relationship is never exhilarating enough. Or something is wrong with his touch. Or, best of all, it's possible to have orgasms on oral or manual stimulation, but not on intercourse. This last has to be stated with the right amount of contempt. The implication must be that other men have been able to do it better. Conducted properly, these tactics can make a psychologically vulnerable man feel so inadequate that he gratefully surrenders his fortune, his principles, and his heart. (Avodah K. Offit, M.D., *The Sexual Self* [New York: Ballantine Books, 1978.])

# *KOTTER V. KOTTER*

*Documentation*
*History of the Marriage*

The marriage started December 2, 1961, under very unusual circumstances; it was put on by her step-parents and consisted of 10 guests and bride and groom; the service was arranged for 7:00 o'clock that evening. I was on time but the bride was approximately 20 minutes late. I was just on the verge of calling it off when she appeared crying and very unhappy, almost as if she was forced by her parents to come to the church against her will, but in any event the ceremony was performed and we were in fact married that evening.

The next 16 months or so the marriage seemed quite hectic with adjusting to each other and the birth of our daughter, Shelly (May 22, 1962), and Anna was showing particular interest in one of my friends who was also one of her old school friends. Her involvement got so intense that it eventually affected our relationship seriously and her disinterest in me prompted her to leave the family home in the spring of 1963 with my daughter, Shelly, less than a year old. Anna and my daughter moved back in with her step-parents and I was left high and dry trying to run my part in the business and overcome the trauma of being rejected by this woman and losing my infant daughter. Months went by with very little communication between the two of us. Anna moved back into San Francisco and resumed a job she had before we were married as a secretary for a stockbroker called Joseph Thompson. Eventually I looking for legal counsel to effect a separation and divorce and ended up with Mr. Davies, who had a law practice in San Francisco, who, rather than separate us, had us both come into his office together and started counselling and in effect talked us into trying this relationship all over again. I went through somewhat of a second courtship thing, with Anna living and working in San Francisco and me living at the family home in South Grove, driving to San Francisco to take out my wife and try to convince her to come home and bring my daughter, who was being cared for by Anna's mother and I believe daycare babysitters, so we could resume a normal life and eventually succeeded in doing this by late fall of 1963.

Upon recommendations of Mr. Davies, we started a joint bank account and I signed over half of the family home to Anna.

The reunion resulted in her pregnancy and eventual birth of our son, Andrew, June 1, 1964. Her interest in her old school friend, however, did not disappear and I was never too comfortable and very unhappy about this situation but I was also trying to build a business and so life went on and I had hopes that she would eventually sort her feelings out and decide to stick with me.

Two and a half years went by since Andrew was born and springtime again, we were going on in our day to day life. Anna had befriended a divorced woman by the name of Wendy Newton, who was an employee at the Plant. This woman was living with a man approximately 70 years of age. Anna and Wendy started travelling together so to speak, which resulted in Anna's absence from the home, usually during weeknights into the early morning hours. I was told that they were attending bingo games in San Francisco. The situation deteriorated between us but Anna did not show any attempt to change this situation. Wendy was also dating Anna's school friend at this time.

Approximately two and a half years after Andrew was born, I came home one Friday after work, approximately 7 P.M. As I walked into the house everything was quiet, there seemed to be some items missing in the house. I eventually found the "Dear John" note which in effect said that she had fallen out of love with me and was hoping that I would be okay and would eventually find someone who would love me the way I deserve. Anna's parents had apparently financed a mobile home for her in San Francisco. All this went on behind my back. By this time, as far as Anna went, she had killed any love, affection or loyalty and left me very suspicious, heartbroken and totally indifferent toward her. Anna's drinking habit by this time had advanced to drinking herself into blackout stages on occasion. I believe she went back to work for her previous boss, Joseph Thompson, who told me she was an alcoholic.

This break-up went different than the first one. I visited her and the children a few times and then went on with my life, once more deserted after having my heart broken for a second time. I went and buried myself in my work in a very depressed state and stopped communicating with her altogether. Six or eight months went by, I was getting well adjusted to my bachelorhood and had overcome the break-up pains and was carrying on in the business with my brother.

On the occasion of Anna's leaving she was employed as a secretary at the Plant, and of course, left everything high and dry so I had to pick up the pieces in that respect also, along with all the other duties I had in the business. It was late in that year, approximately late November/early December, I was living alone, had been all through that period, about 11 P.M. one night there was a knock on the door, there was Anna with my two children, Andrew and Shelly: they looked a sad sight. She asked if she could come back home on any terms to see if we could work it out just for a while. The sight of my kids standing out in that cold and rainy winter night, I half-heartedly agreed to it on a temporary basis because my love and feelings for Anna were completely gone but my love and affection for the kids was very strong, so I thought for the sake of the kids I would give it one more try. Under these circumstances, with no love for Anna on my part, we started living together once more. She eventually resumed her job as secretary at the Plant, bumping my sister-in-law out of that position eventually. Anna worked at the Plant and my children were cared for by nanny's and babysitters, etc. Anna was doing the payroll and banking at the Plant and therefore was writing her own pay cheque. Her wages were close and I think eventually more than most men were earning in the Plant. We continued with separate bank accounts after the second reunion and the bank account situation was really never discussed any more. Anna's wages seemed to be quite sufficient in a situation where everything else was found. The money she was earning went entirely for her own personal use and pleasure, which consisted of several sports cars, a Sprite English car, a custom-built dune buggy and eventually now, a 1974 Corvette. I always had a new vehicle in the yard all those years, 1964 Pontiac Station Wagon, 1965 Oldsmobile, 1968 Oldsmobile, 1969

Oldsmobile, 1971 Oldsmobile, 1974 Eldorado. The family vehicles were always at her disposal. She used them until she acquired the 1974 Corvette and started driving it instead of the family car. I would suggest that there were no financial problems at any time. I was paying for repairs to the home, all property taxes on our joint properties, holidays, domestic help. Very early in our marriage Anna established the fact that she hated all housework, including caring and changing diapers for the infant children and would rather work at the Plant, which is exactly what she did.

Anna's drinking was getting worse as the years went by. The late sixties and into the seventies she developed a pattern of going home at noon and started drinking a half gallon of white wine almost every day. Her job at the Plant was getting more sophisticated all the time, where she was no longer required to work eight hour days and on certain days would leave the Plant often after doing the banking in the morning—10:30 a.m. and would not come back to work at all, but her pay was always calculated on a 40 hour work week, which she received until she eventually abandoned me and my three children approximately the second week of April, 1976. The children's ages at that time were Simon 7, Andrew 11, Shelly 13.

Anna's drinking was getting more serious all the time. Everytime we went out to banquets, parties, friends, dances, etc., she would eventually make a fool of herself by drinking too much and falling down and throwing up. I would try to discourage her from drinking too much, which was of no use. The more I talked, the more she drank, so eventually outings were getting less and less. The last two years, 1974, 1975, she would frequently be passed out by supper time, lying on the chesterfield in her own vomit. The kids would be terrified to see their mother lying there as if she were dead. I tried everything to get Anna to take a look at herself so she would realize what she was doing to herself and the four of us. By this time she was getting quite overweight—puffy appearance—she was neglecting herself completely hair, makeup, etc. and was getting very unattractive in all aspects. We would have constant arguments about her drinking, which would sometimes result in pretty ordinary language on both sides. In December of 1975, I suggested amongst other things for her to try A.A. to see if they could help her. She was very reluctant about admitting to herself that she was an alcoholic but she finally went to an A.A. meeting and continued to go for about five months. The changes in her at that time were quite noticeable. She started to clean herself up, lost some weight, bought new clothes, hair-dos, wigs, make-up and was exclusively occupied with herself. In other words, A.A. nights she would leave after work, get back at one or two o'clock in the morning. What I am trying to say is first we had a person who was drunk and somewhat absent from her role as mother and wife, and now we had an A.A. member who was absent from the home once again. She would have to go to weekend rallies, so she would be gone for one, two, sometimes three days at a time: all this did not help our situation any. In March of 1976 we decided to take the kids for a vacation to Hawaii. Anna, by this time, had made a few men friends in A.A. who she was writing to daily. I think one of them turned into a romantic relationship. We returned from Hawaii on a Friday night. Saturday morning she disappeared immediately and did not return until that evening and acted very guilty. I suspected she spent the day with her friend." She left the family home approximately one week after our return from Hawaii.

She disappeared one Monday morning; I did not hear from her until that week on a Saturday night. Approximately 11 P.M. the 'phone rang and she told me over the 'phone that she had finally found what she had wanted all her life, which was her freedom and love.

She had met a man, apparently, the day after she left the house, fell in love with him that night, rented an apartment in Surrey on the Wednesday of that same week, bought furnishings, dishes and all the necessary items to equip a house at Sears Stores, accompanied by her new lover, Jason Brown, and commenced living together with this man that very same day. She told me to call her parents and they could help me get accustomed to my single parenthood for a few days and again wished me good luck and hoped I would find someone real soon so I could get on with my life. The furniture for her new apartment was paid for with money she had in her personal bank account, approximately $4,500.00. So here we had a woman, new apartment, new Corvette car, new furniture, new lover, all in three days after leaving her family.

However, this romance did not hold up too well: about three weeks after this meeting, it appeared her friend Jason Brown had walked out and she had expressed the desire to come back home and see a shrink. So now we have a woman with an apartment in San Francisco, a husband and three kids in South Grove, visiting back and forth, seeing a psychiatrist sometimes together, sometimes on her own. So he suggested to her to get into a hospital and dry herself out for a while because after she left the family home she started drinking combined with drugs and was back to her old routine, drinking constantly.

She signed herself into the Bay Centre Psycho Ward, stayed there approximately six weeks, met a new boyfriend on the ward, who was in there for drug addiction and attempted suicide. She left the hospital with this new boyfriend, Jim Sorenson. They moved from the San Francisco apartment to a new location in South Grove, where they lived together until September, except for a trip they took together to Arizona to visit Jim Sorenson's parents. September I had found a live-in housekeeper, June Matthew, who was looking after my home and children. I had been looking for a larger home to house this live-in housekeeper and my family. Anna phoned me one morning, wanted to come home, was better now, realized she had been wrong and was positive after all this she would be able to manage the home and the children again.

Moved into large home in September of that year. She was taking drugs, M.D.A. 10 caps a day; kept on seeing Jim Sorenson, who was supplying her with these drugs; drunk and stoned all the time. I kept the housekeeper because I realized she was not interested in house, children, or me. Left the home in January 1977. She moved intoanother apartment after another stay in the Bay Centre Hospital. Emerged out of hospital with new boyfriend, Charles Milne, bought a house at Shasta Lake, wanted divorce and settlement. I told her to get a lawyer and tell me what she thought she wanted, so I left it up to her. She went to Mason, a lawyer in San Francisco. My lawyer, her lawyer, myself and Anna had a meeting, discussed the Agreement. Anna agreed at that meeting she would supply me with the evidence needed to effect a divorce, which she eventually did. We signed the Agreement and everybody lived happily ever after until now. I lived up to the Agreement 100%. Charles Milne lived there off and on all this time. My children would talk about Charlie and sometimes a man called John who I never met. Charles Milne would pick up my children and his own and take them over to Anna's house for weekend visits. It sure seemed to me that he was living there under a common law situation.

Mason, Jonas and Armstrong, Psychiatrists

4th May, 1976

Consultation

Re: Mrs. Anna Kotter

This 33 year old married woman was referred to me by Dr. Tanner because of feelings of depression and anxiety related to marital difficulties and excessive drinking. I examined Mrs. Kotter in my office on 21st April, 1976.

Mrs. Kotter complains of being tense and worried all the time. She feels depressed, has crying spells—feels that life is not worthwhile, feels frustrated all the time, feels that she cannot cope with any more emotional demands upon her and that she just cannot keep going the way it has been over the past months. She complained of stomach upset, vomiting spells, pounding headaches, sleeplessness, lack of appetite, and weight loss. She also feels that she has lost interest for her husband, including sexual interest, and for her family. It is as if all her good feelings towards him and her three children have disappeared. She feels, in other words, emotionally flat and just wants to be by herself and not bother with any other needs. She feels resentment against them, gets easily irritated at them, and becomes hard on the children. She has contemplated suicide but it was while she was seriously contemplating this alternative, that she decided to join A.A. She is also scared of some other alternatives such as terminating the marriage, or at least walking out on the family for a time. She has decided not to take any drastic decisions until she can sort out her own emotions.

Most of Mrs. Kotter's distress stems from the difficulties she has experienced in her marriage for the past 14 years. The marital relationship has been characterized by constant bickering and arguing, drinking and separations. On her part, she complains that the husband has always looked on his job, the family business, as his God. By this she means that for him his job has the basic priority over any other needs, her needs or the family needs. He works long hours every day of the week and spends also long hours during the evening trying to transact his business. He claims that he is a social drinker and that drinking is part of doing business in his line of work. From her point of view, he just likes to drink and to spend a good time with his buddies, instead of being home helping with the family. For years, she has felt neglected and frustrated, she has felt that he does not love her and she has tried to dampen down her feelings of frustration and dissatisfaction by drinking. Her drinking has usually been confined to the home, and especially in the evenings, but she has always taken care that her children do not see her intoxicated. However, for about a year prior to December, 1975, she started losing more and more control over her drinking, started to experience frequent blackouts, had begun to go home at noon time from her work at the family business, in order to drink at lunch. As in any marriage of this sort, she played a game of "cops and robbers" regarding the hiding of liquor from her husband who kept looking in every corner of the house to prevent her from drinking. She claims that she has had enough of lying, cheating, hiding and making excuses for her drinking, not only to her husband, but to herself and this is the reason that she finally looked for help from A.A.

The problem facing her now is that while she has found some fulfillment and contentment in A.A. she has found that her involvement there has created resentment from her husband, who feels jealous about what she is doing, and about her contacts with male members of the A.A. He resents being left alone babysitting, and puts up a great fuss whenever she has to go to her meetings. On her side, she claims that she never created a problem when he was out every evening drinking with his friends. A further contributing factor to Mrs. Kotter's distress is the fact that her husband, at least superficially, and for the time being, has decided to change his ways regarding the family. To please her, he decided to stop drinking altogether and to spend the evenings at home. He claims that now that he is home, and now that he is not drinking and spending his time with his friends, everybody in the family should be happy, especially Mrs. Kotter, as this she has given as the very reason why she drinks. Mrs. Kotter claims that such a drastic change has confused her and that she does not know how to cope with it. The fact that she is not over happy at his change of behaviour makes her feel guilty, and this causes the two of them to enter into long drawn out conversations and discussions about their marital life, her previous shortcomings and the present difficulties. These discussions, she claims, drain her of all her energy, and make her tension and anxiety increase, as well as her feelings of guilt and depression.

Mrs. Kotter is the older of two adopted sisters. The father was a rather passive individual that let his wife take all decisions and management of family life. The mother is described as an authoritarian and domineering person that allowed nobody to cross her decisions. Mrs. Kotter always felt extremely afraid of her, learned to keep things inside herself and suffer alone. There were many restrictions in the family, and although she always had plenty of physical commodities and was given more than she needed in material possessions, she felt unloved and unwanted and misunderstood. She married at an early age, not only for reasons of love towards her future husband, but also because she wanted her freedom from what she felt were tyrannical parental restrictions. She feels now that her husband has turned out exactly like her mother, namely what he decides is what is done. As with her mother, she has been afraid of him and has felt that he takes her only because she is needed in the family and not because he loves her as the person she is. The marital relationship has been a tense one. The husband himself is a dependent person, somewhat immature. These characteristics, coupled with her own personality shortcomings, has developed into a mixture of "give aways" and "holding backs" in their interacting. As the husband says quite pointedly, the two of them have never been able to be at the same level of happiness and understanding. They both use their feelings and have learned to manipulate each other in order to gain emotional advantage over the other. Thus, when one is happy and relatively stable emotionally, the other is depressed and clinging. This prods the other into being more loving and understanding and when this happens the seesaw action takes place, whereby the one comes down feeling depressed and guilty, while the other regains a better level of stability. This seesaw type of relationship whereby one is down while the other is up, or vice-versa, develops when a dependent hostile interaction becomes the modus operandi and ways of resolving problems of marital adaptation. Both partners are acutely aware that they are, or have been so far, unable to break the pattern and live a better adjusted marital life.

Mrs. Kotter came neatly dressed to both interviews. She was somewhat slow in entering the office, had a drawn face with haggard marks under her eyes, and sat in a dejected position, her head leaning down and her shoulders stooping downwards with her hands just hanging off her lap. Her voice was slow and complaintive while describing the way she was feeling. On many occasions she was on the verge of tears. It was noticed, however, that as the interview wore on and she started talking more and more about her husband, she became boisterous, raised the level of her voice so that she was practically shouting. Also it was noticed that while discussing her pattern of drinking, she sometimes chuckled, and then her sad expression disappeared and she even laughed wholeheartedly on one occasion. Her mood was then appraised as moderately depressed while her affect was conceived as being labile or "mercurial." She denied any immediate suicidal ideation, but it was felt that being at her present level of emotional instability, such a way of acting out could not be entirely discounted. Also the possibility of going back to drinking as a means of resolving her acute emotional distress was seen as being quite likely. This, as a matter of fact, was very frightening for her, as it has already been implied by her husband that he will force her out of the family if she continues drinking as before. Apart from her depressed affect and mood, her feelings of tension and anxiety and her long lasting personality difficulties, there was no other evidence of gross psychopathology.

Diagnosis:
1. Neurotic depressive-anxiety reaction in a passive-hostile personality.
2. Alcoholism.
3. Marital dysfunction.

Recommendations:
1. Immediate steps should be taken to curb the present level of anxiety and tension, to improve her sleeplessness, and her depressive feelings. This can only be done on a short term basis with medications of both tranquilizer type and anti-depressive type. Care should be taken not to prescribe anything that would get her easily habituated.

She certainly has all the personality characteristics to become habituated to medication, the way she has been addicted to alcohol.
2. I would recommend and have prescribed for her Surmontil 12.5 mg HS #10 and Stelazine, 2 mg lod and lhs #16.
3. To continue in A.A.
4. To be seen along with her husband at the beginning to sort out basic problems in her relationship with him, while at the same time, supporting both her and her husband.
5. In the long range, it will be advisable to do some marital therapy but this would have to wait until the present emotional conditions subside.
6. If the marital condition continues to be so volatile, then it would perhaps be necessary to induce some temporary separation by placing Mrs. Kotter in the hospital or in a half-way house. This would be done only if the foregoing recommendations fail to produce the expected beneficial effects.

"Mathew A. Jonas," M.D., D.Psych.

*Bay Centre General Hospital*
*Psychiatric Nursing History*

Ward: 3 WB
History: Hosp. # 644
Adm. Date: Feb. 5/77

Patient: Kotter, Mrs. Anna Age: 33 Doctor: Dr. Tanner

This 33-year-old married woman, a patient of Dr. Tanner, came to my office in an acute state of tension, anxiety, agitation and restlessness. She was crying uncontrollably, sobbing and sighing and in between expressions of distress, indicated that she was feeling extremely guilty because of her inability to have any further feelings for her husband and her wish to separate, while at the same time, realizing that she could not do this to her family. Mrs. Kotter has been drinking a bottle of wine a day and sometimes more. This will not be Mrs. Kotter's first admission to Psychiatry. I understand that this will be the third time that she comes for similar feelings and also as a way of drawing her out. The marital difficulties have always been present, but so have been her feelings of depression and her alcoholism. Following her last admission six months ago, however, she did much better, went to work, came back home and the drinking stopped for a while. She claims, however, that over the past two months, things have become bad again. The husband, believing that things have settled down, bought a large home and the family lived in hope that Mom would remain at home. Slowly, she could not cope again with the high demands placed on her at the husband's expectations that things will work out for the better between the two of them. Mrs. Kotter states that whenever he tries to approach her and whenever he does nice things to her, she feels extremely guilty because she has no further feelings for him whatsoever. There are no sexual relationships and, actually, she feels a physical aversion to his advances. This has increased a tremendous guilt complex within herself, feeling that she is the one to blame for the family unhappiness and feeling that she just cannot continue burdening the family with her distress. She has thought again about separation, but this has already been attempted in the past and she believes that again, that would be giving further hardship to the family.

ON EXAMINATION: Mrs. Kotter was extremely restless and agitated, as indicated, sobbing, sighing and crying. She spoke in short sentences, but spontaneously and coherently. The content of her conversation was depressed and such was also her mood and her affect, although, on occasion, her level of depression would marginally improve and she would smile. There were some suicidal ideas. There was no indication of any thought disorder or perceptual difficulties or any memory impairments.

At this time, the most important thing is to settle Mrs. Kotter as soon as possible. I don't think that this will take too long and then we will have to start the process of seeing whether there is any alternative at all to Mrs. Kotter's distress. Some minor tranquilizer medications and anti-depressants will be added to the regime.

"J. Tanner, M.D."

JAT:rl
dictd: Feb. 5/77

*Bay Centre General Hospital*
*Psychiatric Nursing History*

Name: Anna Kotter
Admission Date: Feb. 5/77
Admission Time: 12:10
Accompanied: Yes No X
Allergies: Penicillin
Medication and dosage at home: None
Medication, time last dose taken: Last drink last night/No pills at home
Valuables:

Watch X
Radio
Purse

Rings 1 w/clear stone
Wallet X to send money home
with husband
Keys

Glasses
Dentures
Other

Date: Feb. 5/77

Complaints: Drinking about 1/2 gal. wine/day. Sometimes not every day, depends on home situation. Drinks "enough to put myself to sleep." Marital situation.

Appraisal: (including problem formulation) Apparently marital situation has disintegrated to what Anna believes—beyond repair as far as she is concerned. States Willy has done as much as he can to hold relationship together. Feels she is being unfair to him. Also states that daughter hates her which is to be expected. Slim blond (bleached) lady, weeping considerably and finding conversation difficult, because of this to express her problems, clarify them and seek adequate solutions on a group and 1:1 basis.

Signature "P. Wallace"

KOTTER, Mrs. Anna
#644 Dr. Jonathon Tanner

Discharge Summary:

This lady, in her late 20s, married, had to be re-admitted as an emergency because of further feelings of depression, tension, anxiety and a further increase in her consumption of alcoholic beverages. She has been admitted to Psychiatry on several occasions because of this symptomatology, which apparently has a lot to do with difficulties in her marital relationship. Following her last discharge, Mrs. Kotter attended my office for some time and did well for several months, but after quitting her follow-up, she remained at home, also quit her job, began drinking heavily and finally it ended up in this admission.

Her condition on the Ward following admission was very distressful, as she kept crying and complaining all the time. She was placed on some Elavil at night and Serax during the day. Slowly, she regained her own self and started participating actively in the different ward activities. She has worked out for Lithium on the assumption that her depressions had shown certain rhythmicity and the feeling that, if the depressive symptomatology could be felt dealt with successfully with Lithium, it would be then easier to deal with her alcohol and her marital problems. The husband was seen regarding these matters. Mrs. Kotter finally decided to stay away from home, at least for the time being, following discharge and this was agreed upon by the husband as well.

Lithium was started.

During her stay, she also had a D & C and also consultation with Dr. Amos regarding some bad corns in one of her feet.

Her mood on discharge was excellent. Her condition had recovered quite well.

Diagnosis:

Reactive depression and excessive habitual drinking.

Prognosis:

For this episode is good, but in the long run, one has to see whether Mrs. Kotter is going to get depressed again and whether she is going to be back to drinking. Again, this very much depends on how the marital situation is going to stabilize.

She will be followed up for Lithium levels at Dr. Tanner's and Dr. Emmerson's office and she is to phone my office for further appointments for her psychiatric follow-up. She has been prescribed Lithium to take 900 mg. a day and Elavil to take 50 mg. hs.

"J. Tanner, M.D."

JT:rl
dictd: March 16/77

*Letter to husband from psychopathic wife:*

December 18, 1978

Dear Willy,

This will be my final communication with you—mainly to wish you a very Happy Christmas but also to say I am sorry and hope you are able to experience the feeling of forgiveness. Not to just say it to oneself but to truly experience it. You see, God has allowed me to forgive myself for wanting to destroy the both of us for the act I performed when I was seventeen. It was my decision and because I acted thru love for you I rationalized and decided it wasn't so bad after all. However it turns out the emotional effect it had on me turned disastrous as we've both been shown. I buried it so deep that even I was unaware of what was the problem. How wonderful it is to be freed of it. The other thing is that *I did* take the money from your Mom's petty cash but because you showed such trust in me—I couldn't bring myself to tell you the truth. I pray she'll forgive me. Please believe me now, the above is not meant to hurt you further but rather done for a selfish reason. I am unable to remove the total burden of it—tho I've tried—by telling anyone but you. And by truly saying I'm sorry. In other words, I guess what I want you to know is God has freed me from the terrible, endless hell I've been in and shown me I was totally to blame. You see, God is the only one who has the right to forgive us. If it sounds I've gone religious, well, I guess I have but found God's love to be the only truly fulfilling love there is. You once said it's just another crutch for me. That's because I am a cripple. God has said, "Seek the truth and you shall be set free."

In closing, thank you for all too many things to mention. I pray for you and the children daily, that you find happiness and peace within, for you see I am now truly grateful to have been a part of your life. God bless.

In His Love,
Anna

*P.S.* I am not drunk writing this! You were also right when you suggested Dad could help me. He's been the biggest human factor involved in my recovery.

*Letter to her children:*

February 28, 1979

Dear Andrew and Simon:

Lovely writing paper heh! Am going to try and get this off to you today. I have not been able to get in touch with you but hope Auntie Rose had called you the other day to explain. I have been very sick with the worst cold I've ever had and unable to do much else but sleep and be babied. Finally, today I feel half human but because I am going with Charlie to San Diego to take some pictures of the room he did last year that we told you about. He has a few things to finish up in there, before the house can be sold. I'm sorry I have not called but even going to the bathroom became an extreme effort. I was also very upset about the business (Diane's) going bankrupt altho I found it a relief to finally be free of the burden. I had a lot of pressure on me for the last week because no one was to know what was happening and I had to remain strong for Diane. She has taken all very hard.

Will probably be away a couple of weeks but pray you will feel that I am always with you no matter what. You two have been very instrumental this past two years for many happy times for me. I hope now that I have a new life. That doesn't mean I am tied to daily work, we will be able to have some times together, perhaps camping in the bus with Charlie.

Anyway, my sweethearts, love you and miss your darling faces immensely. Take a moment to love each other—sometimes that's all we have. Shelly has moved—her new address is 146 Rockwell Street, Los Angeles.

I will for sure be back for Simon's birthday and if my voice is ever returned will phone soon.

Love and Hugs
"Mom"

(New name being Tinkerbell or "Tink" for short)

March 21, 1979

*Simon*—I suggest you let Andy read this to you. Some parts you probably won't understand now but I ask you to tuck this letter away and when you are older perhaps you will understand why I was not able to be with you two during your childhood. For that—I am sorry; but I had no choice.

Love,
"Mom"

You'll have to watch the numbers on the pages—typically it's confusing—I tried to reread this and I even got lost!

*Andrew*—The enclosed note will release your funds in the bank. I had hoped you would keep the account open and save it for a rainy day—however slim the chance is that you will indeed ever have a rainy day (financially anyway). But, the choice is yours as is the case in all areas of our lives. As requested (even if it's boring) read Simon the enclosed letter and tuck it away to read again when you are both older and can understand what this hundred pounds of jangled person (called Mom) is trying to say on this day, twenty-first of March, 1979. You are my children, (no-one can take that away, at least) and I love you.

"Mom"

March 21, 1979

Dear Simon: My Child at Spring

Happy birthday my dear Simon. The enclosed pictures is my all-time favorite of myself and my children—I have looked at this picture every day I've not been able to be with you. Your dear faces have been a great encouragement to me—you are all beautiful and truly God's gift to me. Ten years old—wow that's neat! Maybe you can put these pictures in your album I gave you at Christmas, do you remember when they were taken? On your seventh birthday in Hawaii—now you are ten. It's neat your birthday falls on the first day of Spring—Spring being my favourite time of the year—it holds such a promise of good things to come.

My only regret in my life today is that I am unable to share in yours and Andrew's daily growth. You see when I left you all, I was very sick—inside my heart. No-one is to blame for this—it was created because of a disease—I simply drank too much, too often. The abuse of alcohol and drugs can make a person very ill—so ill that in fact you have no choice to which way your life will go. My only hope for you children is that you never find it necessary to let alcohol or drugs run your life! The price you must pay for your weakness is too great. In a lot of cases it even means death. I hope you are not ashamed of me as your mother—for I love you dearly and that is mainly why I left you to your father—I was incapable of looking after you properly. This tragic story, however, has a happy ending, for today I am well and very happy. You see, I believe today God has been looking after me since birth thirty-six years ago. I wanted to give up many times but God had better ideas for me. He is making me healthy and happy, I believe, so one day soon I may help people who were or are as sick as I have been. Don't get me wrong, I am not a "Bible thumper" as Shelly says, but I do believe in a loving God. Even God had to sacrifice his only Son (Jesus) for us to live happy fulfilled lives. Jesus died so we may believe his teachings about life. God only wants us to be the best possible people we can be. He is not a punishing God but he disciplines us through our own mistakes. I want you to realize that the Lord is always with you, to teach you, to forgive you, to protect you, and most important to love you. Whenever you feel lonely or fearful you can always talk to God and he hears you. Even if you don't understand any of it, if you ask he is there. God, however, expects us to be good people and when we trust in him totally as our teacher one soon finds that nothing in life is impossible if you are willing and try. Charlie and I don't attend any one church because they, in most cases, try and change things around to suit themselves. The Bible alone teaches us all we ever need to know. It can be used like one would use the yellow pages of a phone book when you need your toilet fixed and have to find a plumber in a hurry. Many people have the wrong concept of God. They believe that if there is a God all they have to do is ask him for a Cadillac and then sit on an easy chair till it happens. It doesn't, they say "see there is no God." In actuality what God does in that case—He pulls up an easy chair along side of you and outwaits you. Anyway, enough of this Sunday School lesson for now.

Since Diane's business had to be closed I have been told to take a long rest. The last month at that job damned near finished me. I had to hide the fact that it was going to close. Anyway, close it did and hopefully I shall never need to work for anyone again (20 years has been enough for this turkey). Charlie and I have been up north finishing his work there and because he had worked almost non-stop for six months there, he too needed a rest. He has started turning the exterior of this home into a castle (mini) with rock (like you helped him get, Andrew), but we can just work on it a few days here and there. Imagine, your Mom in a castle!! I have always been accused of living in a fantasy world, so why not hey? I already have my prince, Charlie bear. Have you seen the castle that's being built on the Highway past Carmel? It's really neat and it's the kind of thing Charlie has wanted to do all his life. We're having a lot of fun planning it out, anyway, even down to a drawbridge and moat.

Was wondering why you phoned Nana and asked her if I was selling my home at Shasta, Andrew—where did you get that idea? I hope never to sell my little house on the prairie—Charlie and I have put a lot of love into fixing it up, to sell it to someone who wouldn't appreciate it.

I am, however, renting it out to some friends of ours from San Diego who want to move here. Charlie and I have work to do all over the State this year so we are using the bus as our home at least till winter. It does create a problem in that it's hard to have you kids for just a weekend. I am hoping we can work something out soon tho because I miss you too much. We are hoping both of you would like to spend all or part of your summer holidays with us. We could play with Charlie's router, heh Simon (remember the mushrooms you dig with it). Charlie can teach you how to use it to make nearly anything you want. Gee, he has taught me so many new things. It's a gas!! I can even bake pies on a wood stove—neat heh! My photography is really improving, I am so excited about the things one can produce with a camera—I just love it.

There is a very wise suggestion that I would like you to ponder (think about) and it is this—if a man comes to you and he is starving and asks you for food, instead of buying him a fish, teach him how he can fish. Thereby, he need never starve again cause he can always catch a fish. Cute heh; of yes, I must tell you of a very exciting possibility in my life. I have been working on a book about the different experiences in my life to this point. It was suggested many times to me that someone else could (by reading the book) learn from my troubles and tribulations and perhaps not go as far down as I did. So far I'm up to about three hundred pages on the rough draft of it and I have a long way to go yet. I have a friend in A.A. who is a publisher and he says he will help get the book published, also have written some neat poems, which sometimes end up to be a new song—when Charlie's on the guitar, Ronny on the banjo and untalented me on the tamborine. Life is a gas believe me, especially with all it's little twists. We can only learn from our own experiences it seems to me, but it seems unfair for the school of experience sometimes can be rough—mainly because we get the test before the lesson (wonder if you understand that). I haven't heard from Shelly since early January and my attempts to get her to answer my letters have fallen on deaf ears. I believe she wants total freedom to learn and grow on her own so she can find her own space to be comfortable in. I only pray she remains strong in her principles and finds a man who can love her despite her faults. I realize now Shelly never got much love during her childhood, which I feel really sorry about. We were always too busy critisizing every move she ever made and so I believe we will not be part of Shelly's life for a long while. I do understand from her letters that she loves us all, she just needs room to breathe (we all do from time to time). Up until 1976 you children must have had a lonely childhood. As I see it now, your father and I were nothing more to you than two people you could call Mom and Dad, and provide you with a bed and some growlies daily. I get very annoyed with myself to have been so blind to your needs. By that I mean, instead of buying you twenty-nine bikes, it would have been much greater to have taken you on my knee and gave you twenty-nine kisses (not in public Simon) and told you twenty-nine times how much I love you. I guess until recently I just didn't have my shit together as Auntie Rose would say. I sure miss her by the way, and ask you to give her my love. How is Matt, Poohbear and Uncle Dan?

Oh, yeah, what I wanted to tell you was that altho I will change the names of the people in my book, you two boys are laced all the way through it. Your cute antics, your not so cute antics, some of your neat sayings. For example, Simon's opinion on his feelings towards Charlie—and I quote, "Charlie's neat, Mom—he's not normal!" End of quote. And Andrew; one being the time when you couldn't speak too clearly yet and we were on our way home from Denny's (must have ate there a whole bunch of times, heh) anyway you requested we stop the car so you could go No. 2, and met a negative response and told you could wait till we got home. I sheer desperation you said, I quote, "Dad, if you don't stop the car, I'll shit my pants." I don't remember the rest of it, but I would almost guess we stopped the car! Remember the time we drove up to Gram's and we nearly peed ourselves laughing singing, "You be the bread and I'll be the butter"? Anyway, once the book is published (how's that for positive thinking) you two characters will be down in black and white. I hope that meets your fancy. Just remember what a riot we had between Christmas and New Year's this year. All those things could only happen to me and the likes of me. For example; most (normal) people fall down the stairs—I fall up the stairs!! Suppose I fell down a few too but remember the up ones and have the scars to prove it. I'll swear I was born under what is known as Murphy's Law—that is after you have patiently made toast, buttered it, with jam on, you slide it on a plate to transport it to where you want to devour it. By this time, you are running horribly behind and might miss your boat. The toast, not once but every time, slides off the plate—*jam side down!* What can I say?

Well, my dear pals—it's time for me to hit the sheets—I know I could sit here all night writing to you—I feel so good being able to write to you, with all honesty and I feel warm inside for I have prayed that God would commission a pair of special angels to protect you from any harm and that perhaps he will *gently* guide you through this journey called life. We all come into this world with nothing but bones, skin and blood—we leave almost the same way, bones and skin—what you do with the space between coming and going is your choice, I only pray you ask for God's love and guidance in your life—it can work miracles and all one's fantasies can become reality—I know this to be a sure thing for it was very simple (only I complicated things) to find a new, wondrous, serene, totally fulfilling life before me—with each day becoming greater and greater. All I had to do was put the cork in the bottle forever, keep my ears open and my mouth closed (ever wonder why God gave us two ears and only one mouth?). I'm only sorry it couldn't have been sooner, but I must always remain grateful for every new day, count my blessings and help others who can't ever be sociable drinkers again to find what I have found—sorrily some die before they can grasp it all. Charlie suggested I keep this letter to you simple and somehow I doubt I have honoured this request but I want you to know that although I can't be physically with you—I am always near and you are never out of my thoughts and prayers. Remember God loves you and so do I. If you need to be in touch phone our number here (826–8468) and etiher Josh or Angela will keep the message until I phone her—usually once or twice a week. One request—please respect your father even if you don't agree—he has had a rough road and please show kindness to his lady friend—I am so grateful you have a good, solid home life now—with everyone of us happy, maybe in the long run it has all been for the better. Oh yes, Simon, you asked at Christmas if I would someday marry Charlie. Well, I have been asked and gave a resounding "yes" as my answer—you see he's neat, he's not normal. But then neither am I so I guess that's what it takes sometimes. Ten years ago, and at this precise hour I was giving birth to my Child of Spring. What a joy, my children, you are to me, and because Charlie cared enough to help me back to reality (it was no easy task for him, I'll tell you) today I am very happy and content with the knowledge that I will die (not for a long time, I hope) sober.

Thank you Simon bear and Andrew bear—Good night, pleasant dreams, God Bless and may the angels watch over you forever and ever. (The above is a prayer Aunt Connie and I used to say every night before dropping off in slumber.) Keep smiles on those wonderful faces and, as Nana says, "Keep your bowels open and everything will work out!" The latter, if I am correct is no problem for a Kotter. Charlie sends his love—Summer, too.

Prayers to see you soon.

Mom XO times ten.

Shasta Mountain
April 1, 1979 (I think)

My dear Andrew and Simon:

If the following sounds like a "bribe"—it is.

Was wondering (and only if you have no other plans) if one—or better yet both of you—would like to come and visit Charlie and I in our mountain home—high in the mountains eight miles outside of Shasta. I hoped you would be able to come for Easter (as I have some neat ideas for a hunt we could all go on). Suggest you could catch the bus in Langley, Thursday after school (you would have to check the schedule) and we would be in Shasta by car (or our neat new, very old "hillbilly" truck, which you haven't seen yet) on Monday, April 16. Think it over, *I will phone Monday April 9,* at 6:00 P.M. to find out your decision.

If just Simon wants to come—we would pick him up at home—but for both of you the bus is very uncomplicated as long as you listen to the bus driver—then, you won't end up in Timbucktu!

It sure is neat here—we shall use this as "home base" till September when we move back to Shasta Lake to start construction on the house there. Charlie is presently down at the coast (left yesterday evening and returns tomorrow) to deliver some of his wares (makes wonderful outdoor tables) much too nice for outdoors, I might add—delivers them and fireplace wood to customers in the valley. We have a super little cabin overlooking miles of valley and mountain—lovely creek runs right behind the bedroom window.

Our offer doesn't include any penny arcades or movies but you would really have a ball I can guarantee. When not working, Charlie has been working on the bus—starting to look unreal and you could help there or play around with his router (he has his portable power plant here also). We have no electricity here and I love it—so peaceful! I am learning all kinds of neat things—can rustle up some pretty mean vittles on the wood stove—including lemon meringue pie, new concoctions of my own. I am sure loving the change of pace—am at present very disenchanted with what society has to offer. That will change in time, I suppose, but for now—I am very, very happy to be a "mountain woman." If I ever find a mountain like this by ocean—only an atomic bomb would get me off.

I sure miss you guys a lot however, and shall hopefully look forward to seeing you soon. Glad you got your waterbed, Simon. No waterbeds here, but the stove is in the bus and you can either sleep there or in the cabin with us—we have tons of bedding—if you come bring only a few change of clothes.

Yesterday Charlie found a baby mouse by the creek and I played with it for hours. Only the size of a quarter, it obviously had lost its mommy. I took 36 pictures of him and had a gas. Even learned from him can you imagine! Had to finally let him go however—only cause Charlie made me for fear we would eventually be overrun. Sure was fun and I should have some adorable pictures to show for my afternoon's fun.

Well, shall close for now. Remember, I'll call on the 9th at 6 P.M. for your decisions.

Your mountain Momma's
love, and hugs
XOXOXOXOXOXO

P.S. Have no phone of course, but there is a phone at the main house down the valley. Will call you from there. If you ever *have to* get a message to me you can call, and tell them to have me call you. No. is 656–3266.
—Just had visit from their two dogs—one of them can count—no kidding—for biscuits, of course.
Oh yes, bring warm coats. Got sunburned three days ago—snowed yesterday. Weather full of surprises here. Neat lake and river to fish in nearby, too.

*Discussion and Summary*

The reader, who is now becoming somewhat more of an expert on psychopathy than the average psychiatrist would appear to be, from careful perusal of the early discussion in this book, including the first cases, can see most clearly that this case is the best example so far of a case history showing virtually every one of Dr. Cleckley's sixteen characteristics of the psychopath as discussed in Chapter 2.

However, it is also obvious that this case most specifically and best illustrates the characteristic Number Eleven, the specific loss of insight, and to quote from Dr. Cleckley in his discussion—specific loss of insight is a psychopathic characteristic.

> He has absolutely no capacity to see himself as others see him. It is perhaps more accurate to say that he has no ability to know how others feel when they see him or to experience subjectively anything comparable about the situation.

In his discussion, Dr. Cleckley points out, quotes and discusses excerpts from the letters of a psychopath to the wife, which are very nearly identical in many places and certainly in the general gist of the letters, with the letters you have just read as documentation in this case. At the end of his quotes on these letters, he makes a very cogent statement, which really wraps up the psychopath's specific loss of insight in one short paragraph.

> There is more in all this than simply false promises and fraudulent efforts to persuade the wife not to get a divorce. There is also indication of inability in his fundamental reactions to size up normally what he has done, what he is, and what he has been.

The case also clearly shows how the psychiatric facilities and services really are unable to deal with the psychopath; we see her slip through the hands of many psychiatrists and many admissions to the Bay Centre General Hospital, Psychiatric Hospital Services, without anyone even intimating that there was a psychopathic or sociopathic element to her problems and that she, in fact, suffers from a basic personality defect, rather than a neurotic illness of anxiety or depression, or passivity or hostility, or any of the other convenient labels that were attached to her on her many skirmishes with organized psychiatry. We also see how a psychopath is really basically untreatable by organized psychiatry since she is in effect so plausible and so clever that she really is not committable for psychiatric treatment and because she is not in effect a perceived physical danger to herself or others. We see here, again, the psychopathic characteristic of suicide rarely carried out, as Dr. Cleckley says in his discussions of suicide in the psychopath, characteristic Number Fourteen:

> Instead of a predilection for ending their own lives, psychopaths, on the contrary, show much more evidence of a specific and characteristic immunity from such an act.

Here we see this woman perpetuating endless psychological violence on her husband, on her children, and on anyone who came within the spider's web of her psychopathic personality. If the psychiatrists had paid more attention to Dr. Cleckley's clear descriptions of the characteristics of the psychopath, and more specifically to the first three characteristics, that is, superficial charm and good intelligence, absence of delusions and other signs of irrational thinking, and absence of nervousness or psychological manifestations, then they may have seen through her histrionic, jaded, fawning, and clever attempts to mislead the psychiatric system as she very well did. Here, we see very clearly a point that will be further discussed at some length in chapter five, when we discuss the psychopath in the family, and that is: The psychopath goes through the family and the chronicle of family life much as a cyclone goes through a mid-Kansas American town, destroying and deforming all things in her path, but herself coming out on the other side of town unscathed and ready to take on the next little hamlet.

In this case we see a marriage starting out under stormy circumstances, in that the wedding itself was under unusual circumstances in that the bride managed to stand up the groom for some twenty minutes, appearing at the last minute, crying and unhappy but carrying on with the marriage ceremony. Even in the first sixteen months of the marriage, this woman begins to put down her husband to the point where she gets involved with one of the friends of the couple to the point where the husband left her after sixteen months, taking with him the daughter. It's interesting that despite the rocky marriage the woman had managed to convince the husband that they had best get on and have a family early, thereby enshrining her rights as mother, a frequent refuge of the psychopath. He carried out a second courtship, taking his wife back, and most interestingly he states, and "the reunion resulted in her pregnancy and eventual birth of our son, Andrew." It's absolutely amazing how very frequently the psychopathic female takes refuge in motherhood, being that she is now totally acceptable, and has, in fact, total control of the father, I quote, "for the sake of the children."

In his statement about the "Dear John" note, which was finally left in the house for him when his wife left him at the end of 1966, some five years after the marriage, is the statement,

> I eventually found the "Dear John" note which in effect said she had fallen out of love with me and was hoping that I would be okay and eventually would find someone who would love me the way I deserve.

Here we see a clear view of the superficial charm and good "intelligence," As Dr. Cleckley has said, "more often than not a typical psychopath will seem particularly agreeable and make a distinctly positive impression." One can be tricked into thinking that this woman truly cared for this man and left him for his sake, so he could find someone to love him as he deserved, etc., etc. This is an indication of unreliability, untruthfulness, insincerity, and marvellous lack of remorse or shame over what she has done to contribute to the marital breakdown. Certainly poor judgment and failure to learn by experience, and a pathological egocentricity and incapacity of love. And here one can quote from Dr. Cleckley's discussion of pathological egocentricity.

> He is plainly capable of casual fondness, of likes and dislikes, and of reactions that, one might say, cause others to matter to him. These affective reactions are, however, always strictly limited in degree. In durability they also vary greatly from what is normal in mankind.

From the same discussion by Dr. Cleckley:

> The psychopath seldom shows anything that, if the chief facts were known, would pass even in the eyes of lay observed as object love. His absolute indifference to the financial, social, emotional, physical, and other hardships which he brings upon those for whom he professes love confirms the appraisal during psychiatric studies of his true attitude. We must, let it never be forgotten, judge a man by his action rather than by his words.

Certainly, as you will see in further perusal of the documentation of this case, when one judges this woman by her actions rather than her words, the alleged statement of caring in the "Dear John" note is a farce. Hereto we see the hooked-husband syndrome again in that after this breakup he still continues to visit her, but finally manages to overcome his depression by burying himself in his work, and after six or eight months begins to get himself organized into his evident bachelorhood when suddenly appearing at the door his Anna with the two children and, quote, "They looked a sad sight." Then here we see again the incredible pathological egocentricity, unreliability, untruthfulness, insincerity, lack of remorse or shame, poor judgment, and failure to learn by experience and specific lack of insight so characteristic of the psychopath. After all the horrors that she had perpetrated on this man, she still asks to come back home and, quote, "On any terms, to see if we could work it out, just for a while." Again the psychopath as mother uses the children in her machinations and as the gentleman states and I quote, "The sight of my kids standing out in the cold and rainy night, I halfheartedly agreed to it on a temporary basis because my love and feelings for Anna were completely gone, but my love and affection for the kids were very strong, so I thought for the sake of the kids I would give it one more try." Here we see how the psychopathic female has the husband constantly under her thumb because she has his children as her hostages in this terrible drama of the psychopathic marriage. Mr. Kotter continues his history of the marriage with his description of his wife's increasing drinking problems, of her half-heartedly embracing A.A. and of her doing the characteristic psychopathic thing, getting involved romantically with members of the organization, where she should be going to attempt to learn from her experiences, but again here confirms the psychopathic characteristic of poor judgment and failure to learn by experience by repeating the same romantic nonsense; she shows her hysterical psychopathic behaviour, her incapacity to love and poverty in major affective reactions in the statement by the husband concerning one of her disappearances, and quote,

> She had met a man apparently the day after she left the house, fell in love with him that night, rented an apartment in Surrey on Wednesday of that same week, bought furnishings, dishes and all the necessary items to equip a house at Sears stores accompanies by her new lover, Jason Brown, and commenced living together with this man that very same day.

This is a clear indication of poverty in major affective reactions and lack of insight.

In the documentation is shown that romance, too, did not hold up too well: how she wound up in the psycho ward and again manages to trap a man into her psychopathic net: left the hospital and moved in with a new boyfriend. Then she continued to repeat the performance until January of 1977 when she had another stay at the Bay Centre Hospital and emerges out of hospital with a new boyfriend, Charles Milne, bought a home at Shasta Lake and proceeded to want a divorce and settlement. This case so clearly illustrates Dr. Cleckley's point No. 11, specific loss of insight, and I should quote,

> He has absolutely no capacity to see himself as others see him. It is perhaps more accurate to say that he has no ability to know how others feel when they see him or to experience subjectively anything comparable about the situation. All of the values, all of the major affect concerning his status, are unappreciated by him.

There follows in the documentation a most interesting factor, and yet most unhelpful to the workings of the Court Psychiatric Report from Messrs. Mason, Jonas and Armstrong, in which we see the primary characteristic of the psychopath, "superficial charm and good intelligence." The psychopath is so plausible in this report we see that she has managed to convince the psychiatrist that the drinking problem is not hers but the husband's. She turned to alcohol because of her neglect and frustration with the marriage and the husband's workaholism, supposedly. It is interesting that the Psychiatric Report is dated 1976, some fifteen years after the marriage in 1961, and Mrs. Kotter seems to have conveniently warped the history to forget that by 1966 her drinking had proceeded to the point where she was having blackouts, as reported by the husband in the first years of the marriage and in 1966 she was beginning her pattern of chasing other men and worsening drinking. She even goes to claim in the Psychiatric Report, and quote:

> To please her he decided to stop drinking altogether and spend the evenings at home. He claims that now that he is home and that he is not drinking and spending time with his friends, everybody in the family should be happy, especially Mrs. Kotter, as this she has given as the very reason why she drinks. Mrs. Kotter claims that such a drastic change has confused her and that she does not know how to cope with it.

Here we see the psychopath's great plausibility at work again in the clever attempt to subvert any positive move on the part of the husband to do something good for the marriage into a negative situation in which he's changed so much that she is now confused. The psychiatrist does at least attribute to some degree her unreliability, her untruthfulness, but he did notice in fact that:

> As the interview wore on, and she started talking more and more about her husband, she became boisterous, raised the level of her voice so that she was practically shouting. Also it was noticed while discussing her pattern of drinking, she sometimes chuckled, and then her sad expression disappeared and she even laughed wholeheartedly on occasion. Her mood was then appraised as moderately depressed while her affect was conceived as being labile or "mercurial."

The psychiatrist documents here but fails to recognize a clear picture of a psychopath. She has general poverty in major affective reactions, very clearly shown in her mercurial emotions and acting out here. In addition we see her specific loss of insight. To quote further from Dr. Cleckley's work,

> There is also inability in his fundamental reactions to size up normally what he has done, what he is, and what he has been.

As we see in the many chronicles of the psychopath that have been given in this work, the psychopathic in her activity in the marriage is completely missed and psychiatric treatment is really of very little use. The psychiatrist comes up with a ball-park diagnosis of neurotic, depressive anxiety reactions and passive hostile personality, alcoholism and marital dysfunction, a diagnosis the next-door neighbour could have come up with quite easily. There is further excellent psychiatric documentation of many of the characteristics of the psychopath, but further points out very clearly that the psychiatric nurses and, in fact, a second psychiatrist, in February of 1977, missed the boat also and despite the fact that there was no diagnosis of manic-depressive illness, they took a shot in the dark and started her on lithium, a drug not only not indicated but, in fact, dangerous under the circumstances in a well-known alcoholic personality, drug abuser.

In the letter of December 18th, 1978, her "Dear Willy" letter wishing him a Happy Christmas, we see that she still shows her specific loss of insight, shows her poor judgment and failure to learn by experience, shows her inadequately motivated social behaviour, her pathological egocentricity, her untruthfulness and insincerity, and her lack of true remorse or shame, in that she goes on again stating that she was acting, and I quote, "through love for you." We also see that she has done what many psychopaths also do and has taken "God" into her life in a hysterical rather than in a religious sense in that He has now become the guiding light in her so-called psychiatric recovery. As we have seen in Case 2, the Molders case, in which all the prayers to St. Jude, etc., etc., God becomes another crutch and excuse for the immorality or rather amorality of the psychopath, and their most despicable conduct.

The letter to Andrew and Simon, of February 28, 1979, is also how the psychopathic treats them, which shows no understanding whatsoever of feelings on her part, excusing her lack of contact with the children by bizarre statement, and quote:

> I'm sorry I have not called, but even going to the bathroom became an extreme effort.

One wonders why she kept the telephone in the bathroom. However, this is so sad that facetiousness possibly doesn't fit, but it shows the total lack of feelings and loss of insight in that this woman should even attempt to use such a hollow and stupid excuse. She goes on with the expected motherhood statements of, and I quote:

> Sweethearts, I love you, miss your darling faces immensely, take a moment to love each other—sometimes that's all we have.

Here again the record so far discussed on this woman would certainly seem to indicate that she knows even less about love than she does about life—incapacity for love.

This is followed by a letter to Simon himself and which she titles, "My Child at Spring." It is so terribly sad to read through these chronicles, which show her really total incapacity to appreciate the feelings of others and, in fact, so clearly shows Dr. Cleckley's statement regarding specific loss of insight in that the psychopath,

> ". . . has absolutely no capacity to see himself as others see him."
>
> It is perhaps more accurate to say that he has no ability to know how others feel when they see him to experience subjectively anything comparable about the situation.

In her letters to the children, she also makes a plea for them to embrace God, etc., and here too one can be fooled by her superficial charm and plausibility into thinking that this woman has, in effect, again some insight into what has gone on in her life and has learned from experience, but when one reads through this, one can see that they are superficial, hysterical, unreliable, and show a total lack of remorse or shame except in very superficial and shallow statements, which I am sure have no impact whatsoever on the brutalized children, except to further confuse them. In fact she goes on to compound the agony of these children by answering Simon's innocent question in the following despicable manner.

> Oh, yes, Simon, you asked at Christmas if I would someday marry Charlie. Well, I have been asked and gave a resounding yes as my answer—you see he's neat, he's not normal, but then neither am I so I guess that's what it takes sometimes.

Can you just imagine what a confusing and heart-rendering statement that is to a young child, who, as all young children in separated families, desperately hope that his Mom and Dad will get back together again, when in fact only asked this question in hopes of it being rhetorical and of his getting a negative answer from the mother and a statement that, Oh, no she would be going back to his Daddy. She shows a total inability to understand the affects of her actions on others, nor in fact, does she show any fact that she cares. This is just another example of the pathological egocentricity.

## The Theta Syndrome

*Elleston Trevor*

> *We all like to be loved, even those who won't admit it. And we are all dismayed by another's hate: It strikes at our ego with almost demonic force.*

New English Library
Times Mirror
1977

## *DONATO V. DONATO*

*Introduction*

This case shows a number of most interesting situations to do with the psychopath. As you will note in Chapter 3, in the discussion of the psychopath and the possible origins of the psychopath in the early years, reference should be had to the facts brought out by the husband concerning his wife's early years, in which he relates her early childhood as consisting of a very cold mother, who never showed the defendant any love or affection, and a father who had a child with a minor niece (a fourteen-year-old daughter of the mother's sister, who was living in the basement of the matrimonial home). The father was charged criminally, convicted, and sent to jail for this episode. And further, an uncle who sexually molested the defendant when she was a young girl. The hatred the defendant had for her brother and the remorse she suffered after his death.

If one could set the stage for the development of a psychopathic personality, this case certainly would support my discussion in the early part of Chapter 3. Whether there is, in fact, a genetic defect in this psychopathic female, Mrs. Donato, is certainly brought into question by the father's psychopathic activities with the niece, resulting in her pregnancy; the psychopathic activities of the uncle who sexually molested the defendant herself as a young girl; and the very cold mother unable to show love and affection, very possibly a woman who herself was a psychopath.

This case also well illustrates the pathological egocentricity, inacapacity to love, inadequately motivated social behavior, the fantastic and uninviting behaviour with drink and sometimes without, and an impersonal, trivial, and poorly integrated sexual identity, all characteristics of the psychopath and all demonstrated here very clearly by Mrs. Donato in her conduct throughout the marriage, as is shown in the court documents and most specifically in the taped encounter, which occurred in the matrimonial home during Christmas of 1978, at which time a surreptitious taping of a conversation between the children and Mrs. Donato was carried out by the father, who felt that he would in the current court system possibly fail in his attempts to show how violent and perturbative his wife was towards his children, and therefore he had the good sense to take a tape, which was subsequently presented in court and which is here transcribed. This tape absolutely terrified the judge and shows the violent and perturbative behavior of this shocking female towards her three children, aged from nine years down to four. In the light of this taped recording's presentation in court, the judge completely swept aside the psychiatrist's report, which was totally misleading, based entirely on hearsay and, I may say, appalling psychiatric and human judgment. In the beginning paragraph of the letter from the psychiatrist, Anthony P.

Travis, who is quoted in its entirety here in the documentation for this case, a short passage is quoted:

*Documentation*

> I am herewith informing you that I have seen Mrs. Donato as a patient since March, 1978. Mrs. Donato has a history of psychiatric illness dating back several years.
>
> (In fact this psychiatrist had committed Mrs. Donato to a mental hospital facility several times during the year preceding writing this letter on July 26, 1979, but he makes great light of this situation here in his report.)
>
> In the past year however, she has been doing exceedingly well and has functioned without any significant disturbance.
>
> (One will note that the taped violence of Christmas 1978, occurs just some six months prior to the doctor offering his learned opinion that she has functioned without any significant disturbance, is certainly a great indication of the total plausibility of the psychopath and the inability of even a trained psychiatrist to determine a true, functional level for the psychopath.)
>
> During the course of my treatment of Betty I have come to know her fairly well and I feel confident from my association with her that she is a responsible and capable mother. There has never been any indication throughout her treatment that her relationship with her children was a significant issue.
>
> (What the hell he can mean by her relationship being a significant issue with her children is a mystery, but it is certainly appalling that a trained psychiatrist can offer to the court such totally erroneous and misleading evidence as in fact this learned psychiatric opinion.)

When this matter finally came before the court on the 6th of May, 1980, the wife, Mrs. Betty Donato, had been once again committed by the same psychiatrist, Anthony P. Travis, to a mental health facility.

Despite this shocking information, the psychiatrist in his second paragraph makes a total and unqualified recommendation to the court, offered as a learned psychiatric opinion, quote:

> I would have no hesitation in recommending her as a suitable parent for custody of her children.

How in God's name can any court deliver a learned judgment with such assistance?

Now, we must further castigate the psychiatrist, because in paragraph 4 of the letter, this is his bald statement,

> I have not seen Mr. Donato during the course of my treatment. I have had several telephone conversations with him *and have had information about him through Mrs. Donato.*

Here, Dr. Travis makes the fatal mistake for his own credibility of giving an opinion, as Dr. Karl Menninger has often said, which is extremely dangerous, i.e., that of the psychiatric state of a patient whom he has never seen, based only on hearsay evidence. Dr. Travis goes on to say,

> His behavior during the course of Mrs. Donato's illness and the recent separation has not given me any competence whatsoever in his ability as an able and consistent parent.

A statement showing the inability of a psychiatrist to correctly analyse the potential danger of the psychopath. Not only does the psychiatrist here falsely elevate the wife, Mrs. Betty Donato, to a mantle of sainthood, but in the same breath goes on to condemn Mr. Donato to be an unfit parent.

The Court delivered the order awarding custody of the infant children of the marriage to Mr. Donato, access was defined and restricted, and, in fact, the learned judge had the wisdom to leave access by the oldest boy to be, in fact, at his choice rather than that of the mother.

*Report of Social Worker*

> *Personal History of Mr. Donato:*
>
> Mr. Donato was born in the City of Montebebelluna, Province of Treviso, Italy, on July 13, 1938. He is the second of five children, three of whom were boys and two girls. He states that he immigrated to the States in 1956 to follow his sister, living then in San Francisco. Mr. Donato was eighteen (18) years old at the time and recalls having to go to night school to finish his education (he completed grade five in Italy). Mr. Donato indicated that this was a difficult period of adjustment for him as everything was unfamiliar to him; however, once he had learned to speak English it became much easier for him here. He remembers his family as being close, happy and religious; he says that he maintains contact with them by letter.
>
> *Education:*
>
> Mr. Donato completed grade 12 attending night school and while doing so he also completed an electronics course by correspondence. During this time he worked mornings at construction sites, road paving projects, factories and various other jobs. He took photographs as a hobby starting in 1958 and has since made it his fulltime profession.

He has been one of the collaborators and photographers of the Italian newspaper, *Eco d'Italia*; he still contributes in these ways to this newspaper. For many years he has offered his services to the Italian community, which acknowledges his professionalism and devotion to his work. Mr. Donato still attends photography courses and workshops whenever he can and he says he is always eager to learn more on this subject.

*Employment:*

Mr. Donato began working as soon as he arrived in the United States. He took jobs in construction, road paving, factories, etc. After completing his electronics correspondence course he worked from 1958 to 1961 on his own as a television repairman in San Francisco. He then worked from 1961 to 1963 for Sears Roebuck as a television repairman. From 1963 to 1967 he worked with The Investors Group as a salesman. In 1967 he moved to New York to work as a photographer for an Italian newspaper, however, the job was not as it had been described to him, so two weeks later he returned to San Francisco. From October 1967 to February 1968 he worked as a television repairman for Zenith TV, and from 1968 to 1975 with General Electric. During employment with General Electric he was also pursuing a career in photography. In 1973 he opened his studio at 4761 Rainier Street, North Grove, California. In 1975 he left General Electric and since then his fulltime employment has been as a professional photographer at his own studio. Mr. Donato states that he is a member of the American Association of Professional Photographers. His present hours of work are Tuesday to Saturday, 9:00 A.M. to 5:00 P.M. However, his Saturday work hours are often irregular as his services are requested at weddings and other ceremonies. His clients describe him as a conscientious and excellent photographer. Mr. Donato plans to remain in this field of work as he finds it most satisfying and suitable to family life.

*Health:*

Mr. Donato states that he has never been sick. He has his regular physical examination without fortunate findings. His family has no history of either mental or physical problems.

*Regilion:*

Mr. Donato is a Catholic. He has strong beliefs and he attends Mass on an on/off basis. Mr. Donato strongly feels that his children should be raised upon his Christian beliefs.

*Financial Circumstances:*

There appear to be no financial problems at present. Mr. Donato stated that prior to opening his photography studio he had some financial difficulty, but that now he manages satisfactorily. He is saving for his family's future.

*Relatives:*

Mr. Donato has only one sister here in the States, Mrs. Ramero; his other sister and brothers are living in Italy. As he grew up with strong family ties, he still enjoys visiting with his sister and her family and his friends, and he feels they have been very accepting of him and his wife and their children. He has visited more often with these people since his wife and he have separated. They have become supportive resources for him, they have offered to help him in his attempts to gain custody of the children. They appear to be stable, happy families who take family life seriously.

*Marriage to Betty Donato:*

Mr. Donato met his wife in 1965 at Stanford while hitch-hiking onto campus. He stated that she was a very nice girl and he liked her company and enjoyed doing things with her as they had common interests. They were married July 8, 1967. Although they had some difficulties, he was happy—he believed that every relationship experienced "ups and downs." He stated that his wife seemed to be going through emotional changes added to the difficulties within the relationship, became difficult for her to cope with her emotions and she was often quite depressed. Furthermore, Mr. Donato feels the birth of Pietro, their first child, may have triggered something in his wife because their real problems began after Pietro was born. In fact she seemed to suffer from depression frequently and often he was the one to do the cooking and cleaning and caring for Pietro. He had colic and was very difficult for Mr. Donato. Then in 1973 Mrs. Donato became pregnant with Nola and after the birth Nola had chronic diarrhea. Mrs. Conato's depression deepened and the marital relationship worsened. During this Mr. Donato tried to keep the family together.

He describes himself as a man with very simple hopes: he wants a good life doing things together with his family, with each member caring for the others. He feels that husband and wife should stand side-by-side and not be put off balance by pushing the other, or one having to be better than the other. His hopes may have had conflict during their marriage: he said that he was open to the idea of his wife working and having some independence and he was willing to share some of the household duties and child caring; however, he probably couldn't completely accept this and a resentment built and hostility arose that prevented them from communicating. Mr. Donato has had the children living with him since January and he feels much better now that he has them under his care and he is sure that he can take good care of them. He feels that their mother's instability does not do the children any good, that they need a stable parent, one who not only cares and gives affection to them, but also one who can take the responsibility of parenting and who is able to make decisions. He feels that his wife has done this only on rare occasions in the past.

*Plan if Custody is Awarded to him:*

Mr. Donato plans to stay in the same house where they presently are living, located in North Grove. The children have developed friendships there and they now like the area. He sees that the religious influence is more to serve as support to the strength of the family than to impose limitations on the activities of the children. Mr. Donato will continue his work at his studio, he will pick the children up from school and will remain with them for the rest of the day. He will be with them on the weekends that Mrs. Donato would not be with them. He will participate, actively or passively, in his children's activities, showing his interest in their involvements. He said that he made this commitment ever since the children came into his life and he will continue to do so. He would also encourage the children to visit regularly with their mother.

*Personal History of Mrs. Donato:*

Mrs. Donato was born in Sacramento, in the State of California, in the United States of America, on July 1, 1945. She had one brother who was two years younger than her; he is deceased. The family always lived in Sacramento. Her mother works as a nurse and her father is retired but was a mechanic. She felt closer to her father than to her mother. She was also very close to her brother who died in a boating accident in 1966. Both her parents shared in taking care of her and her brother, but she felt that they favoured him. Mrs. Donato stated that her parents had high expectations of their children and encouraged them to be independent and to get a good education. Mrs. Donato visits her parents often and says that their relationship is better today than it was a few years ago.

*Education:*

Mrs. Donato attended grade school and completed high school in Sacramento in 1964. She then attended Stanford University where she received a Bachelor of Science degree in Occupational Therapy in 1967.

*Employment:*

Mrs. Donato was employed as an Occupational Therapist at North Grove Mental Hospital from 1970 to October 1972. She has done much volunteer work with the Community School and as an Occupational Therapist at Bay Centre General Hospital; she is presently involved with volunteer work at the hospital.

*Health:*

Mrs. Donato is in good health at present, but has had some health problems in the past.

*Religion:*

Mrs. Donato is Protestant and she attends the North Grove United Church. She has always encouraged her children to attend church and to say their prayers and study their church lessons.

*Financial Circumstances:*

Mrs. Donato is receiving social assistance funds at present. When she resumes employment she will earn an average wage and will be able to support herself and the children, with some help from Mr. Donato.

*Relatives:*

Mrs. Donato has her parents who live in Sacramento and an uncle living in Los Angeles and another aunt living in Carmel.

*Marriage to Nino Donato:*

Mrs. Donato met her husband at Stanford University in 1965. She said that at the time they needed each other, she was alone, but that mostly they had common interests. They saw much of each other for the next two years, then they were married July 11, 1967. Mrs. Donato found herself occupied with Pietro, he had colic and this brought her much distress. Problems continued and Mrs. Donato was not able to accept her husband's attitude to family life, that is, the husband as the head and controlling person in the family. She felt that her need for independence and freedom to make her own decisions was not possible in this relationship. She was first hospitalized in August 1969 due to her depression, she remained in hospital for some time. In April 1973 she had her second child, Nola; she was a good baby, but a few months after birth Nola developed chronic diarrhea. When coping with Pietro became difficult for her, Mr. Donato would take over, this also occurred with Nola. This left her feeling alone and isolated. Mr. Donato would not give her his attention and she learned that although he is a kind, loving person, he has strong feelings about how to raise a family and she felt that he was not accepting her as his equal. When their third child, Marchello was born, the marital relationship became even worse. Mrs. Donato had to seek help from a psychiatrist, as she had done in previous times. Mrs. Donato said that they always suffered from financial difficulty as Mr. Donato did not manage his income well and had various debts and this bothered Mrs. Donato considerably. Because of marital problems and the "ups and downs" of their relationship Mrs. Donato had to leave her children and her home; she could not cope with the type of lifestyle she lived within throughout their marriage.

*Plan if Awarded Custody:*

Mrs. Donato plans to move back to her home, where Mr. Donato and the children presently reside. She stated that she will require maintenance funds from her husband for the children and herself. She said that she will transfer Nola back to the Community School because she does not have a car and it would be too difficult for her to pick Nola up after school from St. Mary's School where Nola will return in September. She feels that as Nola has a good teacher at the Community School, and as she has many friends there and her brother also attends the school that Nola would adjust well there. She plans to be with her children as much as possible and take part in their activities. She will accept the children visiting with their father and hopes that the conflict between her and her husband will be resolved because she feels that it affects the children detrimentally.

*Children for Whom Custody is to Be Decided:*

*Pietro Donato:* (Born: July 11, 1968)

Pietro is a bright and active 11 year old child. He will be attending the Community School in September. He has been upset by the conflict between his parents. He stated he would prefer to live with his father because he does not "run away" as his mother has done on many occasions. Pietro said that his mother took good care of him, but never took care of the house. He said, "It was always messy around our house, now it is much better."

*Nola Donato:* (Born: April 14, 1973)

Nola is a young and gentle girl, she is very quiet and sensitive. Her desire is to see her parents reunited and she appears very disturbed over their conflict. She will return to St. Mary's School in September, if her father receives custody, or she will attend the Community School if her mother receives custody. Nola loves both her parents very much and says that it is very sad that they do not like each other anymore.

*Marchello Donato:* (Born: October 18, 1975)

Marchello is a happy and active boy. He is quite easygoing and it is easy to be with him. He likes to visit his mother and has been doing so since January 1979, when his parents separated. His young age appears to have let him escape the problems of conflict between his parents and he therefore shows none of the problems and sentiments of his older brother, Pietro.

*Evaluation and Conclusion:*

During the course of this investigation it has become quite apparent that both Mrs. and Mrs. Donato love the children and want to ensure they grow up to be happy, well adjusted people. They have both shown a willingness to co-operate in this investigation.

Mr. Donato feels that he will be able to offer a stable, consistent environment for his children and has indeed arranged a plan consistent with this. The home he has chosen is the one they are presently living in; it is located in North Grove. Relatives and friends who were interviewed gave support to his ability as a father and have offered their assistance. His employment is stable and he is thought of quite highly by the community and his fellow photographers. His commitment to family life and the raising of children is very strong and his plan is certainly one that will provide a stable, happy home for the children. He feels that he has tried very hard to relate to the children as individuals and not to let his ideas and feelings interfere. On the other hand Mrs. Donato feels that she has always been very close to the children and has done most of the caring for them.

She worked for two years during the marriage and if she did not feel satisfied as a housewife, she did remain home to take care of the children. She further said that she could not accept custody of the children being awarded to Mr. Donato as he would disregard her opinions and feelings on how their children should be cared for. Both parents have positive contributions to make to the lives of their children. The only negative factor appears to be their conflict in relation with each other: each fears that the other will try to control them and deprive them of having a good relationship with the children. It appears that this mutual suspicion is a factor that will be resolved in time and indeed must be resolved if they expect the children to be free from the effects of it. Whichever parent has the children must maintain open communication with the other parent and encourage this from the other as well. Each spouse must be accepting of the positive factors of the other's ability as a parent

In conclusion, I would like to state that it is extremely difficult to make a decision as to custody when both parents try their best to be good parents and try to be active and involved with the children. It is my opinion that Mr. Donato has made his move out of his genuine concern for his own happiness and the happiness of the children. As Mr. Donato is of a happy disposition, his chilren relate to him in this way and they themselves are bright and fun-loving. The children have good feelings for their mother and they enjoy doing activities with her. I find, however, that the children are closer to their father and function well at home with him.

*Recommendation:*

My first recommendation would be to suggest joint custody of the children between the parents, and the terms ordered by the Court.

However, since there does not appear to be a possibility of reconciliation between the parents, my second recommendation is that custody of the children be granted to Mr. Donato, with liberal access to Mrs. Donato.

It is felt that Mr. and Mrs. separated in an attempt to find a happier situation for themselves that would also benefit the children. Mr. Donato has been very understanding and has found that he can relate to his children in a positive way. The children appear to benefit from this. Their continued regular contact with their mother is a vital contact for them and Mrs. Donato also. The mother and children enjoy being together and Mrs. Donato is a very positive influence to their lives.

Respectfully submitted,
"Peter Drews"
Family Court Counsellor

At this point may I point out that from the beginning of her mental instability, Dr. Wilson, our then family doctor, Dr. Pike, her psychiatrist #1, Dr. Paragon #2, and then Dr. Truest #3, Ann Hart, Brian and social workers that I spoke to, as well as the defendant herself, attributed her problems to the very poor upbringing in her family, i.e., her mother was always very cold and could never show any love for her. Her father having had a child with his *minor* niece, and as a result of this he was put away in the psychiatric ward at Bay Centre General Hospital. His brother having molested the defendant sexually when she was a young girl. The hatred that the defendant had for her brother, and the remorse she had after he drowned. Her mixed feeling she had about our last son, Marchello. She, by her own admission, could not love him until he was about 2 years old.

*Taped Encounter—Christmas 1978*

N = Nino B = Betty P = Pietro N = Nola M = Marchello

1240 P Was talking to someone.
1243 N Stop it, Pietro.
1287 P Get away from me.
1288 B Go and fuck yourself.
1289 N If you touch him one more time.
1289 B He touch me and that's the second time (*blurry*).
1290 P Get out of my way (*blurry*).
1291 B I will not stand for that.
*Marchello and Nola start to cry.*
*A few words were interchanged among N, B & P (blurry).*
1293 P I'll kill her.
1294 N He was sitting there before you.
1295 B And I was sitting here.
1295 P You were too.
1296 N Idiot.
1296 B Oh! Call yourself an idiot.
1296 P Oh! Fuck off.
1296 N Pietro! No more bad words. *(This was the first time I heard Pietro using such words.)*

*M & P said something blurry.*

*B said something blurry then Pietro said "oh-h-h."*

1300 B Okay, kid, you asked for it! You asked for it!

1302 P I'm ready! I'm ready! I'm ready!

1303 B O.K. You'll get it tomorrow. Let me tell you.

1304 M *Said something blurry.*

1305 B I will so!

M *Said something blurry*

1305 P I'm ready.

1306 B I'm not going to tolerate that kind of behaviour.

1307 P I'm ready and I'm going to MURDER HER.

1308 B Sure, and you have been murdering the kids on the soccer field, haven't you?

1309 P I have not.

1310 B *says something (not clear) then proceeds by saying,* I have heard what you have been doing at soccer games. One little thing and you'll get mad and you'll *(blurry)* up. Bob speaks to you two or three times every game.

1313 P You want a bit.

1314 P Oh-h-h. Bull shit.

1315 B That's what I'm told.

1317 B He cannot control. He can't *(blurry)* together.

1318 P Ah! Shut up.

1320 P I'm not going to sit in the same room with that idiot.

*Pause.*

1333 B And you are no father either. Sending a child to her room during her birthday party crying.

B Nola's last birthday. You better believe it. You were here? And a five-year-old told her mother. Her mother said how was the party. The child said, "You know what? Nola's father spanked her, made her cry and sent her to her room." Because the child would not sit on the chair.

1344 P *Barely heard.*

B Oh! Fuck yourself.

P Ah! You.

1345 N Pietro, stop it.

P I don't have to. I'm going to murder her! I'm going to murder her! I'm going to murder her! I'm going to murder her! I'm going to kill her! I'm going to kill her! I'm going to kill her!

1350 N *Heard in the background telling P to stop it. At this point P was on the floor, B was on top of him.*

1350

P Let go. Let go of me. I don't need you *(to B)*. I'm going to murder her, I'm going to murder you *(B)*.

N *Said something to the effect that if she didn't let P free N was going to call the police.*

1353 B Oh! Thanks, your name and my name will go down in their record.

*At this point N points out to B that her name is already in the State Police record as she was picked up the time she escaped from the Mental Hospital.*

1411 *B & P arguing*

1420 N Shut up! Leave him alone.

There were witnesses. Kicked her mother away from Seymour Village.

1435 N I'm not talking to you.
B Gee whiz. I can't wait to get rid of you.
1450 P *(screaming).*
N Stop it—leave him alone.
P *(Second scream)*
N Leave him alone—Leave him alone, please.

N Let go!
1465 B Oh shit! You said . . .
B Pietro, he has been saying all along: Your father will be so upset over this situation that it could kill him. He could have a heart attack. He keeps saying that. And what did he do? He phone himself last night and told him. What a dirty—bastard. *PAUSE.*
1537 N Your vulgar language has been recorded tonight. Did you know that?
1710 B Go and fuck yourself.
1712 N *Blurry*
1727 B *Blurry*
1746 B Were you there when he talked to Grandpa Pietro? Were you there *(Pietro screams)* when he talked to Grandpa?
P *(Started to cry)* I'm not saying.
B I want Yes or No. Were you there when he talked to Grandpa?
P Nola, say nothing. Don't say anything. Nola, don't say anything. Don't say anything.
B *(to Nino)*—Did he *(Dad)* say that Mom had gone away?
1754 P Don't say it, Nola! *(Repeats four or five times).*
B Did he tell Grandpa that I had gone away?
P I'm not going to say.
B Is that what he said?
1760 P I say what I said.
B You are a liar, too.
P Daddy.
B You are a liar! You're a liar. You are a liar just like him. If you care about your Grandpa you'll tell what he said to him.
P Get out of here.
B If you care. If you care about Grandpa you'll tell me. What did he say to Grandpa?
*(At this point she starts pounding him.)*
P *Screams.*
N *Screams.*
M *Screams.*
N Get away from him. Get away from him.
N *is heard calling the State Police.*

Anthony P. Travis, M.D.
Psychiatry

July 26, 1979

Mr. Peter Drews,
Family Court Counsellor.

Dear Mr. Drews:

*Re: Betty Donato*

In accordance with our telephone conversation this week and per Mrs. Donato's written permission, I am herewith informing you that I have seen Mrs. Donato as a patient since March 1978. Mrs. Donato has a history of psychiatric illness dating back several years. In the past year, however, she has been doing exceedingly well and has functioned without any significant disturbance. During the course of my treatment of Betty I have come to know her fairly well and I feel confident from my association with her that she is a responsible and capable mother. There has never been any indication throughout her treatment that her relationship with her children was a significant issue.

I would have no hesitation in recommending her as a suitable parent for custody of her children.

Her present treatment is of a supportive nature. As mentioned above, she is doing extremely well and considering the serious difficulties that she has experienced in separation from her husband her adjustment is exceptionally good.

I have not seen Mr. Donato during the course of my treatment. I have had several telephone conversations with him and have had information about him through Mrs. Donato and through his contact with Mrs. Ursula Muller, North Grove Family Services, and Mr. Henry Walker, social worker at the Psychiatric Day Centre. My impression from these sources is that Mr. Donato is a very erratic, unpredictable and emotionally unstable individual. A great deal of Mrs. Donato's emotional difficulties relate directly to her very troubled relationship with him. His behaviour during the course of Mrs. Donato's illness and their recent separation has not given me any confidence whatsoever in his ability as an able and consistent parent. Should you wish more information about Mrs. Donato, I suggest you contact Mrs. Muller and Mr. Walker.

I hope that the above information is of assistance to you. Should you have any further question, please do not hesitate to contact me.

Yours truly,

"Anthony P. Travis, M.D."

APT:rl

*Court Order*

*Donato v. Donato*

> THIS COURT ORDERS that custody of the infant children of the marriage, namely PIETRO DONATO, born the 11th day of July, 1968, NOLA DONATO, born the 14th day of April, 1973, and MARCHELLO DONATO, born the 18th day of October, 1975, be and the same is hereby granted to the Plaintiff, NINO DONATO.

*Discussion and Summary*

The reader needs no extensive discussion of the point made in the presentation of the Donato case. The documentation stands on its own as a shocking revelation of the terribly misguided judgments that can be awarded by the court when they depend on such faulty, foolhardy, irresponsible psychiatric evidence as was presented by Dr. Travis. Once again reinforcing Dr. Karl Menninger's thesis and advocacy before a meeting of the American Psychiatric Association that:

> Psychiatrists should form no part of the decision-making process of the courts of this land.

# THE SAWYER CASE

*Introduction*

In the very early conflict in this marriage, as detailed in the life story of the victim, there is the new wife, very desperate to early establish dominion over man in the style of "The Wife of Bath," telling him after three or four months of marriage that either his mother move out or she would move out, thereby forcing the mother out. One also can see her lack of remorse or shame in that Kate keeps going on and on talking about how other friends acted towards their wives without any appreciation whatsoever how other friends' wives may have acted towards their husband's, their responsibilities towards their mothers. Even at this time, she had this man cowed to the point where he was unable to render any financial support to his mother. He proceeds to submerge himself in his work, probably both to earn the funds required by the psychopathic female but also to escape from the uninviting behaviour at home. Early in the marriage begins the humiliation on the *Odessa,* there is the statement that Kate held "court" over the other passengers, talking loud and contradictory. Here are three typical characteristics of the psychopath, poor judgment, pathological egocentricity, fantastic and uninviting behaviour with drink and sometimes without. Her pathological egocentricity and the fact that they spent four months in England with the wife not the least bit interested in any of the tradition or history or the sights, in fact the poor chap didn't even get to see the Crown Jewels, as his wife wasn't interested. There is a very interesting confirmation in this in her comment about the Coliseum in Rome, totally lacking in any historical appreciation.

This man steadily accepts his wife's constant pressures to run life the way she sees it and she totally dominates him and, in effect, finally makes this cowed husband accept her psychopathic view of his worthlessness. Her fantastic behaviour continues all through the discussion where she begins to constantly embarrass and harass the husband in public, alienating him from his friends, denigrating any of his accomplishments, even to the point where he notes in December 1974, where she kept "comparing me very poorly against my colleagues to the extent that I began to believe her." The situation is best summarized by the last paragraph in his statement in which he states, "I could not carry on as I felt myself going down a very long slide to an early grave."

In the history of the wife, as related to the husband, there is some indication of the roots of psychopathy in the fact that the mother did not appear to care about this child, and was raised by their servants, she had many quarrels with the mother, who interfered constantly with the attempts of this girl to socialize and, in fact, the notation here that the father was a heavy drinker and finally died of a heart attack, is probably an indication of the father's response to this woman's, Kate's mother, psychopathy, which Kate absorbed from her mother and perpetrated on her husband, Mr. Sawyer.

And now to the details of documentation of this marriage; there is the case history as the life story of Mr. Sawyer in his own words, plus his appreciation of the history of the wife, as he related it, plus a most interesting psychiatrist report, which shows her relentless domination and psychological attack on this man, reminiscent of the attack on the father in Strindberg's play of that name.

*Documentation*

In this present case history, firstly, the life story of the victim:

I married Kate on the 16th day of June, 1962. At the time of the marriage I was living with my mother, who was in desperate financial straits. She and my father had adopted a girl, and at that time my two nephews were also living with us as my sister was in the USA and immigration difficulties dictated no recourse.

We moved into an apartment in the Kai Yuen Terrace in Hong Kong, and after three or four months, my wife flew into a rage and said either my mother went or she will go.

My mother left with the children and lived in various single rooms in the Colony.

At that time, Kate kept talking about how my other friends acted toward their wife, etc. She would not listen when I tried to tell her about the financial realities. I was unable at that time to lend any financial support to my mother either for fear of another outraged reaction.

The marriage continued along with me submerging myself in my work, and no communication (spoken) between us. Communication was her yelling at me.

She then went on a series of tactics designed to humiliate me.

We were on board the MV *Odessa* in May 1964, on passage from Hong Kong to London when one evening she "held court" over the other passengers; talking loud and contradictory. I was the recipient of some very curious glances the next day.

We spent four months in England and she was not interested in any of the "sights." We were in the Tower but I was unable to view the Crown Jewels as she was not interested.

An example of the comments I had to swallow included a very seriously asked question concerning the Coliseum in Rome. "Why don't they tear it down and build a new one? This old ruin smells of horse piss!" I tried to explain about the several thousand years of history associated with the place and did not get through.

I never did get to see the Sistine Chapel, which was the object of our going to Rome, due to her objection. All she had to say about that visit was to give me hell because I was reluctant to pay for a ride on a horse-drawn carriage as she had spent most of our money in England buying children's clothes, which was fine, but also purchasing some other garbage.

I settled into a quiet life and gradually my friends drifted off, I have since found, due to their reluctance to associate with her.

In about 1966, we started talking about leaving Hong Kong. I had wanted to visit the States first, then we could decide whether to make our final move. She vetoed that idea and put on severe pressure to "go now"!

We were accepted by the American Immigration, and in the round of farewells from my friends, Kate started acting up.

One particular incident in the home of my friend John Rivers, who I had known since we were five years old, she quite deliberately and without provocation set about making accusations about another friend's family in all our presence. Everyone was very embarrassed and I lost another friend then.

We came to America in June 1967. On the day before the Eugene Air Show in 1967, we had arranged to attend with another family who had come over on the ship with us. She took exception to a remark I made about buying some Kentucky Fried Chicken and started scolding me loudly. The other family begged off going to the show the next day.

We started house hunting and she kept giving me hell as we could not qualify for mortgage for the first house we saw. She kept talking about buying a new car which I resisted as I felt our small resources was better utilized in the purchase of a home. I bought an older car and she never gave me a moment's peace about it.

I started going to night school to upgrade my education and she resisted that, saying I should be at home helping her with the housework. I would go to work, come home and bolt my supper, clean up the children to ready them for bed and leave for school.

In 1968, my father came to the States. He saw what was happening and asked me, "This is a life?" She would not let him smoke in the house, so he would stand outside in the garden in October for a cigarette. He left the States after two weeks. After he left I got scolded by Kate as I would not accept a thousand dollar loan from my father to purchase a car. She would not accept that $1,000 does not buy much of a car, and I had no means of repayment.

In July 1968, I took some exams from my night school courses. Being unfamiliar with course numbers, I signed up for the wrong exams and did not do well. As she read all my mail, she had a field day telling everyone, including my children, I was a failure.

I had joined the Jaycees and Round Table in Hong Kong and was quite well regarded by them. In San Francisco I joined the Rotary but she objected, and I had to leave them in early 1969 for peace in the house.

In September 1969, my mother and adopted sister came to America. I had hoped to be able to keep them in America as they were living in a room in Hong Kong. After a week, my wife said she's got to go. There was a big quarrel and the next day when I got home from work she had taken our youngest daughter and left. I looked at every motel on State Street trying to find them but was unsuccessful. I was worried as she had no money. Two days later she returned, and never spoke until my mother left.

In November 1973, she got really wound up about one of my

friends. We had a big fight in front of our children and she took off again for a few days.

We went on a motoring holiday in April 1975, and she scolded me in front of the children in the car all the way.

In December 1974 she took particular delight in goading me about my past unsuccessfull attempts at promotions, and kept comparing me very poorly against my colleagues to the extent that I began to believe in her.

In August '76, we went to visit her sister in San Diego, and all the way home she spoke of the imagined delights of divorce.

In January '76 she scolded me for looking for a place for my mother. Throughout that year she said, "If you're a man you'd leave. You got no guts."

I put up with all her tirades, until December 1976. On the 22 December I heard that my mother was in hospital for an operation. I was concerned and she gave me hell for it.

When I got home from work on 23 December 1976, she had left again. I went to her hotel and tried to talk to her. We went to the dining room of the hotel and for about an hour she berated me in a loud voice about everything I had ever said or done. I left her finally as I couldn't take any more.

She returned home on Christmas Day and gave us (me and the children) hell for imagined wrongs.

I took her out to dinner at the Seafood House in March 1977 and on a chance remark about my friend Gord Johnson, she took the opportunity to launch into another tirade. She would not eat her supper and I hadn't paid the bill so I was stuck for a very humiliating hour.

In April 1977, I was attempting to change the kitchen sink, and to arborite the kitchen counter. I met nothing but resistance from her until I finally left the house for three days to the tears of my children. She spent $350 for a plumber to finish the job. Never gave me any credit for attempting to do the work, saying all I cared was for the money.

On 31 May '77, I mentioned I was going out for an evening with some people from work. The resulting quarrel led to me leaving.

In all our years of marriage she had never praised me for anything. She stated in a factual manner I smelled like a goat—I stank. I was no good in bed. I looked weird, etc. I was a failure, no good husband and provider and a lousy father.

I finally had enough. I had wanted to stay to provide a steadying influence to my children until they were older, but I could not carry on as I felt myself going down a very long slide to an early grave.

Here follows the history of the wife as related to the husband by her:

She gave me her date of birth as 7th October, 1941. Her father was a lecturer at the University of Hong Kong and she was his favourite child. She was referred to as "the goose" as she had a "big bum." Her father died when she was quite young and she felt let down, very disappointed. Lately she told me she felt betrayed. He called her "Biba."

Her sister, Jane, was her mother's favourite and when her father died, Jane got all the attention and money for whatever she wanted.

When she was about five years old she said she fell off her bicycle and knocked her front teeth out and spent some time at the Batilda Hospital, which is one of the more exclusive general hospitals in Hong Kong. While there she met a young Dutch boy who was a good friend and apparently still is.

She went to the French Convent School, at the time she was not a Catholic.

When she was about 14 or 15, she was very good friends with a boy named Brian Warden. Warden's family were going to New Zealand and wanted her to go with them, but her mother refused permission, which was a disappointment.

She talked about her sister's boyfriends, how Jane would have her boyfriends in and they would be fed by mother. How her oldest sister Pat was always going out with American sailors, etc.

She told me during the Japanese Occupation they lived somewhere on the Peak, and her parents had enough food for them.

Her father was a heavy drinker, drove his car too fast and finally died of a heart attack.

She was very good in school.

She was of Persian, Chinese, and Spanish extraction.

Her mother came from a very wealthy family and had lots of property in Peking, which was all confiscated by the Communists.

She was of the opinion that men found her attractive. Some of her friends wanted to bed her. There was an older man who wanted to photograph her in the nude. They took her out and gave her good dinners.

She had many quarrels with her mother.

She was raised by the servants as her mother did not care. Her mother was a nurse.

During the war years, they were living quite well and her parents took in two other girls whom they raised as her "sisters." Her father was her mother's second husband and Pat was her half-sister. She never told me what happened to her mother's first husband.

When her father died, the relatives came and grabbed his possessions and did not leave them too much of a legacy.

When she graduated from high school, she went to work for an uncle, then with a shipping firm where she did very well.

She never had any holiday trips or went anywhere.

She joined the WREN Reserves, and heard the other women talking about men, which disgusted her. She resigned after about a year.

She told me very little else about her childhood. There was a gap from the time she was hospitalized until she was about 14 or 15 when she talked of Brian Warden a lot.

He reports that their problems began at the start of the marriage. She was pregnant at marriage but they would have eventually married and this was not the precipitant cause. The marriage began in the Crown Colony of Hong Kong where both parties lived with their British civil service families. He was a gas distribution engineer for the City and at the time of marriage he supported his mother who had been deserted by his R.N. father. He felt his new wife rejected the mother-in-law being supported and this began their difficulties. He reports they were short of money due to low pay but when he tried to take higher education at night she rejected this and wanted him at home. He finally emigrated to America and found his credentials not as expected and his education not as well accepted. He reports he tried many years of trying to upgrade himself in the face of her resistance to him spending time and money in the pursuit of higher qualifications. He claims he did take schooling for three years but found her harassment of his efforts too much. She claimed he was a failure and wasting his time at school and jealous and possessive. He claims she'd complain about all his efforts in housework, making breakfast or doing house repairs and rennovations. He felt she gave him no support or credit and put down his friends and family. He described her rages and total rejection of his opinion on any subject. He admits he is quiet and passive so that he did not fight back. She complained that he "stank" physically from the start of the marriage and that was used as the reason to reject sexual intercourse. While she didn't turn to other men she would downgrade him by comparing him to what other men could be sexually. He doesn't believe she was unfaithful, but since separation he claims she has had an affair with a twenty-two year old student.

Mr. Sawyer initially reacted in the marriage with passivity. He states he began to accept her view that he was dump and hopeless and he became quite inferior about seeking promotions in work, felt unworthy as a man, father and husband. He claims that the "last straw" for him was her attacks on him, in front of the children. He admits she looked after the children physically but he felt they were criticized by her and never praised as she cannot give such support to anyone. He admits he turned to work to get satisfaction and did attain a supervisory job in the stores area of the Gas Division. While he tried other outlets like Kinsmen Club she objected vehemently and he had to give it up. He described getting up in the morning on his own and coming home to dinner by himself with no real sharing, conversation or connection. He had grown up Roman Catholic and when he tried to return to any religious connection she would downgrade his beliefs and bring Jehovah Witnesses and Mormon proselytizers into the home.

Mr. Sawyer is a sensitive, rather passive, serious, concerned man who now feels much better to be out of the unhappy marital situation. The stresses he felt in marriage were the rejection of his mother and being denigrated by his wife, through her inability to allow him to study or work towards career progress. He was very disturbed by her hostility as he is very sensitive and was particularly concerned about the failure of his children to get much praise, encouragement or support. The lack of sharing, affection, sexuality, etc., was very disturbing to him but verbal attacks on his children and religious beliefs were very distressing. He reported that his wife left several times and returned but she rejected his attempts to get professional help for the marriage. He felt that she believed he was too passive and would never leave and that her reactions of hostility since separation are due to her surprise he would so act.

While Mrs. Sawyer may or may not have consciously acted towards him as he describes, it is clear that the effect on him would be severely traumatic due to his serious, concerned and passive nature. His action in leaving was clearly to free himself of an intolerable situation he could not change or get her to accept any help to change. It would seem to me that her repetitive behavior and attitude, as described by him, would constitute mental cruelty. It certainly required him to obtain psychiatric help (Dr. Harrington) and medications.

### *Discussion and Summary*

As you will see from the documentation, this case certainly illustrates very clearly the psychopathic nature of the wife, Kate, as earlier discussed in the introduction. There is her constant battle to attain dominion over man in the style of The Wife of Bath, seen by her being very early in the marriage at war with this man's mother, somewhat reminiscent of the war in which it is suggested she might have wished to have with her own mother, but failed to win, with the power of her own mother very likely that of a psychopath as well. Her mother had driven her father to drink and an early heart attack. There is her poor judgment, her pathological egocentricity, her fantastic and uninviting behaviour with drink and sometimes without. Then too, her unreliability, her untruthfulness and her insincerity; her lack of remorse or shame; her poor judgment and failure to learn by experience; her inadequately motivated social behaviour; her general poverty of major effective reactions; her specific loss of insight, and all of the other major characteristics of the psychopath as laid out by Dr. Cleckley and discussed by me in Chapter 2. The case can best be summarized by the statement that the unrelenting drive of the psychopath to attain dominion over her man has cowed him to the point where he has, in fact, began to accept her view of his worthlessness, as he states in his early discussion, "kept comparing me very poorly against my colleagues to the extent that I began to believe in her." This poor husband finally awakens and proceeds to a divorce with a very sad two last paragraphs in his initial discussion of his life story with this psychopathic wife, Kate, and I quote, "In all of our years of marriage, she has never praised me for anything, and stated in a factual manner,"

> I smelled like a goat—I stank. I was no good in bed. I looked weird, etc. I was a failure, no good husband and provider and a lousy father.

I finally had enough. I had wanted to stay to provide a steadying influence to my children until they were older, but I could not carry on as I felt myself going down a very long slide to an early grave.

Sad, Sad, Sad.

# *CHANCELLOR V. CHANCELLOR*

*Introduction*

This case history illustrates conduct by the wife so bizarre, so relentless, and so completely lacking in social remorse, as to be explainable only in terms of the female psychopath. The documentation provided by the husband in the form of the marital history shows very clearly the bizarre sexual conduct of this woman whom, within a year of the marriage, drags home some pizza parlour king and introduces him to her husband as a friend. The husband begins to see the light in that he seems to realize that, and as he states, "They were together quite often."

However, this husband is a fine example of "the HUSBAND as a VICTIM" in that he carries on throughout these early disaster even to the point of finding his wife in Harold's basement suite, a fine citizen of Shakey's, he being the Chief Chef. The witless chap goes on to state that, and to quote John Forest, "That at a later date told me that he had had an affair with Shirley, he never came around after that." One would sincerely hope not. He had already been replaced by Dear Harold, then comes Mark and his line, and and on it goes, until a note is made that their daughter, Cheryl, was born October 4th, 1967. Very shortly after that, dear wife Shirley is off to another pizza palace and there meets a new Lothario, Achille. She then goes onward and upward in the world to move into the topless dancer role at the Slippery Mermaid. The dear husband carries on and moves the family one more time and, "To get away from everyone, and sort of start over." Here we have the endless hope of the victim husband that something good will come of this marriage.

Readers can peruse this missive for themselves, but note that the psychopathic female managed to wind another child into this marital relationship sometime between the "Slippery Mermaid" and her leaving him. See how she really had a totally egocentric outlook on the world in that she indulged in her bizarre sexual activities, totally ignoring the child and only using the children on occasion and on whim when she needed some evidence of her motherhood, either personally or to show her friends. Note the letter from Cheryl Chancellor written in 1980, a young girl of twelve, which was written to her father's lawyer in the divorce proceeding. This letter is a terribly sad chronicle of a child's description of a psychopathic mother, and it ends with a very sad sentence, and to quote, "And that is all I have told and there is probably more, but I don't know any more," and signed by Cheryl.

The last letter in the documentation is a letter from Achille, one of the boyfriends from the Pizza Parlour, to Shirley, at a time when she still was Mrs. Chancellor, a mother of a baby less than a year old. In this letter, which purports to show an undying love between Achille and the said Shirley, we again see a clear documentation of the workings of the female psychopath on a male, who in this case happens to be one of a string of boyfriends in this disgusting tale. She has this fellow so wrapped around her finger with her plausibility and her supposedly warm sexual relationships that he is just beside himself and even fails to see her use of her children as a safety valve in the relationship (when she cooled the relationship with Achille by saying she wanted to go back to her marriage and give it another try, "for the sake of her children"). He seems to be a rather sane chap caught up in this psychopathic madness and he gives a very stern and caring lecture to her, about the way he thinks things should be if she is truly interested in salvaging her marriage. He goes on to proclaim his love for her in stating that he would never do anything to harm her; he offers, "When you realize what you are doing, no matter what the circumstances, I will be there to pick up the pieces. This is a promise to look after you and help you for the rest of my life." Here again we see the utter plausibility of the female psychopath, who manages to enslave any man upon whom she sets her eyes and her "heart." It's almost as if he needs to take a beating from this woman in penitence for the break-up of his own marriage. At any rate he seems to have most of his marbles in order, but he persists in chasing a phantom—the phantom of the warm, loving, wonderful, caring person, which Shirley has managed to instill in his mind as the perfect image of her, an image that the reader can see from perusing this documentation is as far from the truth as one can get.

*Documentation*

*Marital History by Mr. Chancellor*

Shirley and I were married on June 14, 1965. Our son Geoffrey was born on December 24, 1965. We lived on West 2nd in North Grove. Shirley started working at Shakey's Pizza about January 1966. Shortly after starting at Shakey's, Shirley brought a customer home with her and introduced him as a friend; his name was John Forest. I started to realize after a while they were together quite often. I worked for Bay Cabs at the time. One morning after I started my shift, I had to return home for something and found the two of them sleeping on the floor together, with their clothes on. I questioned Shirley about the incident and she denied anything. Gary Burns, a friend of Shirley's and John Forest, told me some time later that Shirley and John would often borrow his pick-up truck and go places together. One night I took Geoffrey to South Grove to visit my Aunt Marion. The next morning when I returned to North Grove Shirley was not at home, so I went to look for her and found her at Harold's basement suite. He was a cook at Shakey's at the time. John Forest, Gary Burns and another girl from Shakey's were all there at the time. John Forest at a later date told me that he had had an affair with Shirley. He never came around after that.

Mark Jervis worked at Bay Cabs the same time I did. He had been charged with assault with bodily harm and was very depressed at the time, so Shirley and I offered him a place to stay while awaiting his court case. We all moved to South Grove at this point, until one day I saw Mark and Shirley driving down Main Street with Shirley sitting right next to him. I questioned Shirley about this later and she denied it. Mark then moved out soon after.

Our daughter was born October 4, 1967. On November 1, 1967, we all moved to 18757—101st Avenue in South Grove, which was across from her mother's and next door to Angie and Ivor's, who later got divorced and used Shirley as the correspondent I believe. We lived at this address for about four or five months. At this time Shirley got a job at a pizza place on the freeway. It was there that she met Achille. I have a love letter written by Achille saying that they did have intercourse together. I myself did not know about Achille until finding the letter after we had separated. She later worked at the Slippery Mermaid in San Francisco as a topless dancer. She told me that she was a waitress because she knew I would not approve of her being a topless dancer. This was about May 1968. Shortly after I found out about her I made her quit.

On about September 1, 1968, we moved to Big Sur to get away from everyone and sort of start over. On October 6, 1968, her mother and I and the two children went to Los Angeles for the weekend without Shirley because she had to work that weekend. When we returned she was supposed to meet us at her mother's, but she didn't arrive for two hours and she was intoxicated. We then got into the car and started home to Big Sur. While heading home on the highway, Shirley wanted out of the car because she didn't want me and the children any more. She got out of the car and I tried to get her to come back but she didn't listen and she left. I found someone to watch the children the next day so that I could go to work. After work that day I went to look for her and didn't find her for a couple of days later at a place that she worked at in Carmel as a waitress. She found a place to live in Carmel called the Cypress House. She said she needed time to figure things out for herself and what she wants from life. And asked me to wait for her for four or five years.

For a short period I moved to South Grove with my Aunt Marion so I had some help with the children when Shirley left. On December 1, 1968 my Aunt and I and the children moved back to the house in Big Sur. I found a permanent daycare mother for both children; her name is Mrs. Slieman in San Francisco. They started going to her in December. Shirley moved all of her things out of the house at the end of October and into an apartment in Carmel; the address was Strait Lodge, Anderson Crescent. She took all the furniture except for a crib, an old couch, highchair and two dressers, she also took all the linen and pots and pans. She re-entered the house a couple more times without permission and took a few more things.

On December 16, 1968, Shirley was supposed to have the children for the weekend and I waited all morning for her to arrive and she didn't show up. I had some Christmas shopping to do so I left the children with my Aunt Marion to watch. At about 2:00 P.M. Shirley's boyfriend at the time, and who I believe was living with her at the time, came to pick up the children. My Aunt Marion would not let the children go with him. His name is Gary and I don't know his last name. Later that night, at about 9:00 P.M., Shirley and Gary arrived at the house to get the children. Geoffrey was not feeling very well and was in bed sound asleep and Lorraine was just going to bed. Shirley came in the house as a guest, then proceeded to get all the children's clothes out of the dresser drawers and take the children for good. I told her she had no right barging in and doing what she was doing. She then started to kick and punch me and tore my shirt that I was wearing in half and bit my arm hard enough that it left a mark for a month. My girlfriend Lil, and Shirley's boyfriend Gary, never interfered in the matter. While all this was going on my Aunt Marion called the police and the two of them left without the children. The police arrived shortly after and I told them what had happened and they have a report on the incident.

On December 30, 1968, Shirley asked me to let her have Lorraine for the weekend. I was told to bring her to Shirley's mother in San Francisco but Shirley was not there when I arrived so I took Lorraine back home with me. I phoned the next day and found that she had spent the night at the Highway Motor Court in North Grove.

About January 15, 1969, Shirley convinced me to let her have Lorraine so I agreed so long as she took proper care of her. About June 1, 1969, Shirley was living in a home with three men and Lorraine and she was sharing a bedroom with one of the men; his name was Ross, the address was 1399—-102 Street, South Grove. It was soon after that Shirley gave me Lorraine back and said she thought Lorraine would be better off with her brother and that I would be able to care for her better at the time.

About June 15, 1979, Lil and I started living together; we all went for a holiday to Seattle, Washington, to see my father. When we got back the two children and myself moved into Lil's apartment at 3421—21st Street, North Grove. The next weekend after we returned the children went for a visit to Shirley's, but she did not return them on Sunday. She wanted to keep both of them. Jack Wiebe, a probation officer for family court in South Grove, who we both had been seeing before, told me that there was nothing I could do to get either of the kids back unless I want to wait for a year to get into court. But in two weeks Shirley called and asked me if I would come and get Geoffrey because she could not handle him or raise Lorraine the way she wanted to raise her with Geoffrey around. She then decided it would be best for all if there was no visiting at all. So until just after Christmas 1978 we didn't see or hear from Shirley. When we did, she was living in the Cove area, working at one of the clubs as a stripper. Shortly after Christmas of 1979 Shirley decided that we should start visiting again. Everything has been going along since then pretty well.

On Saturday, April 19, 1980, I got a call about 1:45 A.M. from Shirley's sister, Sheila Mason. She said I had to come and pick the kids up from where Shirley was living at the time with Ivor Kent at 10th Street, South Grove, behind Archie's Grocery, where they have been living since about February 1980, because there was some sort of trouble. I left at about 2:00 A.M. and went over to Shirley's and Ivor's. I met Ivor there and asked him what had happened. He said Shirley got mouthy and he had slapped her in the face. I phoned Sheila from Ivor's and Shirley's and she said I had to bring the kids to Shirley's mother's place in San Francisco, because that was where Shirley was. So I did, to save any trouble with Shirley. There was a small party going on at the time but the children were put back to bed when I arrived with them. Shirley also tried to get me to stay the night there, but I returned home to bed. I got home about 4:00 A.M.

Letter from Cheryl Chancellor, age 12, to myself, as her father's lawyer in the divorce proceeding.

February 28, 1980
Thursday

I want to live with my dad and my knew mom because I love them very much and I have a perfect family here, and I can't leave them. The reason why I wanted to live with my real mom is because she told all these bad things about my dad and gave me the more reason to run away. Then she asked me if I do house work and I said yes because my mom and dad work and I get responsibilities because I'm older. And she ask what do I do and I said vacume, clean the bathrooms, kitchen, and the floors. And floors and she said that my knew mom was making work like a maid wich is not true. Because my mom and dad work hard all day and then my mom comes home and cooks dinner for all of us. And mom and dad may get mad at us sometimes but that is only when we are bad. But every child gets screamed at or hit sometimes. My real mom told me that when Dad and herself were young and they were merried at the time she would tell me that dad wraped her. And broke a lot of things. And then she said that dad broke alot of furniture and she had to pay for it but that is wrong because it was in my dad's name so he would have been the one to pay for it all. And then mom said Dad bashed in the walls of the apartment but then it was in my dad's name at the time. And then she told me that she had to pay for it. When Martin and I were children she used to lock us out of the house for hours. And all that time she would sit and talk to a Spirit on her shoulder. And the nabours would tell my dad that is how he found out. But I can't remember what dad did. And when my dad came home he would have to cook his own meal. And when she was pregnent with Martin I think it was. My Granny looked after her well my dad was at work. And my granny went grocery shopping and cooked the meals for her and for my dad when he came home. I'm not sure if it was me (Cheryl) that was if I was in my mom. Anyway Granny even did all the housework. Well after I was born Granny had an operation sometime after that. And she stayed with my mom and dad, mom did not cook one meal for Granny and for all that, what Granny did for her mom. Mom would not do anything for granny. An my Granny only stade there fore 2 days. The only time she really pade any attention to us is when other people were around. I can remember 1 day when she locked me out of the house that was in Bayridge. But there was alot of other times. But I can't remember because I was so young. And my mom told me if I lived with her I was aloud to do anything I wanted to. Like, go to disques, roller skating, movies out with boys, and I was aloud to go to bed with boys to and then she said I would have to go on birth controle pills. But I would not. Anyway, the thing I do with my freinds I go shopping, movies and roller skating. And then she said I would have to go on a diet to be as skinny as herself but if I weighed like her I would be a tooth pick because I am so tall 5′8-1/2″. And anyways she said that there would not be very much to eat. I guess that is what it is that she might use me for child wellfare. Then she said that dad was useing us for money because of child wellfare. And then mom said that dad used brutal force on her for only getting his own way. But I know it is not true because dad told me that he would sware on the holy bible that he did not do that. And Mom called my new mom a raving lunatic well both my dad and my knew mom came to pick me up from the house. That is all what my mom told me except one more thing that, when mom and dad were talking on the phone she asked if he was going to give me money for clothes dad said no because mom was trying to get money off dad and when mom hung the phone up she told me that dad said no and she said that dad does not love me anymore. And one more thing mom said that dad was going to beat me like dad to her but I don't think its true anymore. Because dad told me that he didn't do it to mom. So that is all I have been told there is probably more but I don't know anymore.

By Cheryl

Letter from Achille, Shirley's boyfriend, to Shirley.

To my dearest:

I know that this is not the best way to express my feelings but there are some things I must tell you which is very difficult when you are unwilling to listen.

Tonight I had to leave so much unsaid which was very important to me. I am very sorry you are angry with me and I hope that you will find enough understanding to forgive me. The timing was bad but it has made it necessary to write this letter as I can express myself enough though you won't listen.

Shirley, the first day I saw you I knew that you were a person I could love. At first there was only friendship, but as time went by it quickly grew into love. I began to feel pangs of jealousy when you left with someone else. These feelings I kept to myself and tried my hardest to hide them. I had no hope that you would love me as I loved you. I had to be satisfied to see you at work and then watch you leave again.

My feelings grew deeper until I could no longer hide them. You will never know how happy I was when you started to return some of those feelings. Still I felt I was too old for you and did not want to burden you with me. I was happy to help you with little things, talk to you, drive you home and be near you. Our friendship grew and I loved every minute of it. At the time I had no one else and you were a new lease on life.

Many times I talked to you, wanted to hold you and kiss you but did not find the courage. I thought it would end a beautiful friendship.

One day as I sat by you in the car I could not help myself and kissed you good night. You responded gently, said goodnight and went home. Before you left you said you would see me again. I was the happiest man alive. All my doubts were cast aside and I felt that you at least had some feelings of love for me.

The first night we were alone in your car and you showed me how the seats went down was the clincher. I could not contain myself any longer. You accepted my advances with love. I kissed you and wanted you so badly. When I tried to caress your body you did not seem to mind. I tried to go a little bit farther and you restrained me. You gently put your hand on mine. I knew that meant no and I respected your wishes. I loved you so much. You did not let my love you then but that restraint meant so much to me. I loved you more than ever and would never do anything to destroy that. That moment created a respect that will never die. If you had not stopped me I might have had mixed feelings and doubts. The qualities of a lovely woman showed. I knew you were a real lady and expressed love in a most desirable way. I will never forget those moments. That was when I became very sure you were for me.

Days went by. I wanted you so much. If I could only get you alone, make love to you and tell you how I wanted you to be mine alone. Some of those days I thought it would never happen. The desire grew within me. I thought of you day and night. It became an obsession. If you rejected me then the results would have been disastrous. You were everything. At that point you still had not made any commitments. I hoped nothing would come between us.

Finally you accepted an invitation to ride with me. We went for coffee, talked and went for a drive. I could not take you back without telling you how I felt. I can tell you now that I wanted to make love to you more than ever. I'm very sorry, but I did not have the intention of ever letting you go. That drive will never be forgotten. You looked so desirable sitting in the seat beside me. I parked.

We kissed and I caressed you with love in my heart. I could not help myself. I never felt so deeply in love with anyone in my whole life. When you took me within you it was an acceptance of my love and you were mine. I don't really know why, but all my life I knew love-making as a bond between a man and a woman that is sacred. Your body against me and your acceptance of my love was what really created a lifetime commitment for me. I love you more than I can say and nothing will ever destroy that.

Telling me that you would be mine forever was how you may have felt at the time. Your mind was confused and I would not hold you to it. I believed that you loved me, but I also respect your love for your children.

When you expressed a desire to give it another try it was a blow that came so suddenly that I could not see things clearly. I tried to accept it but it seemed impossible. There was a time of deep depression, lack of food and no sleep. I had lost all there was in my life. What really made it worse was that you created the impression that there was no more hope for us. That was softened somewhat by your concern and your expression to be lifelong friends. You wanted to have time to think things out and make an honest try at your marriage. I believe you are a very sincere and sensitive person. The fact that you try to make a go of a marriage to someone you do not love is only to your credit. I love you for it. Even in failure you still try because at one time you made a marriage vow and feel you have not tried hard enough. Give it all you have or you will never be able to leave a happy woman. You must know you did everything you could for your marriage. If it still fails then your mind will be at peace knowing it was not your fault.

I accept this and know that some day it will mean more to you. Your efforts only make you a bigger person in the eyes of everyone. Some time your husband will see your attempts and respect you for them even though he may appear not to notice.

My love, I must explain about tonight. I waited for two days to explain something to you. We have coffee for fifteen minutes and you must go home. All it was for me was utter frustration. I'm not very good at explaining hurt feelings. You were over tired and I'm very, very, sorry I kept you. I had no intention of delaying you from going home. If you had come with me as I had suggested I would have gotten you back on time. When you did not believe that, I took it as not trusting me. From someone I love it is hard to take.

I do not wish to end it all for us. My actions, I feel, are destroying any love you may have for me. Please bear with me. Forget any negative reaction you may have now. It is my fault and any anger you may feel is not necessarily real. It is because I forced myself upon you against your will. I will never do that again. Maybe you understand that to me it was extremely important but I needed more time. I'm sorry, love. Some day I will make it up to you.

A few days ago I was very depressed. You explained your reasons and I accepted them as best as I could. For the last couple of days I tried to get things back to the way they were before I told my wife and daughter. I feel I made an honest attempt and made some headway. Tonight I tried to explain my intentions. So you see, what was a moment of boredom for you was the result of two days of thinking for me. I'm sorry, I could not explain tonight. Here is what I have in mind, love.

You are married with two children, with hopes of salvaging your marriage. I don't know whether you sleep with your husband much, but if you don't, you are not making an honest attempt at happiness. Happiness takes two people who work as one. The desires of your husband have to be met or you are causing him to wander. If your loving is not deep enough he will go elsewhere. This does not mean he does not love you. I think he can satisfy himself with others but still come back to you. This can only mean that he loves you more than the others. None of this is any of my business but I must tell you so that you understand.

On the other hand I know that you love your children. You say you do not love your husband. You are not the type of person who would tie someone down without love. Therefore you must have loved him before. If this is true you fell out of love somewhere along the line. There must be a way back if he still loves you.

If you are not satisfied at home, you too, will go elsewhere for fulfillment. Don't let this bother you because it may be the only thing to save your marriage. If you do not get what you want out of marriage it can only cause more resentment and ultimate failure. If you fill in the gaps with whatever is missing at home it may just carry you through a rough period until you can rebuild the happy home life you so desire. I know of no other woman who deserves it more than you do.

This takes us down to me. I married out of sheer love. I made a vow I intended to keep for the rest of my life. Over the years things went wrong. I've been hurt many times and managed to get over it. There comes a time when you can only *say* you forgive and forget. Some things you can forgive but you can never forget.

The breakup of our marriage happened before you ever came along. We have been creating an impression that did not exist. My wife was a cold person in childhood because of personal experiences. When I married her I thought it could be changed. We managed very well but a person with no compassion cannot feel the same. They can make an attempt but cannot succeed. It's like a person with no legs trying to run.

Because I pryed into your life I offer you mine. I have not slept with my wife for months. There is no desire or the necessary love. I will not leave her stranded though. I will help her out of this marriage with no defamation and even help her get started again. She is a good woman. She cannot be blamed for wanting a free life. That's what she wanted when I married her but I would not listen to her then.

Now us. I fell deeply in love with you. I never felt the same about anyone in my whole life. I cannot go back and start over, but if I could I would know what true love is. This I owe to you. I went through life not knowing. I'm trying to prevent you from making the same mistake, but I guess you have to learn the hard way.

It will pain me badly to hear you say in a few years, what you should have done. Please do me the favor of thinking it over.

Shirley, I love you. I would not do anything or say anything that I know would harm you. When you realize what you are doing, no matter what the circumstances, I will be there to pick up the pieces. This is a promise to look after you and help you for the rest of my life. You have given me more than you realize. At times I get very moody because of the way you broke the news. I'm sorry that I came on so fast. I really believe because of my impatience I may have turned you off a bit. The loss is all mine.

Please realize that I am at the stage of accepting you as a very good friend, if that is all there is. If there is more at times I'll accept the facts and I know that I can give you anything you desire without any hang-ups. Just remember that I love you more than anything else in the world and will wait for you. It is no use saying there is no hope because there is always a slim chance. You will remain the same person to me no matter what happens. You have a right to a happy life and I will help you achieve it. If it is with someone else you only have to tell me. Don't say anything now until you have things straight. I'll try to keep my hands off of you when others are around and create the impression that we are only good friends. That is what you want and I will try to please you.

I still have the case of beer I bought for you. We must split it soon. Maybe Fisherman's Wharf? That seems like a good place to get plastered.

How about a night on the town? We can maybe get a few friends to come along if you wish. Just go out and have fun. How about a dance or a movie? I'm free for you any time. If I have something else planned I'll cancel it for you. Remember my life is in your hands.

Take a chance of going in my car some night. I'll put any promise I make to you against the loss of ever seeing you again. That's how sincere I am. I'll talk to you about anything you want, help you whenever I can.

One thing I will never forget. The first loving from you. You have much to offer and I hope that will never end. I will not gamble our future on forcing myself upon you though. You will have to let me know if you want to because I want you to remain sincere all your life. I won't take it as a sign of hope any more though, because to me it is love. If in the future you should want to live with me just let me know. I will not restrict your freedom. I feel that I could make you *want* to stay with me. That is a lot better than staying because you have an obligation. My love is very deep and ever-lasting.

One last thing. I am devoted to you by choice. You are all I want and I will never need anyone else. Don't feel any obligation on your part as you must do what you must. If there is any part of love from our past memories or experiences you wish to preserve, please let me know.

Love part time is better than no love at all. Part of your love is better than all the love anyone else has to give.

If you don't want me to love you anymore, don't tell me. Please don't avoid me unnecessarily. I like it when you sit and have coffee with me. Smile as you walk by. Today I feel good when you just nudged me even. It lets me know that all is well. The only thing that bothers me is that I must love you silently. It is a strong desire to let the whole world know. From now on everything is secret. I understand your desire for such an arrangement.

From now on you have the ball. I only ask that you come to me for help if you need it. Anything you desire. If at all you don't agree with any of this just let me know tomorrow.

Just remember that I love you dearly and intend to remain true always. I'll forever cherish your loving as a seal of lifelong partnership. Even if you stay with your husband. I received from you a much cherished memory that will remain with me forever.

Your love forever,
"Achille"

*Discussion and Summary*

This case history is an illustration of conduct by the wife so bizarre, so relentless and so completely lacking in social remorse, as to be explainable only in terms of female psychopathy. All that is required to summarize is what I'm sure the reader now appreciates, that he has just read a chronicle of a female psychopath in full flight.

What is remarkable is that this conduct is not in itself extraordinary today. In the last five years, this has become almost the norm, with so many young married women. There is one point to make, however; in the hundreds of women being the subject of observation, one theme seems to run throughout the whole of this type of conduct, and that is each of them are possessed of an IQ so as to suggest that each of them is barely able to cope with social problems and her own problems. There is no way that education or any other educational incentive is going to change that problem, nor is there any way in the terms of psychopathy that any other restraint is going to change the conduct that emphasizes such a problem and leads to such family havoc and social havoc, without due regard to the consequences in any way, shape or form. Attempts at treating the psychopath are in essence futile and the situation in the psychopathic marriage and divorce really does boil down to creating coping methods; coping methods for the husband, for the children, and for society as a whole, to attempt to handle the moral wreckage created by the female psychopath.

With three young children, a mother-in-law, father-in-law, brother, not to mention his wife, all under the same roof, Paolo Marini viewed his family responsibilities as a martyr valued his tormentors; without them he would be nothing.

# THE HANKS CASE

## *History of the Marriage*

I met Mrs. Hazel Hanks and her daughter Cindy in San Francisco in 1952 and at that time she was living with her mother in Hillside East in a rented place. She was separated from her husband, Henry Hanks. I was in San Francisco at that time working for a few months; my home was near Bay City, where my brother and I were partners in the mink farm.

Hazel and I went out together a few times. Until I went back to my mink ranch.

In 1953, February, I bought my brother's piece of the mink and moved them to another ranch on the peninsula until I found a ranch in Walnut Grove which I bought for $6,000 in July, 1953. Three and a half acres with mink sheds and a large freezer and a two-bedroom house on the property.

Hazel and I were going steady then, so she moved out to my place as a housekeeper, $40 per month—she had Cindy with her and her mother came out for the weekends most of the time; we would go out for the evening and take in a show and eat out and I paid for it, the $40 was not very much; I spent money on them in other ways.

The mink herd was small so I didn't need any help on it so she just had to look after the house. She had very little money as she had been only working part-time in different restaurants as a waitress. However, she did have furniture, probably $100 to $150 if you had to buy it used as you could get a lot of furniture cheap in those times. I had about $4,000 at that time. As Hazel was not divorced I rented a small cabin where I stayed at night as everyone on the road knew everyone else. I wanted to keep her name clear as things were different in those days.

Haze worked at Sears as a gift-wrapper in the Christmas season; she became divorced from Henry Hanks in 1954, and later we became engaged. In 1954 to July 1955 our relations began to fall apart; she would go into the wildest rages over some small thing like not picking her up at the bus station, or if you wouldn't do something she wanted you to do. When she was in those moods she would lie about me, steal, stop cooking or cleaning the house, sometimes just stay in bed for a day or two. In the real bad spells she would move out to one of the neighbours, whoever would take her in for the night, or she would go out in the valley to some of my good mink rancher friends. Anything to hurt me as I had a good reputation with family, friends and neighbours. In a few days she would be back home, and as I loved her and her little girl, I would take her back hoping everything would be alright. Finally she went into one of her rages and went to let the mink out of their pens; I stopped her and carried her back to the house. On the way she had scratched my hands so I went to the Bay City State Police, showed them the scratches. They came over, talked to her and told her she would be in serious trouble if she let the mink out, and to move as soon as her girl finished the school term, and for me to hold her housekeeping money. So she left in 1953 and moved to Los Angeles where she went to work for Sears. She had taken her ring off some time before she left, but kept it. About 1956 I paid off the mink ranch. Over the next seven years we did not see each other very much; perhaps once or twice per year I would send her or Cindy some money, mostly to buy something for Cindy. She left her job in about '61 I believe and was on Social Assistance until she married Harry Klein in 1965. In '62 or '63 she had to go to the hospital so sent Cindy over here to me at the mink ranch. I sent her to the high school in Bay City and kept her for some months when her mother came and took her back as she was home again in 1964. I sent Cindy to Los Angeles as she had finished high school in Bay City as she stayed at the Bay City boarding there; it was about $1,000 which I paid.

Hazel was in Los Angeles and Cindy was at the Bay City so I did not see very much of them that year. Cindy did not go back as she met a Jack Ruston and they were married, her present husband. Hazel was left alone in Los Angeles on Social Assistance and no help from Cindy so she married Harry Klein and they moved to San Francisco.

My mother passed away in October 1965. She left me three-quarters of the estate and one-quarter to my brother. As my brother sure could use the extra money, I had everything split one-half by one-half and I never regretted it. My brother passed away in 1971 but his wife was putting the money to good use. I do feel angry now that someone who doesn't deserve it should want me to split it again after my mother passed away.

With the same old furniture, they had moved out some years ago. When Hazel moved in in 1966 with practically nothing and broke up with Klein, her second husband, don't think I would ever sue you Jack. For that matter I had not even brought the subject up. Mother, her estate about $23,000 cash, lot 3839, 172 acres, sold for $156,000 in 1973. Lot 557, 18 acres, sold for $43,500 in 1971. Jewellery, some gold, nearly all given to Hazel, not split up, one gold watch quite old.

By December 1965 my resources was about $10,000 in bonds and in bonds about $7,000. In the bank also the value of the property had increased to about $30–40,000 and the mink had increased to about 320 breeders, with about 1,000 pelts to sell at a value of $15 per pelt. The grinders, mixers for feed, 10 ton freezer with a value of about $20,000, also there was ten long sheds for the mink.

Hazel had nowhere to go after she broke up with her husband in 1966. She was not on good terms with her daughter Cindy, or Cindy's husband. I had hoped that over the years things had improved but soon the same old faults started with a new one thrown in; jealous of my family or close friend, she was on a companion deal with me, had only housework to do. Did not have any work to do on the mink farm as I had lots of hired help, only needed help if some emergency, she added the hired hands time every two weeks. The rest of the book work I did, ordering feed and keeping the breeding records of the mink. She had free use of the money. I was an executive in the mink breeders' association so naturally I let Hazel dress well. She never went to any of our monthly meetings but did go to our banquet and winter mink show. However, I believe now she kept a little more under control as she seen the property and my mother's increasing in value each year. I sold my farm for $55,000 to Bay Realty in 1971. As I had been high point winner in the mink show the last couple of years I sold quite a few of my mink as breeders.

However, the sheds and most of the 1,500 wire pens were burned or buried in the ground as just then there was a slump in the mink business.

Hazel and I moved to Seagull Cove in the Bay area. I have lived near there before and my sister-in-law was there, also my niece and nephew and their families and some good friends. I could use my late brother's salmon boat as it had a salmon licence on it. I was buying a piece of property in Seagull Cove but Hazel didn't want it, said it was too near my relatives, they were half mile across the water. So I stopped the lawyer from making up the papers on it. I bought a double-wide mobile home, all new and furnished in Seagull Cove, that was farther away from my relatives, on Lot 22 and bought the lot next to it, Lot 14. She became a common-law wife here and had my name, but by the winter of 1972 moved back to San Francisco and stayed with some people there. However, by January 1973 she was back here again. When she left on these spells she would not take the bus but would hitch a ride with her things so it would look like I threw her out. I always gave her money. Spring 1974, moved out again, stayed with some woman, she had been married three times, perhaps some were common-law, had two children, was not even forty years old, hired a lawyer in San Francisco to sue me. I told her to go ahead.

The doctor was taking tests as they thought I had lung cancer in both lungs. Hazel came back and said she knew she would feel secure if we were married, some of my friends thought so too, so we were married on her birthday, 1974, in San Diego. I paid her lawyer $150, I thought she must have cleared her earlier marriage to Klein up. Some years earlier I had taken her to a lawyer I knew in San Francisco; she had some of Klein's papers to someone he had married in Germany. He had gone back to Germany to get a divorce from this German woman but it was not a legal paper in America so Hazel said hers was not legal to him; it was just on the books and would be a lot of trouble to get it off the books, she said the lawyer said.

Less than three months after we were married her friend, the one she would stay with when she left me, was getting married to her common-law husband number three and wanted me to stand at the wedding. It was August 1st long holiday and I did not care to take the ferry to town in the long holiday. However, I told her she could go. She went into a rage and left and didn't come back until late September. I think that really shocked me as getting married had not changed anything. I gave her money while she was away.

Over the next few years things were not good. If I asked her to clean the house I would be choking with the dust and cat fur. She went into a rage if I cleaned it myself, she said I was doing it to show her up. Another thing she knew I disliked, if I were talking to someone she would keep interrupting me, such as, No Doug it was not July it was August, time after time. She knew I hated to be nagged at the table and you could not stop her. A couple of times I moved out to the nearby motel and stayed a couple of months. I came home each day to feed the animals and maintain the home. After a couple of months she would beg me to come back. For a while she would be okay.

There were six or seven women around her own age here but she never seemed to get close to them. They worked for the local hospital and belonged to the Old Age Pensioners, but she never went with them. I took her shopping here a couple of times a week or to anything that was going on at Walnut Grove. Also we went to San Francisco for a day or two quite often. Went for a couple of weeks for a trip to Canada or to the Midwest in the summer, also about three weeks to the Mountain States in the fall. She was not too bad when we were travelling if she had me all to herself.

Her sister was slowly dying in Omaha so I gave her the money to go back to see her. Her mother and sister told me the same thing I knew about her, she went into wild rages over some little thing, also she would say she was sick. The doctors said they knew that about her and there was nothing wrong with her. I have seen her terrible sick in bed and perhaps someone comes she liked and she would be up, cook dinner, eat a good meal and no more sign of sickness.

I have had her to my own doctor, also to Dr. Tummell, a psychiatrist. He said I am not getting the truth from her. I had her to a psychologist but he said the woman was favouring me.

I hope you can get something out of this, I told you it would not be good.

Jack Wilson

*Discussion and Summary*

Here we see the psychopathic female, in her mid-forties, having wreaked havoc in two prior marriages, now embarking on a third marriage, which she proceeds to destroy, and the marriage under discussion being that given here of Wilson/Hanks. It would appear that the three old strikes, you're out, which might apply here, are unlikely to apply to the female psychopath in that following the successful prosecution of this marital battle, she will undoubtedly go on to her husband number four and perpetrate the same psychological and physical havoc.

Here we see a common characteristic of the pscyhopathic female in operation in that her engagement to Mr. Wilson begins very shortly after her divorce in 1954. In the documentation provided by the written submission of the husband, we see her fantastic and uninviting behaviour in that their marriage begins to fall apart immediately upon their engagement and we see the woman, Hazel, going through a series of marriages. She left his engagement and ran off to Los Angeles to go on Social Assistance until she married her second husband, Harry Klein, and that marriage, of course, did not work out and after one year it fell apart. This witless gentleman took this woman back with the statement, "I had hoped that over the years things had improved." Here we have the endless hope of the hooked husband or suitor that things will improve. As he goes on to note, "but the same old faults started," and she proceeded to go on and destroy this marriage, which was in fact a common-law one, and jumped out and moved to San Francisco in 1972, but came back in 1973, moved out again in 1974 and this gent was still persuaded by her utmost plausibility to go on and remarry her despite her dismal track record, of which he had intimate knowledge of the past some twenty years. Quoting from his dismal statement in his submission, "Hazel came back and she said she knew she would feel secure if we were married, some of my friends thought so too, so we were married." How this gentleman can avoid the label of himself being a crackpot is beyond comprehension. After he lived through all of her psychopathic acting out, her lying, her cheating, her histrionic returns, her leavings, etc., and then went on to marry her. Then in the divorce proceedings he proceeds to write a very clear treatise on the female psychopath, obviously unrecognized by him, as she is unrecognized by society as a whole at this moment in time.

In summary, it is apparent that there are here so many very clear characteristics of the psychopath, written by the husband's own agonizing handscript, with no coaching from anyone, and this writing shows the rage, the antisocial behaviour, lying, stealing, cheating, the total irrational histrionic behaviour, the lack of empathy, and the total lack of an ability to see the consequences of her actions. In addition it very clearly shows the inability to learn from experience as these episodes were repeated over and over again.

In addition, and possibly most important of all, it shows the terrible trap in which a man in this kind of a marriage finds himself, in that he attempted to do the honest and honourable thing by continually putting up with her psychopathic behaviour, trying to excuse it amongst his friends, and trying to do anything he could to make the marriage carry on, for in effect it was doomed and he just could not see it, thereby embracing the role of hooked husband/martyr for more than twenty years.

In *Of Human Bondage,* by Somerset Maugham, he is masterful in his inclusion of this typical case of the psychopath in literature, but I propose, does it show the importance of dealing with impressions of psychopathy as found in a practising lawyer's or physician's office, i.e., the crucible of human existence? In this, the most intimate of forums for the discussion and revelation of the anguish of human relationships, Dr. Cleckley has basically not seen the vast importance of the female psychopath. I submit that he has been denied the opportunity of confronting nose to nose and eyeball to eyeball the everyday torment, horror and turmoil of the American family as is seen in the everyday goings-on in the lawyer's or doctor's office in our modern society.

One further point to be made is that Dr. Cleckley notes again and again that the male psychopath appears to come from what is a well-integrated family home: I would submit that these family homes, which are called "well integrated," are, in fact, family homes that are well camouflaged. This camouflage is only stripped away in the tempestuous urgency of the goings-on in the office of the lawyer dealing with matrimonial problems, or the general practitioner dealing equally as intimately with these vexing family problems. It is evident throughout the psychiatric literature on the psychopath that it focuses on the male; I submit that this again is due to the fact that the academic and intellectual approach to psychopathy has centred on the psychiatric institutes and on the prisons, where one finds a large proportion of the population can be labelled as psychopaths. In an eyeball to eyeball, nose to nose confrontation with the American family as it exists and as it disintegrates today, I would ask you to consider that the female psychopath is equally as important in modern American society as is the male. In fact, when one considers the reasons for the disintegration of the American family as it was once known, I feel that the female psychopath has truly shown herself to be the X Factor.

It must be pointed out here that none of this discussion is to be taken as a criticism of either Dr. Cleckley or Dr. Reid, who have both written eminent works on the psychopath as seen from the academic and intellectual point of view. However, it is apparent that the role of the female psychopath in the disintegration of American society has largely been ignored.

One further point that should be made here is a very glaring difference between the male psychopath and the female psychopath as to Number Sixteen of Dr. Cleckley's characteristics of the psychopath, i.e., the failure to follow a life plan. It is advanced here that the female psychopath truly shows a very marked divergence of this singular characteristic from the generally accepted male psychopath's generally accepted failure to be able to follow any life plan. The female psychopath appears to have a single overwhelming life plan, and that is the same life plan previously alluded to in the quote from Chaucer's "The Wife of Bath's Tale," that is, dominion over man.

## THE HARMON-LAMONT CASE

*The Compleat Psychopath*

This remarkable case involves two consecutive marriages breakdowns in a very short time—both of which clearly demonstrate all the characteristics of the female psychopath in full flight. In short, she shows very clearly all of the psychopathic characteristics to wit, poor judgment, failure to learn by experience, pathological egocentricity, total lack of remorse or shame, untruthfulness, insincerity, unreliability, superficial charm and good intelligence, general poverty in major affective reactions, specific loss of insight, unresponsiveness in general interpersonal relations, fantastically uninviting behaviour with drink and sometimes without, and a sex life which is impersonal trivial and poorly integrated. In addition, it is rare to see such a clear indication of a psychopathic female's life plan. In Chapter 3, it was pointed out that here in the area of a life plan, the female psychopath appears to differ markedly from the male. In the literature, a salient characteristic of the male is noted to be lack of a life plan. In this Harmon-Lamont case, we see a clear indication of a female psychopathic life plan in operation on two unfortunate gentlemen. In the short space of three years, this woman achieved dominion over man through the martyrdom of motherhood, not once, but twice—total victory in both cases, one ending in suicide of the unfortunate victim and the other in capitulation.

The late edition of the *San Francisco Post Examiner* of the 23rd of August 1971 contained the following item:

> Dateline: Walnut Grove, California. Headline: PROMINENT DOCTOR'S DEATH. The proprietor of the Canvass Back Inn, a motel in this suburb of San Francisco, being alarmed at not seeing the guest who had checked into one of his quarters for the past week and not having seen the guest's car moved during this period of time, became alarmed and called upon the assistance of the State Police to enter the room of the guest and upon entering there were found the partly decomposed remains of a man who was soon identified as Dr. Dennis Harmon, a prominent eye specialist practicing in San Francisco and well-esteemed by his fellow practitioners in his specialty. It was apparent the doctor had ended his own life through an overdose of sleeping pills, a good many of which were scattered about the bed upon which the remains of Dr. Harmon lay. No motive has been ascribed to the suicide of Dr. Harmon who leaves a widow, Maureen Jane Harmon and four children, all of this city.

*Curriculum Vitae of Dr. Dennis Harmon, Deceased*

Dr. Harmon was a Bachelor of Medicine, Bachelor of Surgery (London), a Certificant of the Royal College of Surgeons and now, up to his death, a duly qualified physician and surgeon, and licensed to practice medicine in California, specializing in the field of ophthalmology and up to his untimely death, had published six articles pertaining to medicine and in particular, the field of ophthalmology, in internationally recognized medical journals, and presently was about to publish other articles in the field of ophthalmology.

The following is a chronological list of the professional training and the posts that had been held by Dr. Harmon:

*1947–53* Guy's Hospital, London—medical student.
*1953–54* House Office (Intern)—Guy's Hospital, London, England.
*Jan. 1955–July 1955* Six months Senior Intern, University of Illinois, U.S.A. (Chicago).
*July 1955–Dec. 1956* General practitioner, Chicago, Illinois.
*Jan. 1957–July 1957* Six months course in Ophthalmology, University of Illinois, U.S.A. (Chicago).
*Jan. 1958–July 1960* Resident in Ophthalmology, University of Illinois.
*July 1960–July 1961* Clinical Fellowship, Retina Service, Massachusetts Eye and Ear Infirmary, Boston, Massachusetts.

*1961–1971* Ophthalmologist, San Francisco, California.

The records also show that in 1942, prior to having anything to do with medical school or medical training, the deceased had enlisted in the Royal Scots Regiment as an Officer-Cadet, attended the Officer-Cadet Training School in India in 1943, and was commissioned as a Second Lieutenant and served with the Fifth Royal Gurkha Rifles and was honourably discharged in 1947 in the rank of Captain.

*The Bereaved Widow*

Not much is known of the childhood of the widow of Dr. Harmon save and except that Dr. Harmon knew before he married her that he was aware that she had been under psychiatric care and understood that she had withdrawn from the Evanston School of Nursing Hospital in the State of Illinois on account of her psychiatric problems. Prior to the marriage, Dr. Harmon had telephoned his wife-to-be's psychiatrist in Chicago to try and find out more details of her mental health background. He recalled the wife's doctor informing him that if he did not marry this woman she would never again be able to have a normal relationship with a man. Dr. Harmon made the fatal mistake in not asking the wife's doctor at that time whether or not she would be able to have a normal relationship with a man if he did marry her. His wife-to-be was pregnant at the time of the marriage and informed him that if he did not marry her, she would kill herself. Obviously, the marriage was tumultuous from the beginning. They were married on the 14th of

June 1958 in Evanston, Illinois, and in 1961 the wife was hospitalized in a mental clinic in the State of Illinois and her attending doctor referred to her condition as pseudo-schizophrenia. Upon her release from the mental clinic, she was treated by electro-convulsive therapy on an out-patient basis. She came to hate the electro-convulsive therapy treatments and until recently had been under psychiatric care in San Francisco.

*The Children*

Of the four children of the marriage, the two oldest have been under constant psychiatric care and the child psychiatrist having told Dr. Harmon that his wife, now the widow, was hysteric or an hysterical woman and the oldest child will pattern herself upon her mother if their association continued, and the child psychiatrist recommended separating the oldest child from the mother by any means that was practical.

*The Road to Death*

At the coroner's inquest, an entirely new slant was placed upon the doctor's actions and, as it turned out, the records show that on July 27th, just a month previously, the grieving widow had made an application to the Superior Court for a divorce and for an order ejecting the husband from the matrimonial home, leaving her alone there with the four infant children. The now widow implied that her husband had become increasingly violent and was verbally abusing her in front of the children and that as a result of her husband's actions some years past, she had to undergo psychiatric treatment and felt that if the husband continued to reside in this house the situation would repeat itself. Further, the husband was constantly harassing her and this was having a seriously detrimental effect on the children, one of whom was atopic and another one of which has had more than twenty operations for a chronic ear problem.

Again the wife put forward before the court constant physical violence against her person.

However, when the doctor answered, he placed an entirely different aspect on the situation and drew to the court's attention that approximately two weeks prior to his wife bringing this motion to eject him from the family home that she, either deliberately or through a loss of control, had put on a disgusting scene. The husband had previously agreed to stay out of the master bedroom at 2:00 o'clock on a Sunday afternoon. At approximately 2:30 that afternoon, the wife was still not using the room and the husband felt tired and entered the master bedroom to lie down. His wife immediately entered the master bedroom and started screaming at her husband and pulled the husband out of bed (he made it quite clear to the judge that he did not resist) and his wife then pulled up the bed clothes that she was wearing, took his hand, and rubbed it on her vagina and said, "See, I have a cunt too, just like the girls in Las

Vegas. Tits," and rubbed the husband's hands against her breasts. This was all done with great venom and hatred. By the time the husband had backed off into the bathroom attached to the master bedroom, his wife had taken a brush and stuffed the handle end into her vagina saying, "See, I have a cunt, but not for you." His wife then went over to the bed, pulled up her clothes exposing her perineum (with knees bent to her chest), and screamed, "Look at the fucking cunt, look at it," then came over to her husband, screaming all the while. The husband, in desperation, lay down again while his wife continued to scream. The husband considered that she was so quite out of control that he went over to her and slapped her left arm twice with the flat of his hand. After this instant the husband left the room and was followed by his wife who hurt his testicles with her hand such that he had to take two strong pain killers and lay down. When this incident was brought to the court's attention and when the previous history of the wife's mental problems and psychiatric problems was brought to the court's attention, the court had no other choice but to dismiss her application for occupation of the matrimonial home.

Seemingly in the contest that is trial by battle, the husband had won a great victory, but within a short period of time—actually a short week after the hearing—his name was in the evening paper as the story was published. By itself, this set of circumstances calls for analysis.

Firstly, the wife's application for divorce, although based upon irreconcilable differences, the background of allegations focusing on violence of social isolation and on alienating and frightening the children, "My husband refuses to take me out socially or says that we can't afford to go out. On occasions when we plan a family outing, my husband usually finds a last-minute excuse not to go. The children are disappointed and I become very upset." "My husband complains about the amount of money spent on drugs which are necessary for one of the children, who is atopic." Here again, we see the psychopathic female using the children as her major weapon in the divorce action.

"On one occasion, in or about November, 1958, my husband struck me during an argument. For a period of approximately two years, my husband would hit me on various occasions until in or about January, 1960, I became unconscious as a result of him hitting me and he became worried and stopped for a while." Here one sees a totally inappropriate effect associated with what she was talking about. Wild, violent arguments to the point of knocking her unconscious, talked about in jocular terms of him becoming slightly worried and stopping for a bit. "On various occasions if my husband is angry with me, he has thrown bowls and plates of food at me." "My husband has struck me in front of the children and they have seen me very upset many times. As a result of this, our oldest child took sleeping pills and spent some time in the hospital."

Here again, using the children as a weapon and the inviolate motherhood she has been massing shows that he has done everything wrong and because of him, all the problems of the children arise—nothing to do with the mother.

Here again, we see the psychopathic female using the imagined ills of the children as the major force in her court approach for division of the spoils. "That I have requested my husband to provide funds for me to move out of the house with the children, for a holiday for myself and the children as a trial separation—my husband has refused to provide any funds." "That I have repeatedly suggested to my husband that he temporarily move out of the house and I have told my husband that if he did so the fact that he moved out of the home would not prejudice any future dealing we might have with respect to the children or property of the marriage and my husband has refused to do so."

Here we have an excellent example of the specific loss of insight that one finds in psychopaths. The psychopath has absolutely no capacity to see herself as others see her. As Dr. Cleckley says, "The psychopath shows every indication in his fundamental reactions of inability to size up normally what he has done, what he is and what he has done." Despite all the evident rate and fury that has supposed to be going on between the doctor and his wife, she still can't understand why he doesn't give her money to support a trial separation or why he doesn't trust her to move out of the house while she promises not to use this move in a prejudicial manner in the future. She is totally unable to understand why he can't trust her.

*Discussion*

There soon follows a second marriage of the woman in question. This marriage being solemnized May 11, 1974, less than three years after the death of the first husband by his own hand, and just a little over two years following the disposition of ample assets as discussed in the preceding pages. The documentation of this, the Harmon-Lamont breakdown and divorce is most instructive since she pleads poverty and demands support from Dr. Lamont for "all of the children of the marriage," even though none of these children were his issue and she was most amply supplied with funds from the first husband's estate to avoid poverty on her own. However, here again we see the victory of the psychopathic female model, "supermother, children above all, husband as employee" routine.

It will be seen in the documentation to follow that the petitioner, Mrs. Harmon-Lamont, asserts that there are problems beginning in August 1974, one short month after the marriage began, that they ceased to cohabit in July 1975 and the divorce petition was filed by the petitioner against this man, her second physician husband, on October 2, 1975. After much litigation by exhaustion, and doubtless an endless string of legal conferences, offers and counter-offers and counter-counter-offers, the second husband finally capitulates—he gives the psychopath what she demands, signs the Memorandum of Agreement and the Decree Absolute is finally granted December 13, 1977. The law has again enshrined the female psychopath's victory on the home front in that the good doctor does in fact wind up providing further funds in the manner of $550 per month for maintenance of the "infant" children, none of whom are infants in the usual sense of the term and for none of whom is he the natural father. She has thus added this cozy income to the ample funds she received from the first husband's estate; thus again the psychopath and her motherhood triumph, the law enshrines one more financial success for the security of her family situation by victimizing her second physician husband in less than three years. Such a battle plan, such speed and success in her continual search for Dominion Over Man.

It is very illuminating for the reader to see what the proceeds of this marriage are to this woman prior to embarking on her second marriage. For this reason, I quote here from material filed in Surrogate Court of this state regarding the finalization of the estate of Dr. Harmon.

> I the undersigned Executor make oath and say:-
>
> That we are applicant for letters Probate to the estate of Dennis Harmon, who does on or about the 23rd day of August, 1971.
>
> That we have made full, careful, and searching inquiry for the purpose of ascertaining what real and personal property and effects the said deceased possessed of, or entitled to, at the time of his death, together with the market value thereof respectively.
>
> The gross value of the said estate, property, income, and interests as the date of deceased's death was $361,648.72.

There follows in this document explicit details as to the assets and market values, etc., and one should note that the good doctor was very well insured to protect his family in the event of his demise. It will be noted on the last page of the court statement that the beneficiaries are the wife, Maureen Harmon, and the four children, all of whom are infant children; and therefore total control of the estate is placed in the hands of this surviving widow. It might be noted also that this amount of money in 1972 would probably be a million dollars today; so this Dr. Harmon had very carefully built an estate and protected it with insurance to take care of his family. Unfortunately, his psychopathic marital relationship resulted in his taking his own life.

In these two consecutive marriages, this woman has provided a "wonderful" chronicle of the female psychopath. The constant reference to the children of the marriage is most interesting since these were not children of the marriage and certainly not "infant" children of any marriage. They were all at this time eight years of age or older. This misuse of the word infant for the furthering of the woman's case is all too common. It is almost absurdly naive for this woman to think that anyone would believe such a chronicle of total disaster would be endured by any reasonable woman upon the initial violent beatings; surely any woman would have left the home forthwith. Surely this whole long sad tale smacks more of Dr. Cleckley's fifth characteristic of the psychopath (untruthfulness and insincerity), than it does of reality. If not it certainly smacks clearly of Dr. Cleckley's Number Eight (Poor Judgment and Failure to Learn by Experience). Certainly, if this woman were being severely beaten, she would then either have left the home or attempted to get a much earlier restraining order than one sees she did here since she claims to have endured all this violence for some fourteen months. Her use of the children in this document is also very peculiar, in that if she really were a concerned mother, certainly at least in February of 1975, after she claimed her husband was beating the boys and pulling hair out of the head, she would certainly at that time have gathered her children and left home. However, we see no attempt to face the realities of the situation and in fact, they did not cease to cohabit, according to the court document until July 13, 1975, some five months after this so-called unprovoked attack upon the children. Here again, we see a good example of the characteristic Number Nine, pathological egocentricity and incapacity for love. This is not only of love towards the husband, but obviously a very crippled love towards the children if she were "putting up" with this sort of activity as she alleged was going on between the husband and the children. There is also good indication of Number Fifteen (Sex Life is Personal, Trivial, and Poorly Integrated) in the almost cavalier discussion of the apparently brutal sex life wished by the respondent in which she goes on in this court document to end with the naive statement that was attempting to explain to this gentleman of thirty-nine years of age, the basic facts of life in that there should be some preliminary to the sexual experience, so that it is easier for the woman.

Here again is a beautiful psychopathic ploy in which she showed that not only had she twisted this man into marriage, but she had also some nine months after the marriage convinced him that he should now adopt her children. One wonders if she wasn't laying the groundwork for her future court action by giving her more power over the said Dr. Lamont, since these children would now legally be his and therefore she would be able to get much higher financial rewards. Here one sees the life plan of the female psychopath, in which they manage to twist, to intimidate, to bully, to manipulate, to alter all facts and history that come within their sphere of influence, to conform with what they wish life to be for them, which is ultimately that they are in total control and all members of the retinue are to fall in line and do as they are told. In addition, it points out clearly the progression of the sins of the mother being visited upon the daughter in that there is the oldest daughter, now sixteen years of age, obviously bent on a psychopathic life of her own.

But here again the psychopathic egocentricity blossoms through and it is noted that the nervous breakdown that she suffered was as a consequence of the death of her father, whereas if one will go back into the original depositions of Mr. Harmon in the original divorce, it was noted that the child psychiatrist back in 1973 had stated that the relationship between the mother, Mrs. Harmon and the eldest daughter, Valerie, was a pathological one and that Valerie should be sent away to private school to remove her from the malevolent influence of the mother: how prophetically true that was. But one notes that here again the psychopath twists the situation, so that the blame is laid nowhere near her bed, but on her dead husband.

> The facts that such claim for custody is founded are that it is in the best interests of the children that they continue in my custody. With respect to access, I am willing that my husband have access to the children, with one restriction, that is that he not be allowed to take them in a car of which he is the driver. The reason for that restriction is that as indicated in paragraph 1(b) of this petition, the respondent has a problem with alcohol and I have personally witnessed an attempt to drive after his consumption of 25 ounces of scotch and six bottles of beer. With that exception and with the provision also that it be at the convenience of the children, I am very willing that my husband have reasonable access.

Here again is the lying and exaggeration of the psychopath. Also her confirmation of her super motherhood in that she no longer wants this terrible wretch in the house as a threat to her and the children, but is willing to grant him access. If he is such a violent and virulent man as she claims, surely no woman in her right mind would allow access willingly so that he can continue his beatings as she alleges. In addition, we see the psychopath lifestyle again. Here life plan is total control. Her use of motherhood is to further this total control of her world as she sees it and she cannot even understand that she should not be able to continue control of this man after she has divorced him, but insisted she could still arrange his life by making sure that there be a restriction against him as to his driving the car with the children. But most importantly, the incredible lack of insight on her part as regards on the one hand claiming he is violent and unpredictable and has beaten both her and the children and on the other hand being, as she states and I quote, "I am very willing that the respondent have reasonable access."

Here again we see the psychopath marshalling all forces behind her in her relentless charge against the feckless husband. She now has not only the Superior Court of California involved, she has the Family Court of Walnut Grove involved and she has the police force involved through the family court. Therefore the attack is now in full swing in all of the open court levels. It should be noted in No. 8(b) in a comment on the financial position, that as of June 30, 1975, the petitioner is now employed with the social services of this province. A great example of the blind leading the blind and also an excellent illustration of Cleckley's characteristic Number One (Superficial charm) and good intelligence. She is so plausible and so capable of putting forth the concept of robust mental health that she winds up engaged as a mental health worker.

Here again she is attacking on all levels in full battle array. Interim maintenance, permanent maintenance, lump sum maintenance, costs and such further relief as to the court shall deem meet. It should be noted here that the financial situation of this woman following the death of her first husband is certainly significantly better than the financial situation of the poor second husband and we will discuss that further when we can put in the probate documents of Dr. Harmon's estate. But she is certainly using the infant children of another man's marriage to abuse the court process through attempting now to scalp her second physician; it is now almost becoming a career. The psychopath in full flight.

Here the doctor very clearly puts forth further evidence for the psychopathic character of this woman in that he states that within a month of the parties becoming married, she threatens a divorce and obtaining as much maintenance as possible from him, which would go along with her psychopathic life plan. Again we see that the woman is criticizing the husband as being financially irresponsible (as she criticized the first husband in the Harmon divorce). In addition, she is accusing him of being brutal and emotionally unfeeling and one suspects that that is certainly present in her to probably a far greater degree than the poor husband and in addition he points out that she derided his sexuality and confirms further that this psychopath shows a shallow and trivial impersonal and poorly integrated sex life. It also is pointed out here that this petition legally doomed this gentleman in that denial of all the allegations, even to the point of denying the fact that they were married and the fact that he was a bachelor when they were married and she a widow, etc., and all the other denials, play right into her hands, so that she can say to the world this man is stupid, he is insensitive, he is lying. In addition, his counter-petition really is only a chronicle of her psychopathic characteristics, rather than any grounds for a divorce counter-petition.

He also is not following what we feel is the greatest ground rule when dealing with a psychopath and that is get out and stay away, but he continued to hang on by denying all these allegations and prolonging the agony.

She has managed to cave this man and his legal advisers in by continuing the principle of legislation by exhaustion, I am sure there were great constant goings on between the lawyers involved and between the two parties and that eventually the husband had to fold his tent and give in. Despite the fact that he had very obviously been sucked into a marriage for financial gain that he had been set up for this situation, even to the point of starting adoption proceedings to formally adopt the children, so that they would then be his legal responsibility, but if one believes all the charges and counter-charges that there was only one month of effective marriage before the violence erupted and yet he surrenders and I quote from page 2:

> And whereas in order to avoid the asperities of litigation, the parties have arrived at the following agreement, upon which agreement the divorce may be set down on an uncontested basis and upon which agreement the application by the wife to the Family Court will be withdrawn.

Shortly after this application was withdrawn in Family Court, this complete psychopath proceeded to apply to Superior Court as follows:

> I respectfully ask that I be allowed to change my name from Maureen Jane Lamont to Maureen Jane Harmon.

Motion granted.

This is the final act in this incredible drama to this moment in time at least. She has now managed to deliver the ultimate insult; not only has she managed to marry him, fleece him, abandon him, but now chucks away his name. She is not crazy and "she sure showed that Doctor Lamont." Here she has also shown the untruthfulness, insincerity, lack of remorse or shame in noting very clearly in this her court deposition that there were no children of the marriage.

Note that on the 17th of March 1978, the now-divorced wife of Dr. Lamont applied to have her name changed back to Harmon, the name of her first husband, who had sought release and relief from this ghastly charade, by suicide.

These two marital chronicles, extending over some five years relating to this woman's marital exploits and problems with her children, show the classic scenario of the female psychopath who goes through life like a tornado through a village, destroying and deforming everything in her path and emerging unscathed herself and even more powerful.

## CONCLUDING REMARK ON THESE EIGHT CASE HISTORIES OF FEMALE PSYCHOPATHY

If tragedy can be considered to be the Fall of Titans or the destruction of kings, if each of the foregoing illustrations can be said to illustrate individual tragedies in the matrimonial holocaust, then the depth of each of these tragedies is beyond description. But each tragic situation illuminates and intensifies even more the suffering and the interweaving of the individual characters involved whose lives together have lacked insight: the wife into her psychopathic character defect, and the husband into his lack of insight as to what must be done on his behalf to rectify an all-encompassing horrible situation.

This work has hoped to show how the multifarious ways in which the ephemeral, transitory, and changeable conditions of life are revealed. In this work, too, we have shown how much trust has been placed one to the other in matrimony and how this trust has been betrayed, albeit unwittingly, by the psychopath who has been impelled onward without conscience. We have shown also the utter blindness in which two partners have conducted their lives. We have shown at the beginning of the marriage how many assumptions of trust and well-being of plans are made by each of the partners and how these assumptions and in fact, the presumptions of doing right, of conforming to an organized social order are all broken and, in the end result, betrayed. It is shown in this work on matrimony how life between two people commences with such joy and then moves to stark, utter ruin, abashed by life as it really is. We realize that, like the Wife of Bath, the female psychopath may eventually gain her "sixth husband," but that fleeting, nebulous concept of happiness will ever allude her. In truth it becomes clear by Chaucer's curious twist that the Wife of Bath realizes that by the very nature of things, love flows from the man to the woman and not from the woman to the man. So the end result is we are driven to the ineluctable conclusion once again, as I repeat over and over in this work, that in truth and by the very biological nature of humanity itself, by the constants of Western Culture, ingrained through centuries of imposition and refinement, of the dictates and mandates of this culture itself, by the eternal quest of man and woman for what each conceives to be "love," there carries within the seed of each, the germ of destruction.

The pitting of man against woman, husband against wife, the marshalling of all the forces of woman to achieve that illusory concept of Dominion over Man, does, as it seems to me, by my very many years of observation, to be as Brünhilde riding in triumph to the mountain peak, there to immolate herself in her sacrifice for "love."

What will come of this I cannot predict. I prefer to remain in the position of the title of Christopher Isherwood's work,

*"I AM A CAMERA."*

# V

# THE FEMALE PSYCHOPATH IN THE MARITAL HOLOCAUST: WHAT CAN BE DONE?

In this chapter it is well to attempt to outline the situation as so aptly put by Dr. Cleckley in his introduction to the book, *The Psychopath,* by William H. Reid, in which he states on pages X and XI:

> Our record, however, does not even indicate that we have even been modestly successful in our efforts to cure ordinary criminals. It is even less impressive in our efforts with the typical psychopath.
>
> We still lack adequate means, social and medical of curing him, controlling him, or significantly altering his self-destructive and socially destructive ways. Because of this, better realization of the nature of the problems must be sought. Even if effective therapy for some sociopathic syndromes is never achieved, such knowledge would help those working in the fields of medicine, psychology, law and education, eventually to develop more appropriate and effective methods of *coping* with the bewildering and tragic consequences of the primary disorder.

Here again, Dr. Cleckley has in a few short phrases stated the definitive state of the art as regards the treatment of the psychopath and the victims of the psychopath in our North American society.

In 1981 Dr. William H. Reid, M.D., M.P.H., was responsible for the gathering together and the editing of *The Treatment of Antisocial Syndromes.*[1] The dedication page of this work reads as follows:

To
Hervey Cleckley
and
Georg K. Sturup
A pessimist and an optimist, both devoted to the understanding and betterment of the human condition, and to Elise.

[1]*The Treatment of Antisocial Syndromes,* 1981, edited by William H. Reid, M.D., M.P.H. Van Nostrand Reinhold Company, 135 West 50th Street, New York, N.Y. 10020.

To thus label the late Dr. Cleckley "a pessimist" only serves to show that the true personal character and the life-consuming work of Dr. Cleckley has eluded the author. Perhaps the following conversation, which I had with Dr. Cleckley in Augusta, Georgia, in 1983, will show that rather than the label "pessimist," the word *realist* should better apply to Dr. Cleckley, his character and his work.

> "Well, Dr. Cleckley, what are you going to do with these psychopathic murderers, these convicted psychopathic rapists, these torturers and others who are incarcerated for crimes for which the name 'brutality' hardly applies?"
>
> "To directly answer that question I must state that I recommend that in order to protect society from the further depradations of the psychopathic, convicted killers and such, that their lives should be ended by execution."
>
> "Then I take it, Dr. Cleckley, that you are in favor of capital punishment."
>
> "I am in favor of capital punishment, not because of capital punishment being correct per se, but because this is the only way that society as a whole can be protected from further depradations of the psychopath. All too often parole boards and the like, who are totally unskilled in the dynamics of the psychopathic personality, will let themselves be convinced by the glibness, by the plausibility of the psychopath and who, once released on parole, in all too many cases, continues his psychopathic depradations against society and the members thereof."
>
> "I take it, Dr. Cleckley, that what you are expressing is the fact that you are a realist. Can you think of any other word perhaps that would express your views any more clearly?"
>
> "No, I like to think that I am a realist. After devoting a lifetime of study into this problem I have to come to this realistic conclusion."

In Dr. Reid's book, of some 258 pages, we seek again some approach to the alleviation of the onslaught of the female psychopath in day-to-day, every day American life. We note in Chapter 10, headed "Treatment of the Female Offender: One Facility's Experience," written by Elissa P. Benedek, M.D., which deals in its ten pages solely with the female psychopath as related to the criminal scene and observations therein being taken from the various state prisons and the prison systems. Not one word in the whole length of the book with respect to the female psychopath in the matrimonial holocaust, so that Dr. Reid's symposium really gives no help or answer to the problem of the marital holocaust. It is well to consider Dr. Cleckley's observations and recommendations with respect to capital punishment and the fear of the continued depradations of the criminal psychopath let loose on society, in light of the extremely popular Clint Eastwood films, the "Dirty Harry" series, including *Dirty Harry, Magnum Force, The Enforcer,* and the final brutal film, *Sudden Impact.* It was the showing of *Sudden Impact* in New York City in the spring of 1984, that critics, to their amazement, found the audiences standing and applauding at the scenes of Clint Eastwood executing summary judgment upon what were obviously criminals.

It is worthwhile, therefore, to attempt to consider the possible coping mechanisms that could operate in society in dealing with the psychopath in the marital holocaust under the following headings.

What treatment is available for the psychopath herself? There is no known cure for a psychopath; not only is there no help for the psychopath in the marital situation, but the only remedy I propose for the victim of the psychopath is to escape, to get out, as quickly and as quietly as possible, leaving behind him, fame, fortune, his heart, and his children who are held hostage against him, and his reputation. His reputation he can regain. His fortune he can regain. His peace of mind and stability he can regain. He can never, however, regain his children; the damage has been done. What the male so often fails to see in the marriage to the female psychopath is that there is no honorable way out. She is the plausible one, she is the one who will be believed by all of their neighbours, her advisors, her multitude of lawyers, whom she will gather around to pursue the husband. He might just as well accept the fact that he must take the quickest and easiest route out, hopefully through a quick and semi-dignified divorce, so that he can begin to rebuild his life again. Martyrdom is not the answer. In fact, martyrdom of the husband is no use in the fight against the martyrdom of the female psychopathic mother.

One can, in some 349 pages of the book quoted above, *The Psychopath, A Comprehensive Study of Anti-Social Disorders and Behaviour,* W.H. Reid, read a most comprehensive review both of research and treatment modalities of the antisocial disorders and behavior. In reading this impressive tome, one rapidly sees the futility of maintaining any hope for eliciting any long-term change in the psychopath. This book goes through all modalities of treatment, from psychotherapy to institutionalization, to electroshock, to a multitude of single and multiple drug therapies, etc. Despite areas in the book where there is some attempt to generate hope that something can be done to change the psychopath, one can certainly see the basic *current,* and that is that the psychopath is fundamentally a personality defect rather than a disorder, one that is basically not treatable, in the sense that there can be any basic change in the personality as such.

The second consideration in this chapter must be, "What can be done for the feckless husband and the unfortunate children held hostages in this drama, during the existence and disintegration of the marriage?" Certainly they deserve the greatest attention because here it is possible to make some viable, preventative health attempts to ease the anguish and the anger and the confusion visited upon children of the psychopath in the marital holocaust. Unfortunately, very often the children of the marriage have from birth appreciated the fact that the psychopathic mother really was less interested in them as children to be loved objects rather than as a completion of her fantasies of motherhood as the only social acceptable role for her. Here, to quote from Kolb, *Modern Clinical Psychiatry,* Ninth Edition, p. 611

> The future antisocial personality is often a child born to parents who did not want him and frequently he or she is of illegimate birth. The mother's own early life and development have been unhappy and her departure from her parents has been motivated by a wish to escape from them. She has few resources to offer others and thus comes to term (the end of the pregnancy) feeling herself deprived. Any suffering with the birth or failures to realize her fantasies in the child serve only to increase her negative attitude toward the infant. Even when the parents are married, their relationship usually terminates in desertion or divorce. Thus the child may have been passed frequently between others or institutionalized. If he remains with the parents he may have been exposed to violent tempers, abuse and a variety of brutalities and sexual abberations that occur frequently in parents addicted to alcohol and promiscuity.
>
> In this type authoritarian goals for the child are not clearly established and are never based on the foundation of mutual affection and tenderness and trust. Attempts by school and other authorities to establish some control for the acts of the child are treated indifferently, open defied, and fought off by the parents. The child is deprived again of other sources for establishing healthy identifications with those maintaining the social values of the community.
>
> Further, both the attitude of parents to outside authority in the child's own resentments are often deepened and embedded.

This is a very distressing passage in that one sees that here in the psychopathic marriage is set the stage for a repetition of the same psychopathic situation: future generations, as the children of the female psychopath are inadequately bonded to her through her own classical pathologic egocentricity and incapacity of love.

There is now the third consideration in this chapter and that is "the support services for the family involved in the marital breakdown and divorce." Although the children may already have been irreparably damaged, as discussed above in Dr. Kolb's work, there is the feeling that certain help from society could diminish at least the turmoil, the anguish, and the anger associated with the divorce process itself as the culmination of the disastrous marriage.

1. *Counselling Services* available for the children and the husband are only useful insofar as the counsellors understand psychopathy and its probable role in the specific marriage in question. Obviously all marriages are not caused by psychopaths and not all divorcing females are psychopaths, but a significant proportion of these are, and I beg that the large majority of these psychopathic females manage to carry out their plausible act in full view of society and society's institution, the counselling services, the schools, court, the medical profession, without tripping any individual to the fact that this is a psychopath at work and therefore a pointless intervention in an inevitable marital disaster.

In these cases, one would feel that counselling should be oriented towards easing the breakdown of the marital situation and easing the situation as best one possibly could for the unlucky children and the spouse.

2. *Halfway Houses* for the children of the marriage in trouble. Foster home situations have been discussed in some other parts of the world; foster home "children's village" types of organized social resources to help the children of disintegrating marriages could, I feel, go a long way towards helping these children develop a better image of themselves; towards their recognition that they did not, in fact, have anything to do with causing the marital disaster and nor can they do anything to make their mother and father stick together.

It has always been my feeling that in a marital disaster such as a psychopathic divorce, the psychopathic female is in no way capable of understanding or meeting the delicate needs of her children. In addition, the male, who has been subjected to the destructive influences of the psychopathic female in going through this kind of terrible breakdown, is certainly *in no shape to handle the children without professional help. Without doubt,* support services for all divorcing families and the children of the disintegrating union in any divorce situation would be commendable. It is mandatory in the case of the female psychopath. She has so confused the marital situation, the relationship between herself and the children, herself and the husband, and the children and the husband, that these children are specifically at very great risk for a long and unhappy childhood, and psychopathy in their own right.

There is a truism as observed by many in the practice of this branch of the law, and that is, "divorce never ends a marriage." This must be changed. The change will require radical surgery to provide final binding settlements and to provide a safe and stable home as far as is possible for the beleaguered children in this tragic mess, rather than having the psychopathic wife provided with the full force of the legal system in allowing her endless end runs at her husband and his finances, even after the legalities of the divorce are "final." Should he happen to be either a success in his job (a triumph after the denigration and destruction perpetrated on him by the psychopathic wife), or should he win the penny lottery, the system allows her to re-open and away she goes again. It never ends!

One further point to consider for a time is the question of custody and visiting rights. There are many theories as to what should be done with respect to custody and with respect to access to the children. With respect to access, there is the work of Anna Freud in the book which she co-authored, *Beyond the Best Interests of the Child.* In this book, she advocates that upon the dissolution of the marriage, the splitting of the couples and the granting of the custody to one or other of the spouses, that there then be no access by the other spouse. Of course, this is a highly volatile suggestion, one also which is not in accordance with the law of the land. It takes a very heavy onus to show why the other parent should not have access to the child. When a divorce takes place and the children are going to the mother, then each father will never ever enjoy these children.

It is in his best interest to get himself remarried and have a family that he is going to enjoy. It must be taken that visiting rights certainly need to be restructured, especially in the case of the female psychopath, whose devious plausibility and dominion over man can warp and ruin children's minds. It may be better to consider that a constant exposure to one parent is preferable to intermittent exposure to two confused and confusing role models while the child is attempting to grow.

For instance, there is great furor over the fact that children brought up by the single female parent will wind up themselves as social rejects, etc., etc. Certainly the wars of society over the countless years would seem to countermand these incidents of total failure. Certainly in World War II immense numbers of essentially fatherless children grew up, in that many of the fathers were away in some armies for six to seven or eight years in the armed forces and the mother, in effect, brought up these children. It is hardly necessary to point out, they did not produce a complete generation of social rejects and misfits.

Where the psychopathic mother has control and custody of the children, she does her damage on them and from these girl children who stem from the psychopathic mother's custody and control comes the next generation of psychopathic wives.

A proposed solution to the problem of the psychopathic wife and psychopathic mother is that of the controlled sociological experiment discussed by Dr. Bruno Bettlelheim in his landmark work, *The Children of the Dream*, published in 1969 by The Macmillan Company. In this work he discusses the voluntary surrendering of children from the very earliest age. These children were the offspring of the survivors of the Holocaust in Europe during World War II who had now come to the new land of Israel, the land of the dream, after 1945. Their children were raised by well-trained child care workers in the company of the children's peers. Visits by the parents were allowed only for "fun" purposes and *none other.* The observations of these children came to an end at the time of the Six-Day War in June of 1967.

It was found, astonishingly so, from out of these *Children of the Dream,* that there was not one case of drug addiction, juvenile delinquency (criminality), mental illness or homosexuality in the Israeli army, which of course included both sexes. One should note that this army was made up of many draftees from the Kibbutzim, who were in great part those children discussed above, raised essentially without the nuclear family.

It was found that the loyalties of the children thus raised were totally given to the peer groups of each, i.e., the astounding conclusion to the whole of the "experiment" was that well-adjusted, conscientious, and viable adults resulted.

They did not need biological parents; they needed a strong support system, which came from the peer group and the child-care workers. *(Kibbutz* means "group" in Hebrew—Author's Note.)

The state must, for the preservation of the next generation, step in and assume some control over the beleaguered children of the psychopathic mother and destroyed father.

To counter the critics it can be pointed out that this sytem would be far less expensive than the current jumble of foster homes, orphanages, social workers, police youth squads, expensive courts, etc., that exist to attempt to handle these children under the current situation. This, then, poses a part of an American cultural dilemma.

Rather than go further into a long discussion of ideals, one must deal with the realities in light of society's current priorities and economics of the social system as it currently exists. In the light of these realities, probably the only quickly available resource of these hapless families would be a quick and dignified divorce. I would like to state that in all cases where justice is delayed, justice is denied, and I would go on to point out that in no case is it so destructive as it is in the psychopathic marriage. The current system allows endless delays in the court process, i.e., a continuation of the marital war, and thereby continuation of the use of the children as hostages in the marital war, thus inflicting terrible psychological damage on them on an ongoing basis, rather than getting the situation finalized and at least allowing the children to begin to deal with one parent, whomever custody is awarded to, rather than being manipulated by both parents and dragged through a mess of two, three, four, five, or even ten years of a fight between the psychopathic female and her husband.

In summary, there remains to offer a measure of advice for the husband involved in the usually prolonged agony of divorce proceedings involving a psychopathic wife with her army of social support, surrounding and supporting her: In short, cut and run. Bail out and pull the ripcord, and hope for a safe landing, especially in light of the current judicial system.

# VI

# THE SUMMARY

*I Am a Camera* —Christopher Isherwood

I have spent thirty-seven years of my life as a family law counsel dealing in the arena of social disorder—the breaking and broken family with all its ramifications. I have also in the course of this work naturally read extensively on psychopathic and sociopathic disorders and, in this reading, I have been impressed with the fact that there is so much work on the male psychopath in the literature: most especially the classic tract by Dr. Cleckley, *The Mask of Sanity,* now in its Fifth Edition, some forty years after first publication in 1941. It has further impressed me more and more each year in my family law practice how so clearly Dr. Cleckley's profile of the male psychopath is mirrored in many of the women I have seen in the course of analyzing thousands of marital breakups.

Since publication of my first book, *Counsel for the Damned,* in 1973, in which I illustrated and discussed the family breakdown rampant in North America at that time, I am sorry to say that such widespread rage and family dissolution has continued, nay multiplied like a cancer in our society, as shown by the statistics given in the introduction to this work and most particularly in the pace-setting State of California statistics.

As I have continued my practice and my reading in the causes of this social disorder, I have developed a germ of an idea—that, in truth, there are clearly definable female psychopaths in this world. The literature, as I have stated, is almost totally devoted to the male psychopath for one very important reason in my opinion. The male acts out his animus outside the home in full view and against the general social mores because that is his traditional role, and he pays the price by way of criminal sanctions or committal by society to mental institutions. In these situations, he has been widely studied, thus producing the body of literature on the male psychopath. The female psychopath, on the other hand, is hidden in the home, where she wreaks total havoc in and on the marriage, in fact accepting, but abusing, her traditional role, that of Mother.

In the writing of this book, therefore, I have attempted to present the first comprehensive thesis on the female psychopath, relating Dr. Cleckley's definitive work on the male psychopath to the female psychopath as I have seen her in full flight, and full of fight, on innumerable occasions in my family law practice. It is hoped that the discussions of the female psychopath and her characteristics, her actions in and on the marriage, the husband, and the children, have laid the groundwork for the reader to see clearly how the eight cases I have presented and discussed in detail show flagrant psychopathy in its female form. In the many thousands of cases I have examined in my office, exemplified by the eight cases given in this work, I have found by listening carefully and attempting to get at the root of the problem, that there seems to be some serious disturbance in the early years of the female psychopath's life cycle. I have discussed at some length the possible roots of female psychopathy in the early relationships of the future psychopath. For instance, one need only inquire into the relationship of these daughters to the father during their youth and the trauma visited upon the daughter by cruelty, drunkenness, violence, incestuous relationships, desertion, philandering, etc., so often found in the fathers of the female psychopath.

In addition, I have pointed out that, in my opinion, the absence of bonding, that is, the establishment of a calm and trusting emotional and physical relationship with one or both parents in the early years of any child's life, may be the *sine qua non* for the development of the psychopathic child and future adult. The effects of a lack of such a common, trusting, bonding relationship early in life can very frequently be seen in the consideration of the many adopted children who become psychopathic adolescents and adults and go on to live a disruptive and disrupting life in our society. I offer this as my observation in the possible etiology of the psychopath as I have seen in my many years of observation of people in trouble in the family arena. It is obviously for those schooled in medicine, psychiatry, and the social sciences to go on and do further research on this tentative offering of mine rather than for those of us in the legal profession to make such definitive pronouncements. It is my hope that this book will awaken just such professions to the existence of the female psychopath and to the necessity for careful and persistent interrogation in attempting to delineate the characteristic psychopathic female in the disruptive marital situation. I'm very afraid that the possibilities for such research into the psychopathic female in marital disaster are nearing the end—not only because of the problems of confidentiality and privilege, but also because we are at the end of an era—the era where conduct during the marriage had any bearing on the dissolution of the marriage and legal considerations of same. I see no-fault divorce as a very dangerous course of action for society, especially in relation to the psychopathic female and her victims, the husband and the children. At least here in this book, I take what may be the last chance to research the problem and lay it before society.

In the eight specific cases that I have culled from my extensive files,

I have attempted to present in an organized manner the psychopathic characteristics shown in each of these cases. I dare say that the reader will find some of this information absolutely shocking! I must point out to the reader that these cases have been drawn from the court depositions and from the histories written for me as counsel by the husbands and others in these psychopathic relationships, the originals of which I have in my office in full support of the documentation discussed in the individual case histories. Following the individual case histories, I have attempted to provide some framework for consideration of the female psychopath in her development from the early years up to the marriage and her then violent, "rebel without a cause," destruction of the marriage situation, where there appear to be very many common characteristics among the individual cases. These common characteristics I have attempted to lay out as a guideline showing a common thread running throughout the marital disasters of these psychopathic females.

As far as treatment for the female psychopath is concerned, I have little more to offer than those writers who discuss the hopelessness of curative therapy in regards to the male psychopath. One may refer specifically to *The Psychopath: A Comprehensive Study of Social Disorders and Behaviors,* edited by William H. Reid, M.D., M.P.H., published by Brunner/Mazel, New York in 1978. In this 349-page hardcover and in his second book title, the scholarly discussion again primarily deals with the male psychopath, and provides careful consideration of all treatment modalities available to modern psychology and psychiatry. The utter hopelessness of any curative results from such treatment modalities is best stated by Dr. Cleckley himself in the introduction, pages X and XI of Dr. Reid's 1978 work.

> Our record, however, does not indicate that we have been even modestly successful in our efforts to cure ordinary criminals. It is even less impressive in our efforts with the typical psychopath.
>
> I feel that this volume will contribute substantially to placing the psychopath in focus. We still lack adequate means, social and medical, of curing him, of controlling him, or of significantly altering his self-destructive and socially destructive ways. Because of this, better realization of the nature of his problem, and how it differs from other problems, must be sought. Even if effective therapy for some sociopathy syndromes is never achieved, such knowledge will help those working in the fields of medicine, psychology, law, and education eventually to develop more appropriate and effective methods of coping with the bewildering and tragic consequences of the primary disorder.

I stress the importance of the word "*coping,*" and I would like to point out that Dr. Cleckley wrote this introduction April 1978, after some forty years of his own intensive considerations of the psychopath. In other words, all of the so-called advances in modern social sciences and psychiatry have done little, if anything, to provide a curative modality for the male psychopath. As Dr. Cleckley so cogently states, one is really talking more of developing coping methods rather than curative procedures. It is my thesis that exactly this situation applies to the female psychopath in our society, in the matrimonial holocaust and out of it. In other words, it will appear that the same curative potential exists in the treatment of the female psychopath, and that is zero. As far as considering coping mechanisms is concerned, I have concentrated on an attempt to provide support services for the family during and after the inevitable havoc and dissolution wreaked by the female psychopath. As we can see, such services in North American society are sadly few and far between, not the least because the female psychopath is not generally recognized to be an entity, much less a basically untreatable one. I have attempted therefore to encourage in this work such recognition by society, and, more specifically, to awaken the medical, legal, and social sciences to this problem and its ramifications because these are the sciences that must deal with the social wreckage induced by the psychopath.

In concluding my consideration of the female psychopath, I have attempted to point out the great danger that the acceptance of the no-fault divorce, commonly called irreconcilable differences, holds for society, in that this situation is discouraging recognition of the female psychopath's behaviour in marriage by making conduct in the marriage of no import in the court consideration of "justice" in dissolving the marriage. I have offered an alternative proposal to the current situation. First, I have attempted to point out, that under the current situation, the only real possibility for a fair outcome in the psychopathic female's marriage, as far as the victim husband is concerned, lies in recognition of the existence of the female psychopath, careful legal preparation by competent counsel, and speedy attendance at court in attempt to shorten the exposure of the husband and the children to the havoc perpetrated by the psychopathic female, all in the hope that this will produce what I consider the basic function of the law—to get at the truth and to provide order in life and society.

In the end, I would offer an alternative proposal for consideration of marital breakdown and divorce, which I hope would provide some measure of fairness for the husband victim. This new alternative would be really a return to the jury system, in that this would embody the use of a ward system of responsible and responsive community leaders to consider the situation of the social disorder attendant upon the marital breakdown in the marital holocaust. I would suggest that such a panel would include a general medical practitioner of some years standing; a minister of the gospel, priest, rabbi; and an accountant would offer, in my opinion, a more humane and responsive approach outside of the sterile legal system, which may, because of a lack of educational opportunity and investigative opportunities in the individual psychopathic marriages, in fact, only legalize a victory for the psychopath that had long ago been won in the home. It is now only enshrined in the law by the court because the victim husband has no way whatsoever to present the real basis for the marital breakdown, i.e., that being, the character and actions of the female psychopath. It is my fond, though probably to be unconsummated, hope that such a system would be adopted at least in some jurisdictions in North America, even on a trial basis.

With this plea for return to justice and fair play for the psychopath's victims in the courts of the land, I rest my case.

> Many people can love those deserving of love: Some play the saint and love the undeserving. And there is a price to pay for all such self-deception.[2]

[2]This is a quote from *The Only Good German,* by Ted Allbury, Mayflower, Granada Publishing, London, Toronto, Sydney and New York, 1978.

Swich is this world; whoso it can biholde, In eche estat is litel hertes reste; God leve us for to take it for the beste!

—Chaucer

# VII

# A TRIBUTE TO HERVEY MILTON CLECKLEY

Hervey Cleckley became one of only four psychiatrists in Georgia in private practice when he joined the Medical College about 1937. His vast knowledge, his innate understanding of people, his gentleness of manner, and his capability of conveying the goodness of the true physician quickly endeared him to patients and students alike. He rapidly advanced to the forefront of American psychiatry. He culminated his psychiatric honors when he recently became a Life Fellow of the American Psychiatric Association. Acclamations of his talents are numerous.

To students who were at the Medical College of Georgia in the 1940s and '50s, these were the legendary years. These were the times when it was said that "Giants walked the halls"—Virgil Sydenstricker, Perry Volpitto, Lombard Kelly, William F. Hamilton, Richard Torpin, Robert Greenblatt, and Ray Ahlquist—of roughly equal stature and taller than most was Hervey Milton Cleckley. His lectures were so entrancing one could hardly take notes. He was a remarkable teacher—a living legend and one whose reputation will persist.

No aspect of psychiatry has failed to be graced by his learning and his pen: psychopathology, psychotherapy, psychopharmacology, electrotherapy, psychological theory—anything dealing with functions of the mind. He wrote dozens of papers in psychiatry and contributed many chapters to textbooks.

He initially became world renowned with the first edition of *The Mask of Sanity* in 1940. He revised it several times, still of the opinion that no one knew the cause of the psychopathic personality and no one knew a cure.

In 1957 he received the Georgia Writers Association Literary Achievement Award for Non-Fiction after he co-authored *The Three*

*Faces of Eve.* It also became world renowned. Both of these books are to this day considered classics in psychiatry. He was one of the few people who lived to see his work adapted to motion pictures by Hollywood.

The third book, and the one that he always believed to be his best and most important, is little known. It is the study of pathologic sexuality done in a straightforward, scientific manner without pandering. He was particularly intrigued by its influence on social, psychiatric, and literary manifestations. He did not reject the pervert as a person—indeed he had the greatest of compassion for these unfortunates. Powerful and persuasive is his conviction that love between man and woman is among the most noble of mankind's emotions. He handled his words with the grace of a fencer, but they fell with the force of a mace. Few copies of this great study, *The Caricature of Love,* are still available.

Doctor Cleckley once said, "If ever I could have a last will and testament, I would more than anything want it said of me that I saw the utter folly of the Freudian theory and did what I could to reveal its foolishness. The Freudian and so-called dynamic theories have set psychiatry back in America over fifty years. Nothing has been more harmful to the mentally sick of this nation."

A number of his later writings were critiques of various aspects of the Freudian psychosexual theory. Two days before his death, he was laughing over an article in the February 1984 issue of *The Atlantic Monthly,* entitled "Freud and the Seduction Theory." He commented that it was no wonder Freud and members of his family had tried to suppress the seduction theory. Doctor Cleckley observed, "What a jamboree!"

Doctor Cleckley was born in Augusta, Georgia, in 1903. He graduated from Richmond Academy, where he was renowned for his athletic prowess. He majored in mathematics and science at the University of Georgia. He was editor of the yearbook *Pandora.* He was a Phi Beta Kappa. His football feats are legend. He played without benefit of an athletic scholarship. The records at Georgia in the 440 meter and in the high and low hurdles he held for many years. He was captain of the track team.

He was selected to receive the highest, rarest, and most coveted scholastic honor offered—a Rhodes Scholarship. He graduated from the University of Oxford with a degree in physiology. While there he became Intercollegiate Heavyweight Boxing Champion of Europe. He also continued his first athletic love—track. In 1926 he entered the Medical College of Georgia, where before his graduation as a medical doctor he was selected for the Alpha Omega Alpha.

He interned and had a two-year surgical residency in Augusta. Soon afterward he became a staff psychiatrist at Lenwood VA Hospital, serving for several years. Here he acquired his psychiatric and neurological experience. Through largely personal effort and study, he prepared himself and became a Diplomate in each of the Boards of Neurology and Psychiatry. After he joined the illustrious faculty of the Medical College, he created the Department of Psychiatry and Neurology. He became a full Professor and Chief of Psychiatry until 1953, when he chose not to accept a proffered full-time appointment (newly created). He did not wish to become an institutional physician but preferred private general practice in psychiatry. He accepted a clinical professorship and finally became Professor Emeritus.

Until now only his achievements have been covered, but little has been said about the man.

He was a person of unusual modesty and deep humility. He was without malice or meanness. He never said nor did a shabby thing. Those of even brief acquaintanceship quickly sensed that he was a person of such character that they were not likely to encounter one like him again. He possessed great wisdom. Soft spoken and of few words, his observations were penetrating. There was a solemnity about him that demanded dignity and respect.

Hervey Cleckley was a deeply religious man. He felt that man's ability to comprehend an all-emcompassing Power was exceedingly limited. Man's efforts were often naive and simplistic. He deplored the arrogance and sweeping dogmatism frequently displayed by various religious authorities, but he believed that man's need for that Power was not only universal but impelling. He never found organized religion adequate for him personally.

He was ever searching for Truth—"it is burnished by criticism, it will shine through all efforts to conceal it or to destroy it."

He possessed "infinite humor and jest." He had merriment and overflowed with mirth. A good joke brought guffaws from him. He took pleasure in harmless practical pranks. He was not beyond joining up his friend, the very proper Virgil Sydenstricker, M.D., to a sexually oriented lonely hearts club. He rarely used wit and would never hold a person to scorn.

He was revered and loved by every person who knew him. He was widely read, loved knowledge, and constantly increased his learning. He was a keen observer of mankind. He was a scholar and a grammarian. His well-studied library filled several rooms. Research along strict scientific principles occupied much of his time. Two papers were accepted for publication last year, and two more are in final stages.

He delighted in poetry and quoted volumes from memory. He had no favorite poem, but certain verse or lines of verse moved him deeply. Among these were "Lepanto," some of Houseman's poems, a few lines of Swinburne, much of Homer, and hundreds of lines from Shakespeare. His literary knowledge was vast. He abhorred the snobbishness often seen among the cognoscenti of literature. He enjoyed a good drink, the presence of friends, enlightened conversation, and the recitation of poetry—to him that was a fine evening.

Despite his interest and attachment to his work, he was glad when the day was over and he could go to his home that he loved so much. He adored his first wife beyond measure. Her death was devastating. It was as if darkness had inherited the earth. He threw himself into revising the fifth edition of *The Mask of Sanity.* Little by little, over the years he recovered his former perspective on life. His second wife, Emily, fulfilled all of his needs, and she came to occupy all things in his affections. No women were ever loved more and I know of no women who gave more in return.

He was a master physician and instinctively practiced its art. His patients treasured his presence. He was never too rushed to spend whatever time was required for his patients or students. He loved people. His capacity for understanding and empathy seemed without end. He was a friend beyond compare.

One must comment on one of many jokes that he unwittingly pulled on himself. Once while he was teaching class, a violent rainstorm came up. He chanced to glance out of the window and saw his treasured convertible becoming drenched, as windows and top were down. He excused himself and hurried madly down to correct the situation. When he got back to the classroom, the students were practically rolling on the floor. In his haste he had put up the windows, but left the top down.

Hervey Cleckley was a true gentleman, the soul of courtesy and graciousness. He had the simplicity of true greatness, the open mind of true wisdom, and the meekness of true strength. Honor was his name.

—Corbett H. Thigpen, M.D.

## HERVEY MILTON CLECKLEY, M.D.

Born September 7, 1903, Augusta, Georgia
Deceased January 28, 1984

*Degrees:*

University of Georgia, Athens, Georgia, 1922–24 B.S. 1924, Math-Science

Oxford University, England, 1924–1926 (Rhodes Scholar) B.A. 1926, Physiology

University of Georgia Medical School, Augusta, Georgia M.D. 1929, Medicine

*Qualifications:*

Fellow, American Psychiatric Association
Fellow, American College of Physicians (Former)
Diplomate, American Board of Psychiatry and Neurology (1940)
Editor, National Board of Editors, *Journal of Clinical and Experimental Psychopathology*

Member, Board of National Advisors, Association for Psychiatric Offenders
Member, Alpha Omega Alpha
Member, Phi Beta Kappa

*Positions:*

Professor, Neuropsychiatry, Medical College of Georgia, Augusta, Georgia, 1937–1955

Clinical Professor, Neuropsychiatry, Medical College of Georgia, Augusta, Georgia, 1955 to present

Chief, Department of Psychiatry and Neurology, University Hospital, Augusta, Georgia, 1937–1963

Consultant, Veterans Administration Hospital, Augusta, Georgia, 1945–1957

Former Consultant, Fort Gordon Army Hospital, Fort Gordon, Georgia

# SELECTED BIBLIOGRAPHY OF DR. CLECKLEY'S WORKS

## BOOKS, CHAPTERS IN TEXTBOOKS AND ARTICLES IN JOURNALS

*Books*

Cleckley, Hervey. *The Mask of Sanity.* St. Louis: The C. V. Mosby Company, 1941.

*The Mask of Sanity.* The C. V. Mosby Company, Second Edition 1950.

*The Mask of Sanity.* The C. V. Mosby Company, Third Edition 1955. (second printing 1957).

*The Mask of Sanity.* The C.V. Mosby Co. Fourth Edition 1964, Fifth, 1972

Thigpen, C. H., and Cleckley, Hervey. *The Three Faces of Eve.* New York: McGraw-Hill Book Company, 1957.

Cleckley, Hervey. *The Caricature of Love.* New York: The Ronald Press Co., 1957.

*Chapters in Textbooks*

Cleckley, Hervey. "The Psychopath Viewed Practically." Chapter 11, in *Contemporary Criminal Hygiene.* (Edited by Seliger, R.V., Lukas, E. J., and Lindner, R. M.) Baltimore: Oakridge Press, 1946, pp. 194–217.

Cleckley, Hervey. "The Psychopath Viewed Practically." Chapter (pp. 395–412) in *Handbook of Correctional Psychology.* (Edited by Lindner, R. M., and Seliger, R. V) New York: Philosophical Library, 1947.

Cleckley, Hervery. "Antisocial Personalities." Chapter 12, in *An Introduction to Clinical Psychology*. (Edited by L. A. Pennington and Irwin A. Berg) New York: The Ronald Press Co., 1948, pp. 249–264.

Cleckley, Hervey. "Psychopathic Personality." Article in *Encyclopedia of Criminology*. (Edited by Branham, V. C., and Kutash, E.B.) New York: Philosophical Library, 1949.

Cleckley, Hervey. "Psychopathic States." Chapter 28 in *American Handbook of Psychiatry* (Edited by Silvano Arieti) New York: Basic Books, Inc., Publishers, 1959.

Cleckley, Hervey. "Psychiatry: Science, Art, and Scientism." Chapter 5 in *Psychiatry and Responsibility*. (Edited by Helmut Schoeck and James W. Wiggins) Princeton, N.J.: D. Van Nostrand Co., Inc., 1962.

Cleckley, Hervey. "The Psychopathic Personality." Chapter in *Crime, Law and Corrections*, (edited by Ralph Slovenko, M.D.) Springfield, Ill.: Charles C. Thomas, Publisher, 1966.

Cleckley, Hervey. "The Psychopathic Personality." Article for *International Encyclopedia of the Social Sciences*, New York: The Crowell-Collier Publishing Co., 1965.

Miscellaneous: Georgia Writers Association Literary Achievement Award for Non-Fiction, 1957.

Introduction to *The Psychopath: A Comprehensive Study of Antisocial Disorders and Behaviors*, by William H. Reid, M.D.

*Book Reviews:*

Cleckley, Hervey. Review of Dr. Frank J. Sulloway's *Freud: Biologist of the Mind, The Atlanta Journal and Constitution*, December 9, 1979.

*Films and Video:*

Cleckley, Hervey M., M.D., L.F.A.P.A. and Thigpen, Corbett H., M.D. L.F.A.P.A., *A Modern Properly administered electroconvulsive Treatment*, 1980.

*Articles in Journals*

Cleckley, Hervey. "Psychiatry." *Journal of the Medical Association of Georgia* 11: (November 1941) 466–472.

Cleckley, Hervey. "Insight as an Aim in Psychotherapy." *Annals of Internal Medicine* 14: (May 1941) 2115–2125.

Cleckley, Hervey. "The So-Called Psychopathic Personality." *Journal of the Medical Association of Georgia* 11: (November 1941) 466–472.

Cleckley, Hervey. "Semantic Dementia and Semi-Suicide." *Psychiatric Quarterly* 16: (July 1942) 520–529.

Cleckley, Hervey. "The Psychosis that Psychiatry Refuses to Face." *Journal of Criminal Psychopathology* 6: (July 1944) 117–130.

Cleckley, Hervey. "The Psychopath. A Problem for Society." *Federal Probation* 10: (1946) 22–25.

Cleckley, Hervey. "A Shorter Psychotherapy." *Journal of Southern Medicine and Surgery* 108: (October 1946) 307–308.

Cleckley, Hervey. "Common Sources of Confusion in Psychiatric Matters." *Journal of the Southern Medical Association* 42: (April 1949) 341–343.

Cleckley, Hervey. "Psychiatric Problems in a General Hospital." *Journal of the Medical Association of Georgia* 28: (December 1949) 471–475.

Cleckley, Hervey. "The Mask of Sanity." *Post-Graduate Medicine* 9: (March 1951) 193–197.

Cleckley, Hervey. "Depressive Illness." *Post-Graduate Medicine* 4: (April 1954) 370–374.

Cleckley, Hervey. "Use of Diazepam as Adjunctive Therapy in Psychiatric Disorders." *Journal of the South Carolina Medical Association* 61: (January, 1965) 1–4.

Cleckley, Hervey, Sydenstricker, V. P., and Geeslin, L.E. "Nicotinic Acid in the Treatment of Atypical Psychotic States Associated with Malnutrition." *Journal of the American Medical Association* 112: (May 27, 1939) 2107–2110.

Geeslin, L. E., and Cleckley, H. M. "Anomalies and Dangers in the Metrazol Therapy of Schizophrenia." *American Journal of Psychiatry* 96: (July 1939) 183–191.

Krusc, II. D., Sydenstricker, V. P., Sebrell, W. H., and Cleckley, H.M. "Ocular Manifestations of Ariboflavinpsis." *Public Health Reports* 55: (January 26, 1940) 157–169.

Cleckley, Hervey, Bowles, Lester, and Mettler, F. A. "Histologic Changes following Metrazol Convulsions." *Archives of Neurology and Psychiatry* 43: (May 1940) 948–960.

Sydenstricker, V. P., Sebrell, W. H., Cleckley, H. M. and Kruse, H.D. "Ocular Manifestations of Ariboflavinosis: A Progress Note." *Journal of the American Medical Association* 114: (June 22, 1940) 2437–2445.

Mettler, F.A., Cleckley, H. M., and Slaughter, R. P. "A Four Year Correlative Plan for Teaching the Nervous System." *Journal of American Association of Medical Colleges* 15: (September 1940) 291–300.

Cleckley, Hervey, and Templeton, C.M. "Prolonged Coma in Insulin Therapy of the Psychoses." *American Journal of Psychiatry* (January 1941).

Cleckley, Hervey, and Geeslin, L.E. "Progressive Muscular Atrophy and Syphilis." *Journal of Nervous and Mental Diseases* 93: (April 1941) 460–472.

Sydenstricker, V. P., and Cleckley, H. M. "The Effect of Nicotinic Acid in Stupor, Lethargy and Various Other Psychiatry Disorders." *American Journal of Psychiatry* 98: (July 1941) 83–92.

Cleckley, Hervey, and Egleston, Dubose. "Some Observations on Cardiovascular Changes in Shock Therapy." *Psychiatric Quarterly* 15: (October 1941) 662–679.

Cleckley, H. M., Hamilton, W. F., Woodbury, R. A., and Volpitto, P. P. "Pressure Studies in Patients Undergoing Shock Therapy." *Southern Medical Journal* 35: (April 1942) 375–381.

Allen, L. N., and Cleckley, H. M. "A New Pyramidal Tract Sign of Great Frequency." *Journal of Nervous and Mental Diseases* 97: (February 1943) 146–151.

Cleckley, Hervey, and Beard, Byron. "Electric Shock Treatment in Personality Disorder." *Journal of the Medical Association of Georgia* 21 (August 1942) 303–308.

Estes, M. M., and Cleckley, H. M. "Electronarcosis in a General Hospital." Read at meeting of American Psychiatric Association, Detroit, Michigan, May 1950. *The American Journal of Psychiatry* 107 (May 1951) 814–820.

Bromberg, Walter, and Cleckley, Hervey. "The Medico-Legal Dilemma." *Journal of Criminal Law and Criminology* 42: (March April 1952) 729–745.

Thigpen, F. B., and Thigpen, C. H., and Cleckley, H. M. "Use of Electric-Convulsive Therapy in Morphine, Meperidine and Related Alkaloid Addictions." *Archives of Neurology and Psychiatry* 70: (October 1953) 452–458.

Thigpen, C. H., and Cleckley, H. M. "A Case of Multiple Personality." *The Journal of Abnormal and Social Psychology* 49: (January 1954) 135–151 (Read at APA meeting, Los Angeles, May 1953).

Cleckley, H. M., and Thigpen, C. H. "The Dynamics of Illusion." *The American Journal of Psychiatry* 5: (November 1955) 334–342 (Read at APA meeting, Atlantic City May 1955).

Woodbury, R. A., Hamilton, W. F., Cleckley, H. M., and Volpitto, Perry P. "The Effect of Metrazol upon the Blood Pressure of Man and Dog." *The Journal of Pharmacology and Experimental Therapeutics* 73: (December 1941) 431–439.

Thigpen, Corbett H., and Cleckley, Hervey M. "Addendum to Multiple Personality." *The New Physician* 9: (May 1960) 5:27–33.

Thigpen, Corbett H., and Cleckley, Hervey M. "Freudian Psychodynamics—Science or Mirage?" *The New Physician* 10: (April 1961) 4:97–101.

Thigpen, Corbett H., and Cleckley, Hervey M. "On the Incidence of Multiple Personality Disorder: A Brief Communication." *The International Journal of Clinical and Experimental Hypnosis* Vol. XXXII, No. 2 (April 1984).

# APPENDIX

**(Schedule "A")**
**Marriages, divorces, and percent change from preceding year: United States, 1922–75**

| Year of occurrence | Marriages Number | Marriages Percent change | Divorces Number | Divorces Percent change |
|---|---|---|---|---|
| 1975 | 2,152,662 | −3.5 | 1,036,000 | +6.0 |
| 1974 | 2,229,667 | −2.4 | 977,000 | +6.8 |
| 1973 | 2,284,108 | +0.1 | 915,000 | +8.3 |
| 1972 | 2,282,154 | +4.2 | 845,000 | +9.3 |
| 1971 | 2,190,481 | +1.5 | 773,000 | +9.2 |
| 1970 | 2,158,802 | +0.6 | 708,000 | +10.8 |
| 1969 | 2,145,000 | +3.7 | 639,000 | +9.4 |
| 1968 | 2,069,000 | +7.4 | 584,000 | +11.7 |
| 1967 | 1,927,000 | +3.8 | 523,000 | +4.8 |
| 1966 | 1,857,000 | +3.2 | 499,000 | +4.2 |
| 1965 | 1,800,000 | +4.3 | 479,000 | +6.4 |
| 1964 | 1,725,000 | +4.3 | 450,000 | +5.1 |
| 1963 | 1,654,000 | +4.9 | 428,000 | +3.6 |
| 1962 | 1,577,000 | +1.9 | 413,000 | −0.2 |
| 1961 | 1,548,000 | +1.6 | 414,000 | +5.3 |
| 1960 | 1,523,000 | +1.9 | 393,000 | −0.5 |
| 1959 | 1,494,000 | +3.0 | 395,000 | +7.3 |
| 1958 | 1,451,000 | −4.4 | 368,000 | −3.4 |
| 1957 | 1,518,000 | −4.2 | 381,000 | −0.3 |
| 1956 | 1,585,000 | +3.5 | 382,000 | +1.3 |
| 1955 | 1,531,000 | +2.8 | 377,000 | 20.5 |
| 1954 | 1,490,000 | −3.6 | 379,000 | −2.8 |
| 1953 | 1,546,000 | +0.4 | 390,000 | −0.5 |
| 1952 | 1,539,318 | −3.5 | 392,000 | +2.9 |
| 1951 | 1,594,694 | −4.4 | 381,000 | −1.0 |
| 1950 | 1,667,231 | +5.5 | 385,000 | −3.0 |

| | | | | |
|---|---|---|---|---|
| 1949 | 1,579,798 | −12.8 | 397,000 | −2.7 |
| 1948 | 1,811,155 | −9.1 | 408,000 | −15.5 |
| 1947 | 1,991,878 | −13.1 | 483,000 | −20.8 |
| 1956 | 2,291,045 | +42.0 | 610,000 | +25.8 |
| 1945 | 1,612,992 | +11.1 | 485,000 | +21.3 |
| 1944 | 1,452,394 | −7.9 | 400,000 | +11.4 |
| 1943 | 1,577,050 | −11.0 | 359,000 | +11.8 |
| 1942 | 1,772,132 | +4.5 | 321,000 | +9.6 |
| 1941 | 1,695,999 | +6.3 | 293,000 | +11.0 |
| 1940 | 1,595,879 | +13.7 | 264,000 | +5.2 |
| 1939 | 1,403,633 | +5.5 | 251,000 | +2.9 |
| 1938 | 1,330,780 | −8.3 | 244,000 | −2.0 |
| 1937 | 1,451,296 | +6.0 | 249,000 | +5.5 |
| 1936 | 1,369,000 | +3.2 | 236,000 | +8.3 |
| 1935 | 1,327,000 | +1.9 | 218,000 | +6.9 |
| 1934 | 1,302,000 | +18.6 | 204,000 | +23.6 |
| 1933 | 1,098,000 | +11.8 | 165,000 | +0.5 |
| 1932 | 981,903 | −7.4 | 164,241 | −12.6 |
| 1931 | 1,060,914 | −5.9 | 188,003 | −4.1 |
| 1930 | 1,126,856 | −8.6 | 195,961 | −4.8 |
| 1929 | 1,232,559 | +4.2 | 205,876 | +2.8 |
| 1928 | 1,182,497 | −1.5 | 200,176 | +2.0 |
| 1927 | 1,201,053 | −0.1 | 196,292 | +6.3 |
| 1926 | 1,202,574 | +1.2 | 184,678 | +5.3 |
| 1925 | 1,188,334 | +0.3 | 175,449 | +2.6 |
| 1924 | 1,184,574 | −3.7 | 170,952 | +3.5 |
| 1923 | 1,229,784 | +8.4 | 165,096 | +10.9 |
| 1922 | 1,134,151 | ... | 148,815 | ... |

## Table A
## POPULATION, MARRIAGES, DIVORCES AND ANNULMENTS, CALIFORNIA 1922–1975

| Date | Population | Marriages | *Rate | Divorces | ** % |
|---|---|---|---|---|---|
| 1922 | 3,991,000 | 47,477 | 11.90 | 9,227 | 19.40 |
| 1927 | 5,147,000 | 53,487 | 10.40 | 14,135 | 26.40 |
| 1932 | 5,849,000 | 43,164 | 7.30 | 14,097 | 32.67 |
| 1937 | 6,528,000 | 69,397 | 9.90 | 20,718 | 29.14 |
| 1942 | 7,735,000 | 76,014 | 9.80 | 22,962 | 30.00 |
| 1947 | 9,832,000 | 94,461 | 9.60 | 45,997 | 48.70 |
| 1952 | 11,638,000 | 78,883 | 6.80 | 36,682 | 46.50 |
| 1962 | 16,638,000 | 114,128 | 6.80 | 48,027 | 42.00 |
| 1967 | 19,232,000 | 150,000 | 7.80 | 63,139 | 42.66 |
| 1970 | 19,680,000 | 172,388 | 8.75 | ***138,953 | 80.62 |
| 1971 | 20,292,900 | 168,049 | 8.22 | 143,464 | 85.36 |
| 1972 | 20,517,900 | 175,918 | 8.56 | 143,793 | 81.75 |
| 1973 | 20,741,000 | 169,319 | 8.13 | 152,367 | 90.00 |
| 1974 | 20,963,500 | 160,882 | 7.60 | 160,613 | 100.00 |
| 1975 | 21,205,900 | 154,803 | 7.32 | 163,801 | 105.81 |

NOTE: California New Family Law Act Commences January 1, 1970.
* Rates are per 1000 population
** Percentage of number of divorces to number of marriages in that year.
*** Initial complaint for divorce; should not be confused with final decrees of divorce.

Decline of Marriage

Since 1922 the rate of marriage per thousand in the population declines from 11.90 for that year to 7.32 in 1975—38.40%

Since 1922 the percentage of divorces to marriages has risen from 19.40% in that year to *105.81% for the year 1975—544%

*Initial Complaint for Divorce

## Population–Marriages–Divorces, U.S.A.
## 1972–1976

| Year | Population | Marriages | Divorces | Percentages |
|---|---|---|---|---|
| 1972 | 208,234,000 | 2,282,000 | 845,000 | 37.00% |
| 1973 | 209,859,000 | 2,284,000 | 915,000 | 40.00% |
| 1974 | 211,389,000 | 2,229,000 | 977,000 | 43.00% |
| 1975 | 213,137,000 | 2,126,000 | 1,026,000 | 48.26% |
| 1976 | 214,500,000 | 2,133,000 | 1,077,000 | 50.00% |

| | | | |
|---|---|---|---|
| Population increases: | 1972-1976 | 6,266,000 | 3.00% |
| Number of marriages decline: | 1972-1976 | 149,000 | 6.53% |
| Number of divorces increase: | 1972-1976 | 232,000 | 27.36% |

Child Population, U.S.A. 1975 .......................................... 70,522,000
Children—Divorced Parents,
10 year period, 1965–1974 .......................................... * 8,609,000 (12.24%)

Commencing in 1974, divorces for that year and each successive year reached more than twice the national total at the beginning of the decade; 1965—479,000.

*Zero to eighteen years of age.

SOURCE: Department of Health, Education and Welfare
National Center for Health Statistics
Health Resources Administration
Division of Vital Statistics.